D0056750

BRAND NAME BULLIES

BRAND NAME BULLIES

The Quest to Own and Control Culture

DAVID BOLLIER

WILEY

John Wiley & Sons, Inc.

Published by John Wiley & Sons, Inc., Hoboken, New Jersey
Published simultaneously in Canada

Illustration credits: page 36 photo by Robert Glasgow, copyright © 2000, courtesy of Creative Time; page 45 copyright © 1994, courtesy of Barry Kite; page 47 copyright © 2000, courtesy of Heidi Cody; page 51 copyright © Andy Warhol Foundation for the Visual Arts, courtesy of Ronald Feldman Fine Arts, New York; page 90 photo copyright © 1998 by Tom Forsythe; page 149 courtesy of Andrew Baio; page 155 courtesy of Ruben Bolling; page 173 courtesy of AP/Wide World Photos; page 193 copyright © 2004, courtesy of Rand Careaga; page 206 courtesy of Mike Keefe, *The Denver Post.*

For general information about our other products and services, please contact our Customer Care Department within the United States at (800) 762-2974, outside the United States at (317) 572-3993 or fax (317) 572-4002.

Wiley also publishes its books in a variety of electronic formats. Some content that appears in print may not be available in electronic books. For more information about Wiley products, visit our web site at www.wiley.com.

Library of Congress Cataloging-in-Publication Data:

Bollier, David.
   Brand name bullies : the quest to own and control culture / David
Bollier.
      p.   cm.
   Includes bibliographical data and index.
   ISBN 0-471-67927-5 (cloth : alk. paper)
   1. Intellectual property—United States. 2. Popular culture—United
States. I. Title.

To Ellen

Contents

Acknowledgments

A central theme of this book is that authorship is not simply a story about originality, but about inspiration, emulation, and collaboration. It is a pleasure, therefore, to acknowledge the many friends and colleagues who played a critical role in shaping this book.

My biggest debt is to the community of thinkers and activists who believe that intellectual property law needs to take better account of the public interest. There are too many people to name here, but you know who you are. At numerous conferences, workshops, and other gatherings, I have learned a great deal that has found its way into these pages. I am especially indebted to a subset of this community, the people associated with Public Knowledge—its president, board, staff, and friends.

Public Knowledge president Gigi Sohn, and Chair Laurie Racine, who is also the director of the Center for the Public Domain, helped me hatch the idea of popularizing the wacky, curious, and infamous stories of copyright and trademark law. Both immediately understood that any serious reform of this complicated branch of the law will require a broader public awareness of what is truly at stake. Both realized how urgent it is to translate the arcane, crabbed discourse of the law into something approaching the common tongue. Stories, we agreed, offer a wonderful path to understanding. As this project took shape, and throughout its nearly three-year gestation, Gigi and Laurie provided me with indispensable advice, research support, and sanity-preserving laughter. Many, many thanks.

Over the past five years, the Center for the Public Domain has been a courageous pioneer in helping to incubate the movement to protect the cultural commons. Its critical, early support for this book is yet another example of this leadership, for which I am personally grateful.

Researching dozens of stories spanning a vast intellectual landscape was no small challenge. I am grateful to have had the assistance of three resourceful legal researchers. Andrew Goldman helped clear the underbrush in the field that I set out to understand better, Richard Yu gave much of his summer in 2003 answering many research queries, and Nathan Mitchler gave me a small mountain of documents and valuable legal advice, and tenacious follow-up research about cases I was investigating.

The circle of helpful contributors reaches wider still. Mary Alice Baish, Peter Barnes, Howard Besser, Johanna Blakley, Alex Curtis, Joanna Demers, Jessica Emami, Ronald Feldman, Jennifer Jenkins, Marty Kaplan, Nancy Kranich, John Mitchell, Elizabeth Rader, Jonathan Rowe, Carrie Russell, Peter Suber, Siva Vaidhyanathan, and Donna Wentworth gave me many helpful leads, documents, and advice. Jennifer Horney prepared a useful first-time survey of stories about the public domain, which assisted my research odyssey. Ann Oliverio and Melissa Ihnat of Public Knowledge took on the formidable task of obtaining copyright permissions, a task made easier with the generous advice of Iara Pang and Daniel Katz.

Still others helped this book come together properly. Fred von Lohmann of the Electronic Frontier Foundation, Susan Crawford of the Cardozo School of Law, and Paul Alan Levy of the Public Citizen Litigation Group gave me thoughtful reviews of the manuscript. Any errors are, however, mine alone. Blanche Brann gave me excellent advice about the publishing industry. Once again, my editor at John Wiley & Sons, Eric Nelson, showed faith in my work and helped shepherd it through a gauntlet of editorial and publishing challenges. Thank you, Eric.

My friends Norman Lear, Emily Levine, and Lewis Hyde have constantly shown me how wisdom and laughter live in the same neighborhood, a truth that I hope is reflected in the following pages. I must thank Norman in particular for sharing so much with me during the course of this book, and far beyond. Some debts can only be discharged by passing the gift along.

My wife, Ellen, has a knack for good book titles that again rescued me at a critical moment. She also helped me remember to bring some complicated abstractions back to earth, where real people live, and to enjoy life away from this project. My teenaged sons, Samuel and Thomas, were blessedly helpful in that regard too, and great fun besides.

Introduction

Mark Twain once sent a Connecticut Yankee back in time to King Arthur's court. What better way to comment on his own times than use the past as an amusing foil?

I have my own time-travel fantasies. What would happen if contemporary copyright and trademark laws were spirited back in history and applied to the output of, say, William Shakespeare, Woody Guthrie, and Albert Einstein? How would these people's creativity be affected? How might cultural history be changed?

For starters, the heirs of the first-century Roman poet Ovid would surely file the case of *Estate of Ovid v. William Shakespeare*. The complaint: Shakespeare, in his tremendously popular drama *Romeo and Juliet*, made an unauthorized use of Ovid's *Metamorphoses*, which is also based on two lovers from warring families. If such theft is not prosecuted, Ovid's descendants warn, there will be no incentive for new investment in future creative works. The consequences for Italy's trade deficit could be disastrous.

Shakespeare's first response, of course, is to kill all the lawyers. He then points out that Ovid himself was a thief. He filched the folktale of Pyramus and Thisbe and transformed it into *Metamorphoses*. In classic Freudian style, the very title discloses the appropriation!

In any case, if Ovid's heirs are going to sue (Shakespeare continues), surely they should also name Robert Wise and Jerome Robbins, the creators of the film *West Side Story*, as codefendants. For that matter, they should also seek damages from the producers of *The Fantasticks*, the immensely lucrative Broadway play, and Maxwell Anderson, for his 1935 drama *Winterset*, which also featured star-crossed lovers from warring families. Let's not forget Franco Zeffirelli's 1968 film version of *Romeo and Juliet*, Baz Luhrmann's 1996 version, and the thirty-two others listed on the Internet Movie Database.

But plotlines aren't protected under copyright law, harrumphs an offstage copyright attorney. Unfortunately, Shakespeare, like most of us, can't be expected to recognize a spurious copyright claim, and he can't afford expensive litigation to vindicate his creative rights, especially when the adversary has deep pockets. (Ovid's family made a *mint* off the love poems.) So long as a lawsuit hovers over *Romeo and Juliet*, no theater company will touch it. Performances drop off and the play slips into obscurity.

So goes my fantasy. The point, really, is that creativity and culture resemble an ongoing conversation. We necessarily draw upon the past and play off each other. We constantly borrow and transform prior works.

An acute tension arises from this fact. The components and meanings of creative works emerge over time from our collective interactions. Works are inherently social. Yet ownership of a particular work tends to be private.

Historically, this tension has been resolved through copyright law. Individual creators are granted limited monopolies on their works, through copyright protection, while the public is guaranteed certain rights of access and use, primarily through a legal doctrine known as "fair use." The system has worked well. In fact, it has been an important tool for encouraging people to create new works and disseminate them broadly.

What is happening today, however—and the reason for this book—is a radical expansion of the scope of copyright and trademark law. The owners of intellectual property, especially large entertainment industries, are asserting sweeping new rights of ownership and control for themselves at the expense of the public and future creators. It is as if Ovid really could shut down Shakespeare. This is a significant departure from the time-honored principles of copyright law, which have struck a careful balance between private control and public access.

It is not easy to talk about this disturbing trend. The details are abstract and embedded in the clotted language of the law. The cases tend to be convoluted and embroiled in arcane interindustry squabbles. Who can begin to keep track?

Stories, I have learned, can help clarify what's going on. For example, it would be interesting to contemplate the fate of Woodie Guthrie's folk songs if a predatory media company—call it Globatron Content—were to acquire his copyrights and aggressively leverage their economic value.

Imagine that Globatron acquires a dozen media subsidiaries in a single merger deal, and then learns that it has unwittingly acquired the copyright to Guthrie's union organizing song "Union Maid." The famous chorus to the song—"Oh, you can't scare me, I'm sticking to the union, I'm sticking to the union till the day I die"—has become so much a part of the cultural landscape, a government arts official once told Woody Guthrie, that most Americans have no idea that he wrote it. A pleased Guthrie replied, "If that were true, it would be the greatest honor of my life."

But Globatron, the new legal "author" of Guthrie's song, has no personal attachment to the song. It is only concerned that its valuable intellectual property is being ripped off. Surely the singing of the song at union rallies constitutes a "public performance," which by law requires authorization and payment. Popular homage is one thing; a failure to pay is another. The company sues the AFL-CIO for abetting copyright infringement. Splutters one Globatron attorney, "And don't get me started about 'This Land Is Your Land.'"

To take a cue from Guthrie, one might well ask about the brave new world being crafted by copyright and trademark law: *Is this culture* your *culture? Is this culture* my *culture?*

We are accustomed to thinking that knowledge and creativity are things we can freely use and share with each other. That is what a democratic society is all about. But increasingly, copyright and trademark law is extending its reach into the most intimate corners of our daily lives and consciousness. We are being told that culture is a creature of the market, not a democratic birthright. It is privately owned and controlled, and our role is to be obedient consumers. Only prescribed forms of interactivity are permitted. Our role, essentially, is to be paying visitors at a cultural estate owned by major "content providers."

What this means is that the creativity and knowledge exchange that we participate in *outside* of the marketplace—online forums, collaborative archives, music remixes, open source software development—are regarded by the law as second-rate forms of culture, if not illegal in some instances. The "authorship" of commercial vendors is given full-armor legal protection, but the creative interests of ordinary citizens and artists are seen as unimportant. Posting online newspaper articles to a Web site has been declared illegal by one federal court. Scholars who share digital journal articles without authorization may be breaking the law. Using trademarks in artistic works may be considered an unlawful "dilution" or "tarnishment" of the mark.

Isaac Newton famously declared, "If I see farther than others, it is because I stand on the shoulders of giants." Newton didn't reckon on proprietary restrictions that might restrict who can stand on whose shoulders, and for how long, before being obliged to put another quarter in the meter.

Which led me to wonder what might have happened if Albert Einstein's famous theory of relativity had actually been inspired by a company's proprietary knowledge. Recall that as a young man Einstein worked as a patent examiner in Geneva, Switzerland, where he reviewed dozens of patent applications. One patent applicant—let's call it Railway Clocks—sought to synchronize the clocks of railway lines in cities throughout central Europe so that trains could depart and arrive on time. According to one historian, this patent application may have greatly influenced Einstein's thinking about the concepts of time and space.

So imagine this (after first recognizing that patent law is governed by different principles than copyright law): after Einstein publishes his landmark paper on special relativity, Railway Clocks fumes that its intellectual property has been stolen, and by a government insider at that. In the ensuing litigation, Railway asserts that Einstein's valuable derivative knowledge could only have been developed through the unauthorized use of Railway's proprietary knowledge. If self-appointed newcomers like Einstein are allowed to appropriate valuable prior knowledge and use it as they see fit—for free!—who will invest in future research? But one might also ask, will future Einsteins have any free knowledge available to them?

The Modern Obsession with Owning Culture

The fantasies I have imagined here may seem faintly ridiculous. But in truth, contemporary copyright and trademark law is replete with tales of the bizarre and hilarious. That's what I discovered as I ventured into the forbidding precincts of intellectual property law. If Robert Ripley were still chasing down the lurid stories that once graced the Sunday comics section—a rutabaga that looks like Abraham Lincoln, a sultan with five hundred wives—he would find many ripe oddities for his franchise in copyright and trademark law. "Believe It or Not!"

For example, if you dare to evoke some aspect of a celebrity—by creating a portable toilet called "Here's Johnny!" or making an advertisement featuring a female robot that turns letter tiles on a game show—you may be violating that celebrity's "publicity rights."

If you're an artist who makes mobiles, the estate of Alexander Calder, the famous maker of monumental mobiles, may prevent you from selling your works in museum gift shops.

If you want to take a photograph of your friends while sitting in a Starbucks, the manager may intervene to stop your Kodak moment (oops, a trademark that doesn't belong to me) lest you replicate the shop's tastefully designed "trade dress" interior.

If you want to paint your own renditions of Mickey and Goofy on your day-care center walls, lawyers for the Disney Company may send you an intimidating "cease and desist" letter.

While the stories in this book may shock and entertain, there is a serious purpose afoot. These tales speak to a radical reconfiguration of political and cultural power in the digital age. They are significant because they are harbingers of our future. As more aspects of American life migrate to the Internet and digital media, the obscure, clunky machinery of copyright and trademark law is gaining vast new powers to reengineer the flow of information, art, and culture in our society.

What was once considered part of the cultural commons, available for all to use, is increasingly being privatized and locked up. The scope of this plunder is remarkable. It includes all manner of text, images, music, fictional characters, celebrity personas, accounts of public events, and even common words. The ownership of culture now extends to letters of the alphabet, distinctive sounds and colors, and even scents. Increasingly, the lawyers tell us. "You may *gaze upon* and *buy* the products of American culture. But don't be so naïve as to think that you can actually *use* them for your own purposes. We *own* them."

Congress and the courts have actively facilitated this dramatic privatization of culture and political rights with little public scrutiny or citizen participation. The resulting empowerment of several major industries—film, music, and publishing in particular—is matched by a corresponding disenfranchisement of ordinary citizens, artists, and posterity. Try to use existing works in a new creation—even in a fleeting, partial way, even for personal and noncommercial purposes—and you enter a shadowy cultural underground, a zone of the illegal imagination.

New creativity is stymied. Free expression is stifled. A boisterous open culture is turned into a regimented marketplace.

What Would Groucho Do?

Faced with the growing absurdities of copyright and trademark law, sometimes the only appropriate response is WWGS—What Would Groucho Say? (The acronym WWJD—"What Would Jesus Do?"—is already taken as a private trademark. But perhaps we can risk using the derivative WWGS.) I suggest WWGS in honor of Groucho's famous correspondence with studio mogul Jack Warner, described in chapter 5. Warner tried to scuttle the title of the Marx Brothers film *A Night in Casablanca* lest it be confused with Warner Bros.' new film *Casablanca*. Groucho pelted studio lawyers with a long series of zany jibes and digressions. Eventually they gave up and let the title proceed.

Where is Groucho now that we really need him? One can only imagine the deadpan riposte that he would deliver upon hearing that Wal-Mart attorneys scuttled a Web site called walmartsucks.com started by a disgruntled customer. Or that Mattel spent millions of dollars on a legal campaign to prevent a photographer from posting photos on his Web site of Barbie dolls in unflattering sexual poses. Or that ASCAP, a performance licensing body, actually told hundreds of summer camps that their campers may not sing copyrighted songs around the campfire without paying a licensing fee.

Comedians are discovering the rich vein of humor to be found in intellectual property. In fact, an entire chapter of this book is devoted to some devastating parodies and practical jokes involving brand-name bullies. For the hapless victims of copyright and trademark law, of course, things are not so funny. Fear and befuddlement are the operative emotions. Ordinary Americans who are accused of copyright or trademark transgressions have a lot in common with the Jimmy Stewart characters in Hitchcock films; they are the innocent Everyman suddenly engulfed in a mysterious web of unseen, complicated forces.

What could be more innocent than teenagers creating their own fan Web sites to celebrate and discuss Harry Potter, the boy wizard of J. K. Rowling's books? But when Warner Bros. (still jealous of its film titles) came out with the first Harry Potter film in 2000, the studio could not abide the fact that teenagers might actually use the name "Harry Potter" in their domain names. Studio lawyers accordingly threatened the fans with legal action for trademark violations unless they shut down their sites.

The McDonald's Corporation has long been legendary for its proprietary zeal. It constantly prowls the world's restaurants and corner carryouts for unauthorized uses of the "Mc" prefix. In San Francisco, it was McSushi, a Japanese carryout. In England, it was McMunchies, a sandwich shop. In California, it was McDharma's, a fast-food restaurant for vegetarians. So it goes that a San Diego–based multinational claims a venerable Scottish prefix as its private corporate asset.

The proprietary spirit is not just a corporate pathology. The respected science-fiction author Ray Bradbury objected when filmmaker Michael Moore named his film *Fahrenheit 9/11*, in a play on Bradbury's book *Fahrenheit 451*. Many painters, musicians, and writers balk when their works are "quoted" even though it is essential in a free society to be able to quote them.

Copyright and the Consent of the Governed

At first blush, it's hard to know if these stories are merely stupid and amusing, or outrageous and alarming. In isolation, each story may seem trivial, the paranoid overreaction of an over-lawyered corporation. And let's be honest: Is the republic really threatened if a teenager can't name a domain name after Harry Potter or a restaurateur cannot name his restaurant McSushi?

The real question, however, is whether free speech and culture belong to everyone or chiefly to commercial interests. Seen in its broader sweep, the emerging landscape of copyright and trademark law has some disturbing implications for a robust, open world of creativity and knowledge. The prohibitions do not just affect single words or domain names, but sweeping fields of creative endeavor, political speech, and cultural commentary. As we will see in the chapters to come, the creeping tendrils of legal control seem to reach *everywhere*.

I still find it preposterous that Dr. Martin Luther King Jr.'s "I have a dream" speech is legally private property. Even though Dr. King's speech has been heard by millions as a news event and has become an historic treasure showcased every year in a federal holiday, King's estate legally owns it and refuses to let it be reproduced without authorization.

As copyright and trademark holders extend their powers in unprecedented ways, it is important for us to learn these little-known stories. They can help demystify the contrived complexities of the law and help us reimagine a more benign order. The What-Would-Groucho-Say strategy can help show how copyright and trademark law is reaching outrageous new extremes. A largely unresponsive body of law can be forced to the bar of public judgment and common sense and, as warranted, be held up to ridicule.

Because intellectual property law has traditionally been a preserve of industry attorneys, not the general public, certain basic questions are typically ignored, such as: How are ordinary people affected when copyright and trademark law is taken to unprecedented extremes? How is a democratic society sapped of its vitality by the overpropertization of its culture? How are new creativity, scientific inquiry, competition, and innovation being harmed by the new expansions of copyright and trademark protection? These questions lie at the heart of this book.

By depicting some of the excesses and abuses on the front lines of copyright law, I hope to make us more confident in asserting that copyright and trademark law must be the servant of the people. *Our* needs and values are paramount and must be protected. Thomas Jefferson once offered advice for occasions such as this: "When a long train of abuses and usurpations pursuing invariably the same object, evinces a design to reduce the people under absolute despotism, it is their right, it is their duty to throw off such chains and to provide new guards for their future security."

We stand at such a crossroads today. We have reached a point at which copyright and trademark law is surging out of control.

The point is not that copyright and trademark law needs to be overthrown. It is that its original goals need to be restored. Individual creators need to be empowered more than ever. The volume and free flow of information and creativity need to be protected. The public's rights of access and use must be honored. We must strike a new balance of private and public interests that takes account of the special dynamics of the Internet and digital technology.

None of this will occur, however, unless we recognize the problem. That is what the stories can help us do.

Brand-Name Bullies

Bullies succeed by intimidation. When they do not encounter resistance, they push as hard and as far as they can. In copyright and trademark law, large corporations, famous personalities, and well-heeled law firms have prevailed for too long precisely because the public does not have much of a role in writing the law, does not know the rights it may have, and does not have the legal resources to fight back. As a result, brand-name bullies have been allowed to inflict incalculable harm on public life, cultural freedom, and personal choice.

Charlatans should not be allowed to misuse a trademark in order to commit marketplace fraud or confuse consumers. But it beggars the imagination why Ralph Lauren should have a monopoly on the word "polo" (at the expense of an equestrian magazine), or why Microsoft should be allowed to prevent a vendor of a Linux-based computer from naming itself "Lindows." (Even though Microsoft lost its case at the district court level, its litigation in foreign nations "persuaded" its competitor to rename its product "Linspire.") Why should the owners of the Godzilla trademark be allowed to root out any uses of the letters "zilla" in the cultural landscape?

I did not make these stories up. They are immortalized in federal case law, documented in the *New York Times*, buried away in the trade press, retrieved from law review articles, culled from the cultural underground, and passed along by friends.

It is an improbable fact that contemporary copyright and trademark law could provoke so much dark laughter. But just remember, it ain't no joke. . . . Believe It or Not!

PART ONE

Art and Culture: Use Only as Directed

Copyright and trademark law is an important tool in incubating new creativity and building a culture. By giving creators a property right in their works, the law stimulates the development of all sorts of new works. What is not appreciated as much is how overly broad copyright and trademark laws can sabotage creative production. Artists necessarily must draw upon works of the past. They also must be able to modify and transform prior works and collaborate and share with fellow artists.

Since copyrights and trademarks are essentially monopoly rights, the question thus becomes: How far should intellectual property protection extend? What is the proper balance?

As the stories of Part One illustrate, the intended balance of copyright and trademark law has gotten seriously out of whack. The chief proponents of broader, longer, and stricter forms of protection are the various "content industries" that produce music, film, photographs, literature, journalism, and entertainment. They like broad legal protection for their works because it makes those works more valuable. Owning the copyright on, say, a Beatles tune for an extra twenty years could easily be worth a fortune. Broader protection also privileges commodified works over "nonmarket" creativity such as folk traditions, public dialogue, art, scholarship, and the works of online communities.

It is a complicated business drawing the lines of protection properly. But the following stories show that appropriate limits for copyright and trademark protection have been transgressed time and again. Part One explores some of the more memorable examples affecting art and culture.

CHAPTER 1

The Crusade
to Lock Up Music

[It] is entirely plausible that two Connecticut teenagers obsessed with rhythm and blues music could remember an Isley Brothers' song that was played on the radio and television for a few weeks, and subconsciously copy it twenty years later.

—A federal court in *Three Boys Music Corp. v. Bolton,*
upholding the subconscious copying doctrine

For millennia, the circulation of music in human societies has been as free as the circulation of air and water; it just comes naturally. Indeed, one of the ways that a society constitutes itself as a society is by freely sharing its words, music, and art. Only in the past century or so has music been placed in a tight envelope of property rights and strictly monitored for unauthorized flows. In the past decade, the proliferation of personal computers, Internet access, and digital technologies has fueled two conflicting forces: the democratization of creativity and the demand for stronger copyright protections.

While the public continues to have nominal fair use rights to copyrighted music, in practice the legal and technological controls over music have grown tighter. At the same time, creators at the fringes of mass culture, especially some hip-hop and remix artists, remain contemptuous of such controls and routinely appropriate whatever sounds they want to create interesting music.

Copyright protection is a critically important tool for artists in earning a livelihood from their creativity. But as many singers, composers, and musicians have discovered, the benefits of copyright law in the contemporary

marketplace tend to accrue to the recording industry, not to the struggling garage band. As alternative distribution and marketing outlets have
arisen, the recording industry has sought to ban, delay, or control as many
of them as possible. After all, technological innovations that provide faster,
cheaper distribution of music are likely to disrupt the industry's fixed
investments and entrenched ways of doing business. New technologies
allow newcomers to enter the market and compete, sometimes on superior terms. New technologies enable new types of audiences to emerge
that may or may not be compatible with existing marketing strategies.

No wonder the recording industry has scrambled to develop new technological locks and broader copyright protections; they strengthen its control of music distribution. If metering devices could turn barroom sing-
alongs into a market, the music industry would likely declare this form of
unauthorized musical performance to be copyright infringement. Sound
improbable? Chapter 1 looks at some disturbingly hilarious attempts to
privatize and lock down music, a cultural form that seems to flourish
most when it can circulate freely.

ASCAP Stops the Girl Scouts
from Singing around the Campfire

You may *think* that it's okay for little campers to sing "Happy Birthday"
and "Row, Row, Row" around the campfire for free, without asking for
permission. But in fact, you *may* have to pay a license to a licensing society known as ASCAP. ASCAP, the American Society of Composers,
Authors and Publishers, is a performance-rights body that licenses copyrighted works for nondramatic public performances. It then distributes
royalties collected from those performances and channels them to the
appropriate composers, authors, and publishers. The system is intended as
a way to assure that creators receive monies for the public performances
of their works . . . even some campfire songs.

But what exactly is a "public performance," and should summer camps
be charged for license fees for widely sung tunes like "Puff the Magic
Dragon," "Edelweiss," and "This Land Is Your Land"? In 1996, ASCAP
decided that since hotels, restaurants, funeral homes, and resorts pay for the
right to "perform" recorded music, and since many summer camps resemble resorts, why shouldn't they pay too? Under copyright law, a public

performance occurs "where a substantial number of persons outside of a normal circle of a family and its social acquaintances is gathered." Like a summer camp.

After reportedly opening its negotiations with the American Camping Association with an offer of $1,200 per season per camp, ASCAP eventually settled on an average annual fee of $257. Most of these camps were "big commercial camps," an ASCAP spokesperson told a reporter—places equipped with dining and recreational facilities that used music for dances and other social functions. For camps that did not belong to the association, the fees ranged from $308 to $1,439 a year.

When ASCAP sent letters to the 288 camps enrolled with the American Camping Association, demanding payment for the "public performances" of copyrighted songs, it failed to check the affiliations of each camp. Unbeknownst to ASCAP, 16 of the 288 camps were run by the Boy Scouts of America or the Girl Scouts.

When Sharon Kosch, the director of the San Francisco Bay Girl Scout Council's program services, received an ASCAP letter demanding $591, her first thought was, "You guys have got to be kidding. They can't sing the songs?" She reconsidered when she found out the potential punishment. "It's pretty threatening. We were told the penalty can be $5,000 and six days in jail."

So the council took a black marker to its "Favorite Songs at Diablo Day Camp" list, trying to determine which songs were copyrighted and which belonged in the public domain. But the council didn't have the means to check its song list against ASCAP's 70,000-page list of 4 million songs. And even if it did, another composer licensing body—SESAC, Inc., which owns the copyright to Bob Dylan's "Blowin' in the Wind"—had announced it would ask camps for its own set of royalties.

The council couldn't shoulder the bureaucratic hassles. It was low on cash and couldn't afford $10,000 in licensing fees for its twenty chapters. And it could not afford to be sued. So the camp simply stopped singing.

The girls of Diablo Day Camp were reduced to doing "The Macarena" (which was all the rage that summer) in silence, without the music. Non-ASCAP or noncopyrighted songs like "Bow-Legged Chicken" and "Herman the Worm" had to be sung instead of "This Land Is Your Land."

A fourteen-year-old camper tried to tell the younger Brownies what had happened: "They think copyright means the 'mean people,'" said

Debby Cwalina. "The people who wrote it have a thing on it. A little *c* with circles around it. There's an alarm on it. And if you sing it, BOOM!"

As if to play into this stereotype of copyright law, ASCAP's chief operating officer, John Lo Frumento, told a reporter: "They [camps] buy paper, twine and glue for their crafts—they can pay for the music, too." And if the little girls sang anyway, he said, ASCAP would "sue them if necessary."

Not surprisingly, ASCAP's arrogance did not play well in the press. "Tightwad bean counters in the music industry descended to a new low this summer," wrote an editorialist for the *San Francisco Chronicle*. "Let ASCAP bullies try to collect their phony royalties. We dare them."

The press had a field day. The basketball player Shaquille O'Neal offered to pay a camp's royalties for ten years. BMI, ASCAP's rival in licensing music, offered to license its three million songs to the Girl Scouts for nothing.

James V. DeLong, writing in the *National Law Journal*, astutely noted that composers do not create their music from scratch; they necessarily "steal" from the cultural commons: "Song writers draw heavily on the efforts of other people, such as those who invented the musical notation used to put songs into marketable form, a rich tradition of folk music written without benefit of copyright, and old works no longer covered. The composers are tapping into a sort of cultural commons without which their efforts would be bootless, and they have no right to appropriate it."

It was also pointed out that Boy Scouts, Girl Scouts, and other youth camps probably do more than any other force to keep old songs in circulation, introducing them to a new generation year by year. Whatever economic value the songs may have, certainly some significant amount stems from this informal sharing of the works via the commons. But copyright champions systematically ignore the "value added" wealth that derives from the unmetered sharing of creative works.

A week after the public furor started, a chastened ASCAP said that the entire affair was a "gross misunderstanding" and that it would not be seeking royalties from the Girl Scouts after all. Said a spokesperson: "I guess we could have researched the list [of camps] better than we did, but quite honestly there isn't a lot of money here."

For all of its PR backpedaling, ASCAP did not concede any legal ground. The free singing of songs by the Girl Scouts remains an ASCAP-granted indulgence, not a legal entitlement. But as this episode showed, the public has its own considerable voice in how copyright law will be enforced—if it can express itself. Or as Bob Dylan put it, in a song that he claims belongs to him alone, "The answer, my friend, is blowing in the wind. The answer is blowing in the wind."

The Blurry Line between Originality and Copying

One of the most persistent difficulties in applying copyright law to music is determining what is original—and therefore deserving of copyright protection—and what is deemed illicit "copying." Copyright law presumes that the originality of a new work—and thus its "authorship"—can be identified and legally defined as property. But in actual practice, no one creates a new song out of thin air. Virtually every new creation draws in varying degrees upon musical tradition and the larger culture, sometimes in highly specific ways. All creators depend upon a cultural commons for inspiration, imitation, and derivation.

The history of music is a story of originality combining with creative derivation. Sometimes a new work seems familiar because it belongs to a specific musical tradition; sometimes it copies key melodies, notes, refrains, or lyrics. For example, "Good Night Sweetheart" (1931) is based on themes from Schubert's Symphony in C and Liszt's preludes. "Love Me Tender," made famous by Elvis Presley in 1956, is based on "Aura Lee" by George Poulton. "The Lion Sleeps Tonight," also known as "Wimoweh"—recorded by the Weavers in 1952 and the Tokens in 1961—is based on a traditional African song.

In "copying" their predecessors, musicians are not necessarily ripping off someone else's work. Often, a prior work is quoted to pay homage, evoke another cultural period, or make fun of it. Mozart, Wagner, Bartók, and Debussy all wrote music that mocked contemporaries whom they disliked. Bartók imitated Dmitry Shostakovich's Symphony no. 7 with a parody that he described as "trumpets give a Bronx cheer; high strings and woodwinds shriek derision . . . woodwinds trail off in giggles; trombones fart, glissando. The whole wind band combines trills with an umpah bass to introduce . . . violins in varied repetition of the Shostakovich tune." Taking this impulse a step further, Peter Schickele, better known as

P.D.Q. Bach, has built a career as a musical parodist using Johann Sebastian Bach's oeuvre.

But imitation is not just a matter of making fun. On the record sleeve of an orchestral recording of his *Sinfonia*, Luciano Berio explained that the third section was composed as an homage to Mahler: "It was my intention here neither to destroy Mahler (who is indestructible) nor to play out a private complex about 'post-Romantic music' (I have none) nor yet to spin some enormous musical anecdote (familiar among young pianists). Quotations and references were chosen not only for their real but also for their potential relation to Mahler."

In drawing upon the blues, rock music carries on the same tradition of reinventing and interpreting the art that has come before. Sometimes the imitations are strikingly similar. Led Zeppelin's "Whole Lotta Love" is remarkably close to "You Need Love" by the blues composer Willie Dixon, and the band's "The Lemon Song" is clearly related to Howlin' Wolf's "Killing Floor." (Dixon actually sued Led Zeppelin and later settled.) Scholars such as Siva Vaidhyanathan have identified many clear lines of musical influence, if not outright imitation, that connect Muddy Waters to Eric Clapton, Chuck Berry to the Beach Boys, and Big Mama Thornton to Elvis Presley. While there is little question that all of these artists were distinctive innovators, it is not always possible to identify precisely who, if anyone, is solely responsible for a given innovation and whether it should be protected through an exclusive property right.

Vaidhyanathan illustrates the profound limitations of copyright law by recalling an Alan Lomax interview with the blues artist Muddy Waters. Asked about the origins of his song, "Country Blues," Waters admits in the course of a rambling conversation to at least five identifiable sources: Waters himself "made it" on a certain occasion; the song was received knowledge that "come to me just like that"; the song may have derived from a similar song by Robert Johnson; Waters's mentor Son House taught the song to him; and the song "comes from the cotton field."

What may seem like a confusing set of contradictory statements is, in the blues tradition, a unified field. Tradition, inspiration, and improvisation are all wrapped up together, making it impossible to tease out with absolute certainty what is "original" in a given piece of music, let alone assign clear property rights to it. As Vaidhyanathan points out, "Blues originality is just very different from the standard European model. Originality in the blues is performance-based. Pen and paper never enter the equation unless the song is considered for recording and distribution. . . . The blues tradition values 'originality' without a confining sense of 'ownership.' In the blues tradition, what is original is the 'value-added' aspect of a work, usually delivered through performance."

If it is easier to discern the creative borrowings that occur in rhythm and blues or folk music than in, say, pop music, that is because these types of music have historically invited imitation and derivation as part of their tradition. By contrast, pop music, as an artifact of the mass marketplace (Tin Pan Alley, vaudeville, the Broadway musical), has grown up with a tradition of strict copyright protection. Outright, explicit imitation is therefore more rare, if not illegal, in pop music, than in the "open" traditions like folk.

Interestingly, one artist who straddles these two musical worlds, and who therefore embodies their contradictions, is Bob Dylan. Dylan is one of the most original contemporary composers yet one of the most inveterate "borrowers" of other people's work. But does Dylan "steal"?

The issue came to the fore in 2003 when a Dylan fan discovered that some lyrics on Dylan's 2001 album *Love and Theft* were almost verbatim lines from a 1991 novel, *Confessions of a Yakuza*, by Japanese novelist Dr. Junichi Saga. (Dylan would neither confirm nor deny to the *New York Times* having read the book.) While copyright attorneys might be shocked at such "plagiarism," folk music fans (and Bob Dylan fans in particular) know that the essence of such music is appropriation and collage. "Allusions and memories, fragments of dialogue and nuggets of tradition have always been part of Mr. Dylan's songs, all stitched together like crazy quilts," wrote the *New York Times* music critic Jon Pareles about the incident. "His lyrics are like magpies' nests, full of shiny fragments from parts unknown."

It was pointed out that the melody of Dylan's first big hit, "Blowin' in the Wind," was based on an antislavery spiritual, "No More Auction Block." Woody Guthrie's tunes drew heavily on songs recorded by the Carter Family. The difference between Dylan and Guthrie is that Dylan is quite proprietary about his songs, to the extent of testifying before Congress on behalf of a twenty-year copyright term extension. Guthrie, as we saw earlier, was only too proud to have his works become so integrated into the culture that his authorship is forgotten.

In the 1960s the folksinger Pete Seeger introduced a little-known innovation that sought to bridge the "community ownership" of a song with the individual "authorship" claimed by a subsequent songwriter or performer. The song at issue was "We Shall Overcome." Seeger had first heard it in 1947 when Zilphia Horton, a white woman who was one of the founders of the Highlander Research and Education Center, had taught it to him. She in turn had learned the song the year before from African American women on strike against the American Tobacco Company in Charleston, South Carolina. To keep their spirits up on the picket line, the women had adapted an old gospel tune, "I'll Overcome" or "I'll Be All Right"; one of the strikers, Lucille Simmons, sang the song movingly as "*We* Will Overcome" in a very slow meter.

Seeger loved the song, but changed the words to "We *Shall* Overcome" ("I think I liked a more open sound," he said) and added some new verses, "We'll walk hand in hand" and "The whole wide world around." In 1952, Seeger taught the song to a California singer, Frank Hamilton, who then introduced the song to Guy Carawan, who in 1959 brought the song back to the Highlander Center and its young civil rights activists. After Carawan taught it to the founding convention of the Student Nonviolent Coordinating Committee in Raleigh, North Carolina, "We Shall Overcome" quickly spread throughout the South despite the absence of a recording of it.

As Seeger recalls in his autobiography, *Where Have All the Flowers Gone*, "In the early '60s, our publishers said to us, 'If you don't copyright this now, some Hollywood types will have a version out next year like 'Come on Baby, We shall overcome tonight.' So Guy [Carawan], Frank [Hamilton] and I signed a 'songwriter's contract.' At that time we didn't know Lucille Simmons' name." To acknowledge their debt to gospel congregations, the Food and Tobacco Workers Union, and others who had "created" the song, Seeger and his friends created the We Shall Overcome Fund under the auspices of the Highlander Center. The fund receives the royalties from the song and makes annual grants "to further African American music in the South."

The fund is just one case in which Seeger has earmarked a portion of his royalties for the musical communities that originated a song. The idea, he said, is to buck the common industry practice of ignoring the collective origins of music. Or as Joseph Shabalala of South Africa's Ladysmith

Black Mambazo has reportedly said, "When the word 'traditional' is used, the money stays in New York."

Should artists be able to strictly control how their works may circulate and who may use them? Copyright law provides a compulsory license that lets anyone do a "cover" version of an artist's song for a fixed fee, which is why so many versions of "White Christmas" and "I Shot the Sheriff" are floating around. But if artists want to sample portions of a song or change it significantly, permission is needed from the copyright holder. As we will see below, this means that only wealthy recording artists can afford to pay the licensing fees to sample works that have come before. The struggling newcomer cannot afford to make a new song using samples of Aerosmith's "Dream On" as Eminem did in "Sing for the Moment."

One must remember that "theft" is a slippery term. Dr. Saga was delighted to learn that Dylan had used lyrics from his novel, and was surely doubly thrilled when *Confessions of a Yakuza* subsequently rose to number 117 on Amazon.com's best-seller list and number 8 among biographies and memoirs. It is, in fact, a recurrent pattern for a new work to provoke interest and sales in a prior work on which it is based in some way. When Paul Simon wrote songs that imitated the style of Ladysmith Black Mambazo—prompting some purists to charge that Simon had ripped off their music for personal gain—sales of Ladysmith Black Mambazo's music soared.

For artists whose work is reused by another artist, derivative works can be gifts as much as thefts. For the culture at large, new creations generally enrich it.

The problem is that copyright law has trouble recognizing imitation as anything but theft. Happily, some progress is being made. Certain forms of imitation such as parody are starting to gain greater legal protection. For years, comedians, disc jockeys, and even *Mad* magazine were being successfully sued for musical parodies, sometimes of the most innocent variety (see chapter 4). Finally, in 1994, the U.S. Supreme Court for the first time gave broad protection to parody as a legitimate form of fair use.

The rap group 2 Live Crew had appropriated the music and title of Roy Orbison's famous song "Oh, Pretty Woman." At critical points in the song, "pretty woman" became "big hairy woman," "bald headed woman," and "two timin' woman." Hilarious, but legal? The district court thought so, but the Sixth Circuit had ruled that the song was "presumptively . . . unfair" because its use was primarily commercial.

A unanimous Supreme Court struck down this presumption, legitimizing a much greater cultural space for commercial parodies than ever before. The Copyright Act of 1976 had enumerated four factors that should guide the courts in deciding if the use of a copyrighted work constitutes "fair use," a legal use of a work by someone other than the copyright owner.* In this case, the Supreme Court held that none of the four fair use factors are controlling in determining whether a parody is fair use. The ruling also recognized that appropriation, even of an entire work, may be necessary for a parody, and thus protectable under the fair use doctrine. For this reason alone, wrote one legal commentator, *Campbell v. Acuff-Rose Music, Inc.* "could very well go down in jurisprudential history as the case that shepherded copyright law's entry into the postmodern era."

While the *Acuff-Rose Music* ruling is a welcome development, it represents only a small recognition that creativity is an ongoing cultural conversation, and that any such conversation requires copying. Literal-minded courts are still likely to regard send-ups that are *too* sly and sophisticated

---

* The Copyright Act of 1976 stipulates four guidelines in Section 107 for determining whether a use of a copyrighted work shall be considered a "fair use": (1) *the purpose and character of the use* ("transformative" noncommercial uses, such as research, scholarship, criticism, and news reporting, enjoy greater protection than commercial uses); (2) *the nature of the copyrighted work* (greater leeway is given to excerpting from factual works than from creative works such as novels); (3) *the amount and substantiality of the portion used in relation to the whole* (shorter excerpts are more defensible than longer ones); and (4) *the effect of the use on the potential market for the copyrighted work* (the second work should not compete in the marketplace with the original).

While these guidelines provide some help to the courts in determining what shall be considered fair use, the House Judiciary Committee in its report on the 1976 Copyright Act acknowledged, "Although the courts have considered and ruled upon the fair use doctrine over and over again, no real definition of the concept has ever emerged. Indeed, since the doctrine is an equitable rule of reason, no generally applicable definition is possible, and each case raising the question must be decided on its own facts." In 2002, Professor David Nimmer offered a devastating empirical critique of the incoherent adjudication of the fair use doctrine, concluding that "the four statutory factors to reach fair use decisions often seems naught but a fairy tale."

as theft. Unfortunately, as currently constituted, copyright law just cannot sufficiently recognize that sharing and collaboration are a natural, vital part of any artistic tradition.

How Illegal Rap Sampling Revived
the Music Business

It is hard to imagine a more powerful threat to the basic premises of copyright law than rap music and its signature technique, sampling. Sampling in some form or another is nothing new, of course. Composers and performers have always taken melodies or rhythms or styles of their favorite songs and built something new around them. But in the 1980s, two diametrically opposed forces began to collide with each other: more record companies began to invoke copyright law to control smaller and finer "units" of the works (distinctive guitar riffs, melodies, and vocals) even as new technologies were giving artists (and the mass public) new powers to make music using *verbatim* samples of those sounds.

Over the past twenty years, digital sampling has enabled entirely new genres of musical collage—hip-hop, DJing, mash-ups—which in turn has made the line between originality and copying very blurry indeed. If dozens of samples can be taken and remixed into a new song altogether, who is its "author"?

Clearly, large-scale digital sampling involves "taking someone else's work" and is generally regarded as a flagrant copyright infringement. But just as clearly the new art forms, rapping and DJing, are acts of considerable creativity in their own right. Moreover, they mimic the very borrowing and creative transformation that has always characterized artistic work. What is interesting about rap music is how this underground, "premarket" musical genre arose over the course of the 1980s and 1990s and became a cultural juggernaut that transformed pop music, entertainment, and fashion. Its ascendance had nothing to do with the copyright "incentives" that are presumed to be necessary for artists to create. Rather, rap emerged and flourished as a fresh and vital genre precisely because it ignored intellectual property norms. Rap was born in a cultural commons, not a market.

Rap sampling is the product of a very different creative ecology than the copyright-based environment responsible for pop music. The pop aesthetic is based on traditional copyright notions of authorship and originality. A pop star presents herself as the sole creator of an original work, and makes only token gestures to acknowledge creative debts to earlier artists and traditions. By contrast, the African American musical traditions—jazz, blues, rap—are deeply rooted in communal sharing and collaboration. A big part of the music is invoking the signature riffs and styles of great masters to communicate one's musical and cultural identity.

"Exclusive ownership of creative materials runs counter to the ethical codes of African-American musical culture," writes Joanna Demers, an assistant professor of music history and literature at the University of Southern California. "Emphasizing the continuity of life rather than the differences between generations, African metaphysics did not conceive of originality as creation from nothingness, since everything had already been created. Rather, originality is to be found in the novel combination of multiple elements from both the present and the past, an idea very similar to the Western definition of craftsmanship."

Demers cites an observation by Christian Béthune that African American culture has always been based on the borrowing and creative reassembly of previous works: "Cut from his roots, the black man on American soil is left only with fragments and debris stemming from heterogeneous worlds: disparate memories of African heritage, hymns and canticles from the Christian tradition, sailors' music learned on the docks, etc. The sole means of reconstructing an original expression consisted in drawing from this inheritance, even if this meant refurbishing these scattered bits using one's own sensibility."

Thus, while performers in the blues, funk, or soul music traditions may contribute something fresh and distinctive, they also like to invoke the musical motifs of predecessors. No one regards this as piracy or imitation. Rather, it is a way to declare one's identity and pay homage to a respected cultural tradition. The impulse to assert a community affiliation—or comment upon another performer—is at the root of sampling in hip-hop, asserts Demers, whose doctoral dissertation is entitled "Sampling as Lineage in Hip-Hop."

Sampling represents a profound threat to the copyright tradition because it threatens to eliminate the "authorship" of a piece of music. Yet without free, unrestricted access to other people's music, it is safe to say that rap would never have developed in the first place. Chuck D and Hank Shocklee, two early rap pioneers, told *Stay Free!* magazine that hip-hop music would never have gotten off the ground in the 1980s if today's copyright regime for sampling had been in place. "It wouldn't be impossible," conceded Shocklee, but, he insisted, "it would be very, very costly." Shocklee estimated that a single sample could cost half the revenues that an album might earn.

If most pop musicians are highly proprietary about the music that they "own," the early hip-hop artists considered every sound in the culture as fair game for their creativity. The first hip-hop samplers developed a technique of "scratching," the manual rotation of a vinyl record back and forth to produce unique sounds from individual grooves. The essence of the music was a real-time performance pastiche using someone's else's recorded music.

Scratching and sampling thus shifted the locus of "originality" from the composer to the rapper and DJ, whose creativity consisted of the selection and arrangement of samples. Said another way, sampling put composers, rappers, DJs, and record producers on a more or less equal footing—as appropriators of other people's music. In rap music, originality was more about an artist's live performance and improvisation, not the notes as written on sheet music.

With the proliferation of sound synthesizers and, later, inexpensive digital audio and computer technologies, the musical palette for hip-hop sampling exploded. Musical creativity became democratized. It became possible for anyone to draw upon hundreds of snippets of sound, modify them in novel ways, and assemble a sonic collage that might just attract an audience. In these dynamics, rap might be considered a musical analog to open source software: a creative milieu that is open to anyone and receptive to merit no matter its source.

For *New York Times* music critic Neil Strauss, writing in 1997, sampling was a refreshing musical development: "Only when plundering and originality come together to create something new does sampling become reminiscent of pop's pre-rock days, when new and vital music came out of the intersection between a good song, a good interpreter and perhaps a good arranger. The same cliché that applies to any remake applies to sampled songs: in a valid, worthwhile version, an artist makes the song his or her own. Examples range from John Coltrane playing 'My Favorite Things' to Frank Sinatra singing 'I've Got You Under My Skin.'"

What began as an underground ghetto art form in the 1970s had by the early 1990s become a $1 billion market. Naturally, as certain songs became hits, questions about who "owned" a given snippet of music became the subject of legal wrangling. After all, a hit rap song was now worth some serious money.

The bigger stars generally tried to pay licenses for samples, largely to placate their record labels, but many other rap artists, perhaps most, did not bother, especially if the sample was short and not a major, recurring component of the song.

Inevitably, major copyright disputes over sampled sounds arose. One notable lawsuit was waged by Tuff City Records of New York City against Sony Music, distributor of Def Jam Records, in 1992. The dispute involved the sampling of a drum track. An attorney for a sample clearinghouse told a reporter, "Everyone takes beats from other songs, adds things over them, amplifies them, does anything they have to do to make their own track. If Tuff City wins, it could mean you'd have to clear everything on a record."

Tuff City lost the case because it could not prove it held copyrights for either the recordings or the compositions. In addition, the court found that the sampled drumbeats were significantly changed and recontextualized from the original sources. The ruling, *Tuff 'n' Rumble Management v. Profile Records*, proved influential because it recognized that music sampling can be done without permission under certain circumstances if the use is a "transformative appropriation."

Another such case involved the jazz flutist James Newton Jr., who was appalled to discover in 1998 that six years earlier the Beastie Boys had sampled six seconds of his song "Choir" for their hit "Pass the Mic," which in turn was later used on the MTV show *Beavis and Butt-Head*. It turned out that Newton's record company had given permission to use the recorded sample, but Newton, as the composer of the piece, had not given his permission. A court eventually ruled that the sample was a "recording," and not a "composition." It held that the three-note sequence that the Beastie Boys had sampled—a C, a D-flat, and a C, with a background C segregated from the entire piece—was such "a small and unoriginal portion of music" that it cannot be protected by copyright. Curiously, this ruling appears to contradict the precedents of previous fully litigated sampling cases, in which virtually any sound—screams, drum beats, odd sounds—counted as an original "composition."

As the market value of rap songs grew, the uncertainty over how to license samples became a more urgent problem, as Vaidhyanathan recounts in his book *Copyrights and Copywrongs*, "Because sampling raised so many questions, labels pushed their more successful acts to get permission for samples before releasing a record. The problem was that no one knew what to charge for a three-second sample."

What emerged was an ad hoc system of negotiated licenses for samples. An influential force was a 1991 federal court ruling that forced rapper Biz Markie to pay Gilbert O'Sullivan for taking the first eight bars of his 1972 single "Alone Again (Naturally)." The judge bluntly declared that Biz Markie's sampling was theft: "'Thou shalt not steal' has been an admonition followed since the dawn of civilization. Unfortunately, in the modern world of business this admonition is not always followed." The ruling made no provisions for fair use of prior works. Understandably, Biz Markie's lawyers quickly settled.

Once the courts had weighed in on the sampling issue, their rulings began to change the very nature of rap music. "Rap music since 1991 has been marked by a severe decrease in the amount of sampling," writes Vaidhyanathan. "Many groups record background music and then filter it during production so it sounds as if it has been sampled. . . . The 1991 ruling removed from rap music a whole level of communication and meaning that once played a part in the audience's reception to it. The Biz Markie case 'stole the soul' from rap music."

As sampling licenses became the legal norm, creative freedom became a privilege that only the richest, most established artists could afford. It also meant that certain types of works would never get produced at all. Public Enemy produced a track, "Psycho of Greed," that was originally recorded for the group's album *Revolverution*. The track never made it onto the album, however, because it sampled the Beatles song "Tomorrow Never Knows," whose owner, Capitol Records, was asking more for the sample than Public Enemy was willing to pay.

An art form that had been open to anyone, especially impoverished inner-city African Americans, was becoming a proprietary genre whose participation required serious money for licensing fees. Once the propertization of music had worked its way down to four-second sound bites, hip-hop had moved far beyond its communal urban roots and become another branch of the music business. By September 2004, the Sixth Circuit Court of Appeals held that even single notes and chords could not be sampled, even if the original sound was unidentifiable. The court sniffed, "Get a license or do not sample. We do not see this as stifling creativity in any way." So much for fair use.

Some commentators have argued that the rise of sampling licenses caused a decline in the verve, inventiveness, and social bite of rap music. Others argue that any music placed in modern commerce simply must abide by traditional copyright norms and that the market helped amplify rap's cultural influence. There is a certain irony, nonetheless, that a musical genre based on illegal, unfettered appropriation became a global force that arguably saved the ailing music industry.

The music historian Demers writes: "Those rappers in the 1980s who sought a musical 'free-for-all,' in which sounds could be sampled with impunity, were probably veering towards what would have been the first postmodern state of copyright law, a world in which no conditions are set on originality and authorship, and thus where all songs, regardless of their constituent material, are equally original." That vision turned out to be a short-lived creative experiment, and perhaps an unsustainable one. Yet it also suggested that the wellsprings of creative renewal do not necessarily have anything to do with copyright law.

The Sequel to Sampling: Mash-ups

Rap sampling may have evolved into an art form requiring a fat bank account and rights-clearance bureaucracy. Yet the urge to create music is a powerful force in its own right. In the past several years, another genre of openly recombinative music—the bootleg remix, or mash-up—has also soared out of the musical underground and thumbed its nose at copyright law.

Like rap, the bootleg craze had its origins with DJs in clubs, mostly in Britain and Europe. Once again, the genre grew out of creative improvisation and performance. But this time, the resulting songs were embedded in MP3 computer files and shared via the Internet. Making a bootleg remix is fairly easy. All a teenager has to do is download a software program like Acid, blend samples from two or more wildly different songs, and then send the crazy remix out to the wider world via peer-to-peer file-sharing programs. The best remixes can quickly circulate the planet like a global virus; indeed, that is how the trend spread from Europe to the United States.

One appeal of bootleg remixes is the unexpected sounds that can emerge from familiar pop music. Who would think that Christina Aguilera's "Genie in a Bottle" could be mixed with the Strokes' "Hard to Explain," or that a Hall and Oates song could be mashed with Daft Punk?

The mash-up verges on becoming a new genre unto itself by bringing together the legendary and the obscure, and the virtuoso and the tacky. Remixes often discover unexpected depth, emotion, and styles in old, familiar songs.

"The more disparate the genre-blending is, the better," writes Roberta Cruger in *Salon.com*. "The best mash-ups blend punk with funk or Top 40 with heavy metal, boosting the tension between slick and raw. Part of the fun is identifying the source of two familiar sounds now made strange—and then giggling over how perfect Whitney sounds singing with Kraftwerk."

Certain recording artists like Eminem and Missy Elliott are especially popular on the mash-up scene because their music can be easily mixed with a wide variety of other artists and styles. Critic Robert Wilonsky writes, "These are amazing songs not because they merely fuse the previously incompatible, but because they render the familiar absolutely, brilliantly brand-new—and they do so without losing the integrity of the two parties suffering through this shotgun marriage." Others have pointed out that mash-ups are actually a way to "dis" one genre of music by contrasting it unfavorably with another, as when Celine Dion is mixed with Sigur Ros or Beyoncé with Nirvana. The pop hit usually comes off as trite when paired with a punk, rap, or hardcore song.

Like early rap songs, bootleg remixes are outright appropriations of other artists' work. But they also reinvigorate lots of old, often forgotten music. In some ways, this is a dimension of the creative process, the reinvention of the old, that copyright law makes little provision for. Clearing permissions can be exceedingly difficult; fair uses are highly limited; and copyrighted songs often do not enter the public domain for more than a century.

It is a thrill, therefore, when a familiar contemporary song is reversioned in an unexpected way. A much-cited precursor to contemporary mash-ups is the 1980s collaboration between Run-DMC and Aerosmith that resulted in a rap version of "Walk This Way." The stunt showed how divergent musical traditions could produce a popular song while drawing fresh attention to an old rock band.

While that was a consensual collaboration, bootleg remixes are, of course, wholly illegal. This is surely one reason they are so popular. They have a whiff of cultural transgression. But like Trekkies who write illicit fan fiction, remix artists have little compunction about using fragments of mass culture for their own ends; their moral license to revamp fragments of pop culture stems from their emotional rapport with them.

In any case, obtaining legal clearances for every sample in a mash-up is next to impossible. A Belgian DJ act known as 2ManyDJs demonstrated this when they set out to produce a commercial CD of bootleg remixes. This required them to obtain copyright permissions for each of dozens of samples that they had mashed together for an album of songs. The album took two weeks to produce; the permissions clearances—involving letters, faxes, and e-mails to dozens of record labels around the world—took nearly a year, and one-third of the respondents refused to grant permission. The crowning irony was that many of the rejections came from the biggest names in the business—the Beastie Boys, Beck, Missy Elliott, Chemical Brothers—whose early careers were built on sampling other people's works. (Of course, it is quite likely that it was really the record labels, and not necessarily the artists themselves, who rejected these requests.)

One band that has become famous for its inventive remixes is Negativland, a Concord, California, band that since 1980 has specialized in music "collages" using borrowed songs from every imaginable source, especially pop music and television shows. With the anarchic zeal of the Dadaists, Negativland's five male members have produced such albums as *Plunderphonics* and *Escape from Noise*. One of the band's most famous music collages, a spoof of U2's "I Still Haven't Found What I'm Looking For," triggered a three-year legal battle (see page 214).

Remixes have become so popular that established artists and their labels seem to be sending mixed messages to rappers who do remixes. A number of rappers, including Jay-Z and Eminem, now release a cappella raps on their singles, in effect inviting others to remix their songs. Glenn Otis Brown, the executive director of the Creative Commons, a group that provides alternative licenses for creative works, calls this "a great example of our two-tiered copyright system. Labels are saying, 'If you do [a remix] on the underground scene, it's OK. But if it's so compelling that people trade it all over the Internet, then we're going to sue you.'"

But can such two-tier treatment survive? Mash-ups may be unstoppable. They are migrating to the mainstream with remarkable speed and popularity. An early sign of this was the illegal remix known as *The Grey Album* made by Brian Burton, a rapper who goes by the name Danger

Mouse, by remixing Jay-Z's *Black Album* with the Beatles' *White Album*. Released on file-sharing networks in early 2004, *The Grey Album* became an immediate, critically acclaimed hit. *Rolling Stone* called it "an ingenious hip-hop record that sounds oddly ahead of its time," and the *Boston Globe* called it "the most creatively captivating" album of the year.

When EMI Records, who holds the Beatles' rights, sent cease-and-desist letters to dozens of Web sites that offered downloads of The Grey Album, a protest was mounted on February 24, 2004—"Grey Tuesday"—when more than two hundred Web sites offered free—and illegal—downloads of the album. More than one million downloads were made, or more song tracks than represented by sales of the best-selling album at the time, Norah Jones's *Feels Like Home.*

The point of the protest, said organizers, was to show how the current legal environment gives the five major record labels a stranglehold over the types of musical creativity that can develop and be sold. "EMI isn't looking for compensation, they're trying to ban a work of art," said Rebecca Laurie of Downhill Battle, a music industry watchdog group that organized the protest. Nicholas Reville, cofounder of Downhill Battle, said, "Remixes and pastiche are a defining aesthetic of our era. How will artists continue to work if corporations can outlaw what they do? Artists, writers, and musicians have always borrowed and built upon each other's work. Now they have to answer to corporate legal teams."

If nothing else, mash-ups testify to the strong, spontaneous surges of creativity that naturally occur among artists and ordinary people even in the absence of intellectual property rights. The real challenge ahead is in finding better ways to honor such open creativity, which in the past has given us jazz, blues, and rap, while allowing artists to enjoy reasonable market rewards from their works.

Copyright Colonizes the Subconscious Mind

In declaring that "originality" is the preeminent trait of a creative work, copyright law often runs up against an embarrassing reality: sometimes great works are brilliant derivations. "In art," wrote George Bernard Shaw, "the highest success is to be the last of your race, not the first. Anybody, almost, can make a beginning; the difficulty is to make an end—to do what cannot be bettered." Without knowingly copying a predecessor, many artists nonetheless end up making remarkably similar versions of prior works. Great art can at once be an original and yet a copy.

Copyright law skirts past this paradox by invoking a Freudian sleight of hand, the doctrine of "subconscious copying." Although the doctrine has been around for more than seventy-five years, it was rarely applied until a federal court ruled that former Beatle George Harrison's 1969 song "My Sweet Lord" unlawfully copied the Ronald Mack song made famous in 1963 by the Chiffons, "He's So Fine."

The subconscious copying doctrine had its origins in 1924 when Judge Learned Hand was confronted by the credible claim of composer Jerome Kern that he had independently composed a song, "Kalua," that featured a passage known as an "ostinato" that was virtually identical to one that occurred in an earlier song, "Dardanella," by Fred Fisher. An ostinato was described to the court as a "constantly repeated figure, which produces the effect of a rolling underphrase for the melody, something like the beat of a drum or tom-tom, except that it has a very simple melodic character of its own." While the sequence of notes used in Kern's ostinato was traced to several classical works, the specific notes had apparently never been used in an ostinato before "Dardanella."

The conundrum facing the court was how Jerome Kern could both create something independently and yet copy it as well. Carl Jung famously theorized the existence of a "collective unconscious" that humans in all cultures draw upon to create strikingly similar myths and motifs. In theory, copyright law recognizes independent creation as an absolute defense against copyright infringement. But in practice, few judges or juries want to believe that the similarities occur innocently. There may be a deep psychic commons in human societies that at times, mysteriously, generates nearly identical creative works. Philosophically, copyright law does not want to hear about it. As Judge Hand declared:

Everything registers somewhere in our memories, and no one can tell what may evoke it. On the whole, my belief is that, in composing the accompaniment to the refrain of Kalua, Mr. Kern must have followed, probably unconsciously, what he had certainly often heard only a short time before. I cannot really see how else to account for a similarity, which amounts to identity. So to hold I need to reject his testimony that he was unaware of such a borrowing.

By invoking "subconscious copying"—the unwitting use of prior artistic works in new ones—the courts ingeniously found a way to punish the infringer without questioning his integrity. The courts could also uphold the fiction of immaculate originality in copyrighted works, and insist that originality trumps its eternal twin, creative imitation and transformation.

The subconscious copying doctrine lay dormant for nearly fifty years after Judge Hand's 1924 ruling partly because it was tethered to several stringent factual premises. A defendant had to have been exposed to the plaintiff's song. The two works had to be "substantially similar." And the period of time between an artist's exposure to the first work and the creation of the second (or in the law's formulation, "the degree of temporal remoteness") had to be short.

But with the George Harrison case, in 1983, these prerequisites for finding "subconscious copying" were relaxed. At trial, Harrison admitted that "He's So Fine" and "My Sweet Lord" did sound "strikingly similar." Even though Harrison had composed his song six years after first hearing the Chiffons' song, the appeals court held that copyright infringement had occurred.

The subconscious copying doctrine was stretched a few cubits further in a dispute between the Isley Brothers and crooner Michael Bolton and co-composer Andrew Goldmark. In 1990, Bolton and Goldmark composed "Love Is a Wonderful Thing," which Bolton recorded the next year. The song ended up as No. 49 in *Billboard*'s pop chart for 1991.

At the time, Bolton wondered aloud whether the song had already been written, asking Goldmark whether they were simply composing Marvin Gaye's "Some Kind of Wonderful." Bolton had good reason to suspect that he may have been treading on familiar ground: there were 129 songs called "Love Is a Wonderful Thing" registered with the U.S. Copyright Office at the time of the trial; 85 of them had been registered before 1964, when the Isley Brothers wrote and recorded a song with that title. (Titles of songs cannot be copyrighted.)

A jury hearing the case of *Three Boys Music Corp. v. Michael Bolton* ended up finding a "substantial similarity" between the two songs. The reasons cited were that both songs shared the same title hook phrase, a shifted cadence, instrumental figures, a verse/chorus relationship, and a fade ending. The court ruled that Bolton and Goldmark were guilty of copyright infringement even though the evidence of their exposure to the Isley Brothers' song was circumstantial. The court found that "it is entirely plausible that two Connecticut teenagers obsessed with rhythm and blues music could remember an Isley Brothers song that was played on the radio and television for a few weeks, and subconsciously copy it twenty years later."

The loosening standards for applying the subconscious copying doctrine are troubling for creative freedom. As one legal commentator put it:

No longer is the doctrine reserved for instances where access [to a prior work] is certain, similarity is substantial and temporal remoteness is low. . . . In light of [the Isley Brothers/Michael Bolton case], it seems that the mere spark of questionably substantial similarity between two works may spawn a flame of inference that a defendant copied a song he might have heard two decades before, and that flame may carry the day. . . . One might ask whether a work created independently of one's consciousness is really "copying."

And so copyright law extends property rights into the vast psychic and cultural commons known as the subconscious. In the wake of the Michael Bolton case, artists are understandably wary about the mere possibility of a subconscious copying lawsuit. Rather than risk huge legal fees and the personal anguish and publicity of such a suit, artists and their labels are more likely to just decline to release a song.

Now that old films, music, visual images, advertising, and ephemera are being resurrected and made available to contemporary consumers on all sorts of media, including the Internet, one can only imagine the train wreck of competing copyright claims that may be justified in the future by the subconscious copying doctrine. One trembles to contemplate the effects on creativity.

Copyrighting "Genetic Tunes"

As biotechnology has learned to unlock the secrets of the human genome and animal cloning, it has raised new questions about who shall own and control the information contained in DNA. While the courts have allowed the patenting of some genetic information, the idea of owning genes or species has been tremendously controversial. Should a private company be able to limit scientists from investigating specific types of cancer cells even if that inhibits the development of new treatments? What are the ethical—or competitive—implications of allowing anyone to own certain animal breeds or clones?

Entrepreneur Andre Crump came up with an ingenious end-run around all these patenting questions: *copyright* your DNA.

Normally, of course, DNA is not copyrightable because it is naturally occurring. It is not an "original work of authorship" as copyright law requires. But what if the long strings of molecules of DNA—the nucleotides comprised of adenine, guanine, thymine, and cytosine, and represented by the letters *A, G, T,* and *C*—could be converted into a musical tune? That tune would be unique and could itself be construed as an original work of authorship and, as such, be entitled to copyright protection.

In recent years, converting DNA into music has become something of a fad. According to *Wired News,* John Dunn, the founder of Algorithmic Arts, and his biologist wife, Mary Anne Clark, have "sonified" the DNA of vampire bats, slime molds, and sea urchins using the company's Bankstep software. They even released an album in 2001 called *Life Music,* featuring such "songs" as "Triose Phosphate Isomerase," "Beta-globin," "Alcohol Dehydrogenase," and "Collagen." The "tunes" have been described as having a New Age feel; one online catalog referred to it as "ambient music."

More recently, scientists at Ramon y Cajal Hospital in Madrid were fascinated with the possible links between music and genes, and so decided to translate DNA code into music by assigning the DNA units *A, G, T* and *C* to musical notes, and then turning DNA sequences into sheet music. It turns out that a yeast gene known as SLT2 has a triplet of nitrogen bases that appears several times in succession. In musical terms, this yields an "ostinato" whose sound is "a very sad part [of the DNA song], but a beautiful one," according to its "discoverer," Sanchez Sousa. Ten of the DNA tunes have been released as a CD, *Genoma Music.* (One wonders who should be considered the author of these "original works.")

But back to Andre Crump. His great insight was to see how the DNA-into-music software could offer an easy way to obtain property rights, via copyright law, for DNA sequences. Not only would an elusive realm of life be redefined as property, the legal protection would last for the lifetime of the "author" plus seventy years (or ninety-five years for corporate owners). In 2001, Crump founded the DNA Copyright Institute to offer

Is DNA an "original work of authorship"? Creative Time commissioned six artists to design paper coffee cups to spark public conversations about genetic research. This one (front and back are shown here) is by Larry Miller.

to identify the unique DNA Profile of a person or animal, and then copyright it. The cost: $1,500.

The idea is to establish a legal basis for asserting ownership of the DNA against any future infringers. "Clients can establish copyright protection guaranteeing legal recourse so that their personal DNA pattern cannot be duplicated in printed, electronic, photographic or biological form," the company claims. Crump warned that the copyrighting may not necessarily prevent someone from being cloned, but at least it would offer a legal remedy.

If that sounds far-fetched, Crump tried to entice would-be customers with dire futuristic scenarios of unauthorized cloning: "Imagine the biggest Tom Cruise fans around the world, fighting over the chance to procure his drinking glass for the possible DNA samples, or attempting to shake his hand so they can casually scratch a bit of epidermis in a DNA collection sortie. Imagine the sale and resale of not only this DNA, but embryos and other mish-mash made from this DNA in both legal and illegal labs."

Crump told ABC News: "Who's the most likely people to be cloned against their will? It's going to be the celebrities. It's going to be the superstar athletes, the superstar models, movie stars, television stars, musicians, singers." By having a copyrighted DNA Profile, celebrities could supposedly protect themselves against the unauthorized use of their likeness, in a quite literal sense. The DNA Copyright Institute also considers the breeders of orchids, cats, dogs, horses, and livestock to be its prime customers.

If the DNA Copyright Institute is one of the most enterprising ventures to commandeer copyright law to protect DNA, it is not the only one. Steven Miller, a high school biology teacher in Oakland, California, has devised what he calls the "poor person's DNA copyright." Here's how it works: Miller takes a photograph of each of his students while the student is licking a postage stamp. Each stamp is then put on an envelope containing the photograph of the student, and mailed to the student. The unopened letters, once received, constitute a kind of common-law copyright, argues Miller, because they represent a fixed expression of original authorship—the DNA of the person (the saliva residue on the stamp), a photograph of the individual, and a dated postmark.

It is too early to know if the courts will in fact recognize these fanciful extensions of copyright law. But why not? Since the first copyright law was enacted in 1790, granting protection to "maps, charts and books," Congress has expanded copyright law to cover etchings, sheet music, piano rolls, artistic lamp bases, sculpture, software code, architectural drawings, the Yellow Pages of a telephone book (but not the white pages), boat hull designs, and virtually any other creative act that can be reduced to a fixed, tangible medium. If a dash of creativity can now be combined with DNA to produce an original, tangible work of authorship, it is hard to discern any principled reason in legal history for withholding copyrights for DNA.

CHAPTER 2

Creativity and
Captive Images

Good artists copy, great artists steal.

    —Pablo Picasso

When you steal, steal with taste.

    —Muddy Waters, upon being told
    that Eric Clapton had played some
    of Muddy's riffs

T he modern painter Robert Motherwell once said, "Every intelligent painter carries the whole culture of modern painting in his head. It is his real subject, of which everything he paints is both an homage and a critique." His insight points to a dirty little secret of the visual arts—its inescapable reliance on appropriation. Who dares call it theft? That is, indeed, the question: Where will the legal boundaries be drawn to define which appropriations will be considered theft and which artistically justified?

Theft and *piracy* are not neutral descriptions, really, but epithets. The words falsely presume a consensus that certain appropriations are immoral. But in fact, the law is a hopeless muddle of arcane distinctions and conflicting judicial interpretations. Even where the law is somewhat clear, its practical application can generally be manipulated by those parties who can afford high-priced lawyers to intimidate the weak and game the system. Which is to say, not the average American.

It is not surprising, then, that visual artists often run afoul of copyright and trademark law. Any serious painter or filmmaker must comment on the images that suffuse her culture, and in the United States, those images are disproportionately advertising images, celebrity faces, corporate symbols, and famous works of art. If Campbell's soup cans, Disney characters, rock stars, and trademarked images are everywhere—on billboards, television, magazines, consumer products, advertisements, and more—then *of course* artists will need to refer to them if they hope their art will speak to the culture.

Appropriation is a standard operating practice for most creators, especially postmodern artists. It is, in truth, a necessary tool in art for social criticism; "art as theft," as one commentator puts it. Roy Lichtenstein, Claes Oldenburg, Robert Rauschenberg, Andy Warhol, and Larry Rivers are among the most celebrated artists of the twentieth century precisely because they appropriated and ingeniously recontextualized commercial images. Their appropriations were not simply mischievous (although they were often that); they were a crucial strategy for critiquing the values and sensibilities of mainstream culture.

Artists such as Keith Haring, Kenny Scharf, and Susan Pitt have used copyrighted cartoon characters in this manner. Sherrie Levine and Richard Prince have made names for themselves by rephotographing other people's work. Jeffrey Koons is renowned for his verbatim uses of advertising materials and parodies of tacky commercial images. Richard Hamilton, Peter Blake, James Rosenquist, Red Grooms, Barbara Krueger, and Jim Dine have used their appropriationist art to call attention to the closed, claustrophobic system of corporate symbols that define our culture. For many of these postmodern artists, the taking of someone else's image without consent—the "piracy"—is the very point. In their art, they deliberately want to subvert what they regard as the pretentious delusions of high art, such as originality and individual authorship.

Appropriationism is not especially new in art. Throughout the ages, artists have studied the old masters and taken whatever motifs or stylistic quotations they needed. No surprise, then, that some of the most notable art movements of the twentieth century—Dada, Constructivism, collage, Bauhaus art, and pop art—are unabashedly appropriationist. But now that so many images in our culture have commercial origins and ownership—they are legally marked off as *property*—the visual arts have settled into a simmering cold war with copyright and trademark law. The owners want near-absolute control over "their property," while artists invariably want to express the fullest range of human reactions without restriction, sometimes in offensive ways.

Are postmodern artists common thieves? The scholar Roxana Badin cautions us: "Appropriation should not be mistaken for plagiarism. By recontextualizing the image, the artist has, in fact, transformed and altered it in an attempt to force viewers to see the original work and its significance differently." When Andy Warhol endlessly repeated an image of Marilyn Monroe; when Picasso invoked and remade Manet's image of a firing squad executing prisoners; when Robert Rauschenberg used Morton Beebe's copyrighted photo in his work *Pull*, each artist was not simply copying; they were reinterpreting the image to make a point. Some appropriations function as homage, others as shorthand evocations of another time and place, still others as ridicule.

Artists who appropriate another artist's work rarely seek to "pass it off" as their own the way a counterfeiter might. Usually the appropriation is meant to transform a prior work into something new and give it new meaning. What copyright and trademark law so often fails to admit is that quoting prior works is not necessarily about imitation or passing off. Artists like to treat prior works as *cultural artifacts*—unique historical objects that can succinctly communicate specific feelings and meanings. The underground cartoonists who constituted themselves as the "Air Pirates" wanted to parody Mickey Mouse as a cynical, foul-mouthed corporate executive because it was a savagely effective way of rebutting Disney's myths of innocence (see pages 106–109). Jasper Johns appropriated the American flag for his seminal painting *Flag* to comment on our emotions toward the flag. Hans Haacke asks us to contemplate the corporate dominance of culture by using the symbols associated with the Mobil Oil Company and Philip Morris.

This chapter explores how copyright and trademark law frequently overreaches to prevent legitimate artistic expression, and in the process impoverishes our culture. Just because a work of art is famous and has great market value is no reason that it should be legally roped off from working artists. The images of corporations and prior art are part of our cultural commons; indeed, they are a part of our consciousness. The law exacts a cruel tyranny when it authorizes copyright and trademark owners to colonize our minds with their images, but then retains the right to control those intimate sectors of our shared culture and personal consciousness as private property. We may look and buy, but we must use only as directed.

By privatizing too much of our shared culture, the law forces artistic creation underground, into the realm of the illegal imagination. It then

arrogantly presumes that it is potent enough to regulate the powerful cur-
rents of artistic imagination—and that such regulation is desirable in the
first place.

Painting Mustaches on the *Mona Lisa*

The law professor Geri Yonover fantasizes about a hypothetical legal case,
Leonardo v. Duchamp, in which Leonardo da Vinci (1452–1519) sues Mar-
cel Duchamp (1887–1968) for his wicked parody of the *Mona Lisa* painting. Duchamp was a famous Dadaist who in 1915 painted a mustache on a
cheap replica of the *Mona Lisa* and dubbed the new creation "L.H.O.O.Q."
The letters are an aural pun: when pronounced in French, they sound
like "Elle a chaud au cul," which might be rudely translated as "She has a
hot ass." In English, L.H.O.O.Q. can be read as an acronym pronounced
"look."

Fair use? In the contemporary legal environment, probably not. Yonover imagines Leonardo suing Duchamp under the Visual Artists Rights
Act of 1990, a law that for the first time in U.S. copyright history recognized the moral rights of artists. Under the law, visual artists are legally
entitled to have their works properly attributed to them and protected
against mutilation and unauthorized modifications. In Yonover's imaginary
lawsuit, Leonardo could persuasively argue to a court that Duchamp's
mustache on the *Mona Lisa* intentionally distorted, mutilated, or modified
his work in a way that was "prejudicial to his . . . honor or reputation,"
which the statute prohibits. Leonardo would charge that the tasteless pun
simply makes the artistic rip-off more scurrilous.

But how should a court judge reputational damage? Yonover wonders
if it should be "that art galleries no longer give [Leonardo] single artist
shows, that the price of other *Mona Lisa*s in the lithograph series have
plummeted, that the *New York Times* art critic now views this series as
banal and an object of derision, that he can no longer get 'commissions'
to do portraits, that he has been asked to resign from the Valparaiso, Indi-
ana, Post-Renaissance Artists Society?"

Parody presents special challenges for copyright law because, in the
visual arts at least, parody tends to require a significant amount of literal
copying; minor quotations cannot evoke the original work. Duchamp's
L.H.O.O.Q. is essentially a stylized bit of graffiti on Leonardo's painstak-
ing work. One can imagine the indignant fulminations that modern-day

lawyers would bring to this "outrage"—"Duchamp is trading upon my client's hard-earned reputation!" "An obscure poseur is making money off my client's commercial success and visibility!"

In fact, something along these lines occurred in 1987 when Jeff Koons, the artist-provocateur, took a picture postcard of a couple holding eight puppies and decided to make a sculpture out of it. Koons sent the postcard, a 1980 image called *Puppies* by the California photographer Art Rogers, to an Italian foundry specifying how it should be turned into a sculpture—its dimensions, materials, the colors it should be painted, some minor changes in the people's expressions.

The resulting work, *String of Puppies*, was described by one commentator as "a couple with clown faces painted in garish colors with daisies in their hair. They are embracing eight gigantic blue puppies sporting bulbous noses. . . . Gone is the 'charming' and cuddly warmth of Rogers' photograph, and in its place is a garish, perhaps horrifying, perhaps hilarious image." *String of Puppies* was exhibited in Koons's show, "Banality Show," at the Sonnabend Gallery in New York City in 1988.

Rogers was not happy with the reinterpretation of his photograph in a different medium, and he sued Koons for copyright infringement. Koons claimed that his sculpture was a protected fair use of Rogers's *Puppies* image, but both the district court and the Second Circuit Court of Appeals heaped contempt on Koons's appropriation. They declared that the sculpture was primarily commercial in nature, and that Koons had acted in bad faith by eliminating the copyright notice on the Rogers postcard that he had sent to the foundry. While the circuit court acknowledged that *String of Puppies* might be an act of social criticism, it found that the sculpture was not enough of a parody to be entitled to a fair use defense: "It is not really the parody flag that Koons was sailing under, but rather the flag of piracy."

Copyright law has long recognized a "parody defense," but if a parody is too sly or subtle for the judicial eye, it is likely to be considered piracy, not art. For example, if the parody does not sufficiently comment on the underlying work (as determined by the courts), then it may not be legal. Generally, the most critical test is how much of the original work the parody uses. Is it just enough to "conjure up" the original in order to make fun of it, or is it a wholesale appropriation above and beyond what is "necessary" to the parody? If the "heart" of the work is taken, courts are generally reluctant to consider it fair use. In the visual arts, of course, appropriating the "heart" of a work is often essential to a parody. Duchamp had to use the entire *Mona Lisa*!

If appropriation and parody are venerable artistic traditions, some legal scholars contend that intellectual property law is fundamentally hostile to the very aesthetics of postmodernism. *That's* why so many lawsuits result! As Sharon Appel explains:

> Postmodernism is characterized by a rejection of the concept of objectivity and certainty, and of reality as static and objective, and an embracing, instead, of a fundamentally subjective world view. . . . Postmodern artists . . . speak in a symbolic language of quotations and allusions. . . . The style and philosophy of postmodernism are heavily dependent upon the practice of Appropriationism, which gives contemporary art its unique and irreverent flair. To the law, appropriation is simply copyright infringement, for which only minor exceptions are allowed through the doctrine of fair use.

Visual parodies, of course, are as perennial as art itself. Edouard Manet's *L'Exécution de Maximilien* (1867)—which itself echoes Goya's *Tres de Mayo*—was parodied by Pablo Picasso in *Massacres en Corée* (1950). The Manet painting shows a group of uniformed soldiers executing the prisoner. The Picasso painting preserves the same general alignment of figures as the famous Manet painting, but the execution in the Manet is far more personal and specific than the abstract, impersonal execution in the Picasso. Writes art theorist Linda Hutcheon: "Here the purpose seems to be to increase the horror and the drama through ironic contrast of plural nameless massacres with individual romantic execution."

Larry Rivers reworked the famous painting by Jacques-Louis David, *Napoleon in His Study*, and named the new version *The Greatest Homosexual*. Roy Lichtenstein drew upon the style and composition of Matisse's *Goldfish* painting by quoting it in the background of his *Still Life with Goldfish Bowl and Painting of a Golf Ball* painting. Tom Wesselmann borrowed the colors, pose, and general outline of Matisse's *Pink Nude* in his *Great American Nude #26*, a parody of erotic pinups.

Illegal works all? By the lights of contemporary copyright law, perhaps. But case law is not an especially reliable guide for the would-be parodist. As one scholar notes, case law about the parody defense is "a body of law that is arguably even more confused and inconsistent than that of fair use in general." The legal doctrines governing parody cannot be predictably applied; the aesthetic judgment of judges is highly variable; and the likelihood of a serious lawsuit by a litigant with deep pockets is unknowable. Artists may be excused for not knowing what is legal or not.

This has profound consequences in itself. Prudent artists will self-censor themselves to avoid legal liability and expensive litigation. Only the fearless, reckless, wealthy, or indigent are likely to test the limits of the parody defense.

Barry Kite, a collage artist known for his twisted social and political parodies, has at least some of those traits. Calling his oeuvre "Aberrant Art," Kite freely appropriates images from famous artworks, news photos, magazines, and miscellaneous commercial sources to create what he considers "visual poems." Kite uses an X-Acto knife and a laser printer to piece together "found images" into hand-colored collages, many of which he later reproduces in art books and greeting cards. He sells much of his work at art festivals around the country.

Kite's best-selling image is *Sunday Afternoon, Looking for My Car*, which combines *A Sunday Afternoon on the Island of La Grande Jatte*, by Seurat, with a vast parking lot filled with cars. A taste of Kite's bawdy style can be found in a collage that combines two watchmen from Rembrandt's *Night Watch* with a massive woman's bottom taken from François Boucher's eighteenth-century nude, *Reclining Girl*, to form a new piece, entitled *Distracted by Intense Conversation and Personal Problems, Captain Frans Banning Cocq and Lt. Willem van Ruytenburgh Wander Up the Ass of Louis XV's Mistress*.

Appropriations of prior works often get a pass in fine art because they are seen as one-off products that will not receive much visibility or mass-market revenue. The story changes if artists decide to commercialize their works through full-scale reproductions, books, or greeting cards. Then the trademark and copyright owners begin to take notice and call their attorneys. In Kite's case, the launching of his greeting card line in 1992 elicited a stream of cease-and-desist letters.

One of the first came from the Vatican's collection agency, the Bridgeman Art Library, in London. "Because I use an image from the Sistine Chapel in one of my collages, *The Sistine Bowl-Off*—which depicts one of Michelangelo's naked figures bowling—they said I owed them a royalty," recalled Kite. "I wrote them back, explaining they were way off-base, that my work, as a parody, is legal under Section 107 of the Copyright Act,

Barry Kite's appropriationist painting *Sunday Afternoon, Looking for My Car* is his best-selling image.

the fair use section. They said my work wasn't a parody." Kite said he ignored them and never paid anything.

Two other images that elicited nasty letters from attorneys were *Grateful Sailor*, which takes the famous Eisenstadt photo of a World War II sailor kissing a girl in Times Square on VE Day, and substitutes for the girl the original Coca-Cola rendition of Santa Claus. Another photocollage, *Naughty Boy*, takes the memorable photo of a Vietnamese soldier shooting a prisoner through the head at point-blank range, but instead of the actual victim, Kite uses a Norman Rockwell image of a naughty boy surrounded by a crowd of gaping Rockwellian townspeople.

"These images are within the collective consciousness and are fair game," Kite once explained to an interviewer. "My work parodies art to make a point, not to make money. It plays with people's perception of well-known art and makes them think. I manipulate the concept, and on one level, the original art ceases to exist." Whether Kite's works should be regarded as "art" (and deserving of legal protection) or "commercial products" (deserving of less or no protection) remains a vexing question.

Both the Associated Press and Time Warner sent Kite cease-and-desist letters charging infringement in the *Naughty Boy* photo. "I thought I'd let them figure out who actually owned the photo before dealing with them," recalled Kite. "Time Warner sent three or four letters, each one on stationery with a bigger letterhead. Eventually they gave up."

Kite regards the whole cease-and-desist ritual as an expensive distraction. His epiphany came when he discovered that an artist had copied one of *his* images. "I had my lawyer send him a cease-and-desist letter," Kite said, "and the guy ignored me. So I said to my lawyer, 'What, no follow up?' And he said, 'Well, we can sue him and then you'll *both* have legal fees to pay.' "

Kite confesses that he "used to quake when going to my post office box for fear of getting mail from lawyers." But then he got past his anxieties and just did what he wanted: "My whole art form is found imagery. I couldn't limit it to just non-copyrighted images." He added that determining who owns the copyright is next to impossible in any case: "Who owns the image—The artist? The museum? The artist's estate? A book publisher? I don't want to be a part of that. Sometimes an artist just has to do what he has to do."

If Kite is nonchalant toward copyright enforcement, it may be because he has "the best legal protection possible—no assets."

Illegal Art to Express Illicit Ideas

Artists tend to be lone wolves, rarely coming together to take collective action. So it was significant when several dozen of them joined together to contribute works to a provocative act of civil disobedience against intellectual property (IP) law.

Billed as "Illegal Art: Freedom of Expression in the Corporate Age," the exhibit toured New York, Chicago, Philadelphia, Washington, D.C., and other cities in 2002 and 2003. While the works ranged from films and videos to songs and illustrations, the common denominator was their actual or apparent illegality under copyright and trademark law. But unlike most infringements of IP law, which tend to be incidental and innocent, the works of the "Illegal Art" exhibit were deliberate appropriations of corporate symbols expressly designed to ridicule and criticize.

The anticorporate point of view was rather hard to miss. Kieron Dwyer produced a parody of the Starbucks Coffee green mermaid logo,

Heidi Cody's installation art *American Alphabet* consists of light boxes of letters based exclusively on letters from corporate logos. The 2000 work was featured in the "Illegal Art" exhibit mounted by *Stay Free!* and the Internet Archive.

renamed *Consumer Whore*. Tom Forsythe's *Food Chain Barbie* photographs featured nude Barbie dolls entangled perilously in kitchen appliances and immersed in food (see page 89). Diana Thorneycroft offered up the *Sesame Street* character Bert hanging from a noose and Barney Rubble of *The Flintstones* with a bloody gash in his head. Heidi Cody made a point about the corporate influence of culture by creating a sampler, *American Alphabet*, consisting of letters taken from corporate logos (such as the "P" from a Pez candy wrapper).

"Illegal Art" was the brainchild of Brewster Kahle, the director of the Internet Archive, and Carrie McLaren, the editor of *Stay Free!* magazine. Their idea was to use "forbidden" artworks to demonstrate just how far intellectual property law reaches into people's everyday lives. It is not permissible, for example, to show Disney characters in naughty sexual situations or to depict Binky the Rabbit (from Matt Groening's *Life in Hell* comic strip) punching the Trix rabbit.

To date, no corporation has sued the "Illegal Art" exhibit for infringements of their copyrights or trademarks. Perhaps they realize that the publicity alone would be counterproductive for their brand images. In a sense, all of the works in the exhibit are stand-ins for countless other works that never got made in the first place because of the chilling effects of copyright and trademark law.

In a twist of synchronicity, at the same time that the "Illegal Art" exhibit was touring, an art exhibit halfway around the world, in Istanbul, Turkey, was exploring the power of the icon in human societies and the necessity of cultural sharing. The exhibit, "Copy It, Steal It, Share It," curated by Michele Thursz in collaboration with Anne Barlow, looked at icons "as archetypal structures, as sources of knowledge that generate an ongoing contemporary dialogue."

A painting in the exhibit, *Financial Times Silhouette*, shows the silhouettes of men and women, as if from Greek pottery, superimposed on the salmon-colored newsprint of the *Financial Times*. Another work, *Play on Time*, shows a video loop of the moon landing of 1969; the cultural reality of the moon landing seems to exist only in the endless repetitions of the NASA images.

The deeper point of "Copy It, Steal It, Share It" is that humans inexorably make culture by copying, stealing, and sharing their icons with one another. It may seem as though "the spirit of culture has been hijacked," writes the exhibit curator, but in truth "the nature of communication is not to be proprietary." Cultural icons are a source of knowledge and a way for people to converse with each other, a process that can exclude no one: "the gesture of borrowing is intact in the practice of communication."

The Untold Legal Story
behind Andy Warhol's Art

Visual artists who want to comment on our highly commercial culture face a special problem: many of the images that they want to quote, critique, or mock are trademarks. Needless to say, corporate America is not about to let just any artist use its valuable logos, cartoon characters, and product packaging. Such imagery is worth literally billions of dollars in consumer goodwill, and small armies of lawyers are dedicated to protecting this cultural turf against trademark "dilution" or "tarnishment." Yet in an open, democratic culture, why should any company be allowed to shut down artistic commentary about imagery that is so influential and pervasive in our daily consciousness?

One of the few great American artists to venture repeatedly into this complex legal-artistic thicket was Andy Warhol. A commercial illustrator who became an artist at the vanguard of pop art, Warhol was fascinated with the intersection of commerce and American culture. By recasting some of the most banal objects and images of everyday life as fine art, he deftly called attention to the genuine artistry and the crass motives of commercial life.

Though Warhol may be most famous for his series of Brillo soap-pad boxes and Campbell's soup can paintings, his art dealt with a wide spectrum of mass culture. He was especially attracted to great American icons from the worlds of politics, entertainment, and business. But because many of these icons—Mickey Mouse, Chanel, Aunt Jemima, the Wicked Witch of the West—are proprietary images, Warhol often had to negotiate special deals with rights-holders in order to make his art. Remarkably, the legal backstory of Warhol's art has received very little attention.

One of Warhol's first attempts to reinterpret someone else's imagery was a series of paintings of flowers that was based on a photograph by Patricia Caulfield. When Caulfield learned of Warhol's use of her photograph, she sued him. He eventually settled, paying her $6,000 and royalties on the print edition of *Flowers*. Ron Feldman, a friend and a gallery owner who exhibited much of Warhol's work, recalled in 2003, "I think it [the Caulfield lawsuit] shook him up. He always assumed that he was able to just take images and transform them into art because he's an artist and could get away with that."

On Warhol's behalf, in the 1980s, Feldman was often the one to investigate the legal complications of an envisioned painting or print. He would discuss the artistic, legal, and economic ramifications of using a given image with Warhol and his business manager, Fred Hughes. For a series that Warhol wanted to paint, *Ten Portraits of Jews of the 20th Century*, Feldman took on the laborious task of locating the rights-owners of each of the photographs on which Warhol's paintings would be based. In the case of Franz Kafka, the photographer had likely died in the Holocaust, but a book publisher held the photograph in its archives and gave permission for a small fee. Warhol made his print of Gertrude Stein from a photograph found in the Bettmann Archives, which he rendered to relate to Picasso's famous cubist portrait. Trude Fleischmann provided, without charge, a signed photo of her famous photographic portrait of Einstein.

If clearing the rights was sometimes time-consuming and difficult, Warhol's *Myths* portfolio required the most work of all. The ten silkscreens of this series—*Superman*, *Howdy Doody*, *Uncle Sam*, *The Star* [Greta Garbo], *Mammy*, *The Wicked Witch of the West*, and others—featured Warhol renditions of American icons. Since Warhol had by this time become a renowned artist, the rights-holders were inclined to grant permission because any Warhol version of their trademarked image would only enhance its commercial value. Warhol's image for *The Star*, based on a studio photo of Greta Garbo by a famous Hollywood photographer, Clarence Bull, required studio permission. Superman's image required permission from DC Comics, a division of Warner Bros.

For his painting of the Witch, Warhol approached Margaret Hamilton, the actress who played that role in *The Wizard of Oz*. At this point in legal history, the persona rights to the character were apparently not strictly owned by either the film studio or L. Frank Baum, the author of the book. (This changed in 1981 when the widow of Bela Lugosi prevailed against Universal Studios in a lawsuit that gave her control of the persona rights to Dracula, which Lugosi had made famous in a series of movies decades earlier.) In the end, Hamilton agreed to model for Warhol in character, provided he made some special copies of the print for her; no money changed hands. The Dracula character that Warhol made for the *Myths* series was not based on Lugosi's version of the character but rather on an employee who dressed up and modeled as Dracula.

For his *Myths* portfolio, Warhol very much wanted to paint Aunt Jemima, the seemingly fictional character associated with Quaker Oats pancake mix, syrup, and oatmeal. Aunt Jemima, of course, was a trademarked version of the racist stereotype—the stout, jovial black kitchen servant whose life appeared to revolve around serving the family of her white master or employer. Quaker had, in fact, based its image on American history. "Aunt Jemima" was the name given to the female counterpart of "Uncle Tom" on Southern plantations.

"We wrote Quaker for permission to use this image in our series," said Feldman. "Quaker sent us back a threatening letter that said if we dared to do that, they would certainly take legal action. They definitely had

Some companies found that Andy Warhol's versions of their corporate logos helped freshen them up. Paramount incorporated some of Warhol's special coloring into a new version of its white-capped mountain logo. Chanel ended up buying the rights to use the actual Warhol version of its famous perfume bottle.

Warhol gambled that neither Van Heusen nor Ronald Reagan would sue for this interpretation of a 1950s advertisement because it would only publicize a joke at their expense.

trademarked their packaging, but they probably didn't want anyone to call attention to the fact that their product had been subliminally changed in the marketplace over the years. Aunt Jemina was no longer a big black-faced lady; slowly over a period of time she had become a thinner, *reddish* faced person—sorta black, but sorta reddish. She was younger and had a more 'with it' bandana on her head."

Rather than risk litigation with Quaker, Warhol and Feldman came up with an imaginative solution. Feldman had seen a charismatic black singer, Sylvia Williams, at the Village Gate in Manhattan and thought she would make a terrific model for the image. With some trepidation, Feldman called her, explained the legal complications with Quaker Oats, and asked if she would pose for Warhol. As Feldman recalled it, "She became fantastically brilliant and energized, and said, 'Are you kidding? You put *me* on the stand [in a court trial]! They cannot own my heritage!' " Williams was incensed that any company would claim to "own" Aunt Jemima and was only too willing to pose for Warhol.

In the end, Warhol changed the name of his print to *Mammy* not just to avoid a legal skirmish with Quaker, but because he concluded that the real myth he was painting was perpetuated not only in Quaker's product but in the character of Mammy popularized through *Gone with the Wind*.

For decades, the most prevalent popular image of Santa Claus in American culture derived from a commercial illustration by Haddon Sundblom, which appeared in Coca-Cola advertisements in the 1930s. Warhol wanted to include this image in his *Myths* series, but again, the rights-holder, Sundblom's widow, refused. (All American children should be grateful that Coca-Cola did not claim a trademark or copyright in this Santa Claus at the time, or the popular culture surrounding Christmas might be different!) Unable to use the "Coke Santa," Warhol ended up hiring a model to pose as Santa Claus. Feldman was disappointed that the image looks more like a pirate than the iconic (Coca-Cola) Santa Claus.

Andy Warhol's biggest coup as an interpreter of commercial culture is surely his series of Mickey Mouse prints and paintings. A little-known fact about Mickey is that his features were an amalgamation of other animal cartoon characters at the time, which Disney animators had skillfully synthesized. "Steamboat Willie," a character in a 1928 animated short, was Mickey Mouse's first appearance. In the intervening years, Mickey has become less of a cartoon character and more of a genial corporate spokesman for the Disney Company. Naturally, the company jealously protects the trademarked Mickey from anyone who might "tarnish" him.

Why, then, would Disney possibly consent to Andy Warhol doing a rendition of Mickey Mouse? Because Disney realized that there could be no better affirmation of Mickey Mouse's iconic status in American culture than for Warhol to "do Mickey." What better lionization of Disney's corporate identity could the company ask for? A Warhol Mickey would affirm Disney's and Mickey's cultural preeminence while giving Mickey a hip, stylized dimension. For Warhol's part, obtaining permission to do Mickey Mouse was the equivalent to "owning" a part of him. Warhol would in effect become a business partner with Disney in owning a special class of Mickey Mouse images.

Warhol was fortunate in being able to negotiate the deal with Pete Smith, an elderly attorney working for Disney who understood these larger implications. At first, Disney wanted a royalty on every sale of Warhol's Mickey images, but Feldman rejected that plan as too complicated and impractical. Ultimately, Warhol paid a small amount of money up front, agreed to make some special prints for Disney, and agreed not to do a sexual or denigrating version of Mickey. Disney in turn provided Warhol with some early images of Mickey from its archives.

Warhol's *Mickey Mouse* is a fairly straight-up version, but with a few artistic tweaks and subtleties, including an unusual cropping. "Andy wanted this to be something you could hang in your kid's room or your living room," said Feldman. "It had to be elegant in many ways, and yet it still had to have the child-like qualities to it. When you look at this, the furthest thing from your mind is commerce. Andy understood exactly what this was about."

Warhol and Feldman shared the rights to the Warhol Mickeys, but Disney had a stake as well. By agreement, Disney could not prohibit Warhol from using the images for his own promotional purposes, but any other uses, such as an advertisement, required Disney's consent. "Depending upon how you look at it," said Feldman, "Disney gave up a 50 percent interest in Mickey Mouse in whatever images Andy made. And he made more than this one! We have trial proofs in many, many colors."

This rare joint ownership in images of Mickey Mouse caused problems for Warhol when he sought to take one print into Japan for an exhibit. Japanese customs officials immediately banned its entry because the rights to use Mickey Mouse's image in Japan were strictly controlled by a Disney licensee there. After intervention by Disney's Pete Smith, the Warhol print was allowed to enter Japan.

The cultural cachet that Warhol brought to Mickey Mouse was vindicated in 1983, on the sixtieth anniversary of the Disney Company. To celebrate the occasion and buff its image, the company published a special advertising supplement in *Life* magazine with Mickey Mouse on the cover—*Warhol's* Mickey. In a rare turnabout, Disney had to ask someone else, Warhol, if it could use an image of Mickey Mouse. Naturally, Warhol consented. He did not ask for a fee.

Unlike most artists who are careful not to mix their art and commercial interests, Warhol consistently got away with combining them. A whole series of Warhol prints, *Ads* (1985), drew directly from corporate logos and advertisements: the Mobil Pegasus trademark, the Paramount film studios logo, a Chanel perfume bottle, a Volkswagen print ad, the Apple Computers logo, a Van Heusen shirt advertisement featuring Ronald Reagan.

Once again, because Warhol was Warhol, the companies involved gave their consent to let him use their trademarks. They realized that Warhol would give their logos and corporate images a cultural validation that no amount of money could buy. He also gave the images that the companies owned an artistic "freshening" that *they* could then appropriate. For example, Paramount's logo, the white-capped mountain set against a roseate sky, was later modified to reflect some of Warhol's special coloring, said Feldman.

Chanel apparently tried to do the same thing in its advertisements, *almost* incorporating a yellow line that Warhol had added to the bottom of its perfume bottle. (The company later bought the rights to use the actual Warhol version in its ads.) Recently, Mobil began reintroducing its Pegasus logo.

As for the Van Heusen ads featuring Reagan—"Van Heusen Century shirts won't wrinkle . . . ever!"—the company had the legal right to prevent Warhol from making his print, but Warhol and Feldman knew that, as a practical matter, neither Van Heusen nor the president would wish to bring unwanted attention to ads that amounted to a joke—the president of the United States selling wash-and-wear shirts.

Warhol was not unaware of the productive synergies that could be had from mixing his art with commercialism. He purchased the rights to use an ad featuring James Dean promoting the movie *East of Eden* to Japanese audiences. The rights-holder, the Curtis Licensing Company, makes money by keeping famous images alive in culture by promoting their use. Warhol's artistic use of the James Dean image was both art and a good business deal.

It can be argued that Andy Warhol's encounters with intellectual property law represent a special case—the exception that proves the rule. His reputation, artistic skill, and market clout enabled him to negotiate with wealthy corporations on an equal if not superior footing. It did not hurt that his images did not directly criticize or confront company products, logos, and characters; any commentary was more subtle, if not straight "reporting" of the prevailing imagery of our times. For artists with other agendas or lesser reputations, the normal rules of copyright and trademark law would apply. But an artist of Warhol's singular stature and artistic philosophy could negotiate around the rules that govern everyone else.

Feldman confesses to be concerned about the tightening noose of copyright and trademark control: "The idea that artists have the right to fair use is more under siege than ever," he said. "There is so much riding on corporate images that protection has been ratcheted up. They want more, more, more. Every CEO that's in these companies is now inheriting either a tired list or an about-to-be-retired list. They have to give [their trademarked images] a good spanking to get value out of them, and they don't want anyone to disparage them. So they're definitely tightening the noose on artists who might make a commentary."

The best artists are not afraid to venture into legal controversy, Feldman insists. But he admits, "Andy was both a regular case and a special case—depending upon how you want to argue it."

The Dubious Calder Monopoly on Mobiles

Does Alexander Calder—or more accurately, his estate—have a perpetual monopoly on the creation and display of giant mobiles? While the law has not rendered a judgment on this issue, Calder's estate has made its own claims to own monumental mobiles, and compliant art museums have legitimized those claims by capitulating to the estate's demands.

The issue arose in 1998 when the National Gallery of Art in Washington, D.C., hosted the debut of the first major showing of Calder's work in twenty-two years. The 270-piece collection then traveled on to the San Francisco Museum of Modern Art, the Whitney Museum of American Art in New York, and the Phillips Collection in Washington, D.C.

The Calder estate attached a significant condition to its loan of the works. For the duration of the Calder exhibition, the San Francisco Museum of Modern Art would have to remove mobiles made by other artists from its gift shop. The stipulation was not needed for the exhibition's visit to the Whitney and the Phillips because each had already removed mobiles from their shops permanently. (The Whitney had a new Calder gallery and the Phillips had two Calder stabiles on loan from the artist's family.) Both museums feared that the public would not differentiate Calder mobiles from those by other artists or would assume that the Calder estate had licensed or endorsed the other works.

Regina Stewart, the executive director of the New York Artists Equity Association, expressed a common artistic judgment when she told the *New York Times*, "Calder basically created a medium." But does that mean he and his heirs or assignees could own the medium in perpetuity? Stewart likened the estate's demands to saying, "Don't use acrylic paint because I'm the first artist to use it."

Ultimately, the ability of the Calder estate to make its demands stick was based on its ability to withhold or loan Calder works. Lori Fogarty, the director for curatorial affairs at the San Francisco Museum of Modern Art, conceded as much when she told the *Times*, "We are sympathetic to the artist who feels his work is being displaced. But ultimately, we were more sympathetic to the Calder family. When we are going to an artist's estate and asking to borrow 100 works and relying on their generosity, we feel very sympathetic."

The lawyer for the Calder estate, Ralph Lerner, tried to reassure the world by striking a magnanimous tone. The estate did not intend to sue other mobile artists, attempt to confiscate their works, or prevent them from selling elsewhere, he said. "We are bending over backward to be reasonable to everybody."

But when other practitioners of the art of mobiles and stabiles cannot exhibit or market their works in the same museums as a Calder, it is no wonder that mobile-making today more or less remains a one-person monopoly. No wonder, also, that it is a moribund field of artistry.

Old Man Potter Locks Up *It's a Wonderful Life*

It is an article of faith in copyright law that "propertizing" a work enhances its value and distribution. A work that enters the public domain is presumptively worthless because no one will have the incentive to do anything with it. Yet the bizarre journey of the film *It's a Wonderful Life* suggests that copyright protection can be a serious impediment to society realizing full value from a visual work.

The Frank Capra movie, starring James Stewart and Donna Reed, was a box-office flop when it was first released in 1946. It was such a dud, in fact, that Liberty Films, the studio that produced it, never renewed the registration for the copyright (then a requirement for copyright protection). The film therefore entered the public domain in 1976.

Or so everybody thought. Scores of television stations around the country began to show *It's a Wonderful Life* at Christmastime because it was a heartwarming tale that cost nothing to air. Soon the film was ubiquitous at the holiday season.

In a strange turn of events, a subsidiary of Spelling Entertainment, which had bought Liberty Films, changed its mind in 1996 about the public-domain status of *It's a Wonderful Life*. Despite the failure to renew the copyright of the overall film, Spelling claimed that the short story that was the basis for the film, and the film's musical score, were still under copyright protection, and that, therefore, the film had *not* entered the public domain. Spelling warned broadcast stations that they risked legal action if they aired *It's a Wonderful Life* without permission.

The similarities between the book and the film are so few that a court may or may not agree with Spelling Entertainment's claim. But since no TV station has wanted to risk a lawsuit with Spelling, the Christmas tradition of airing *It's a Wonderful Life* (without worrying about paying copyright tribute) essentially ended. No court has ruled on the actual legal status of the movie's copyright protection, so the film may still be a public-domain work as far as anybody knows. But for practical purposes, given Spelling's asserted ownership and apparent willingness to go to court, *It's a Wonderful Life* has been snatched from the public domain.

It's as if Old Man Potter had actually taken over the Bailey Building and Loan Company and put George Bailey out of business. Another Christmas classic comes to mind—*How the Grinch Stole Christmas*.

CHAPTER 3

Appropriating the People's Culture

[F]ew, if any, things . . . are strictly new and original throughout. Every book in literature, science and art, borrows, and must necessarily borrow.

—Justice Story in *Emerson v. Davis* (1845),
which first recognized the fair use
doctrine in copyright law

I s it legal to have sexy daydreams about *Star Trek*'s Captain Kirk and share them in writing with others? Can a company appropriate a folk tradition and then claim it as private property? Do the members of online gaming communities have any moral or legal rights in the fictional characters and artifacts that they create? This chapter explores the strange anomalies that occur when copyright and trademark law becomes so dominant that ordinary "people's culture"—the everyday creativity and sharing that occur in human communities—becomes stigmatized or illegal.

For most of human history, the human imagination has been unfettered. Creativity has arisen and flowed among people, and within communities, without anyone claiming stories, songs, or images as private property. The idea of anyone *owning* whaling songs, folk stories, or quilting patterns would strike the people of the eighteenth and nineteenth centuries as absurd, or at least antisocial. Indeed, such communal ownership and sharing was and is part of the beauty of folk music, fairy tales, classical myths, ethnic dances, handicrafts, and native traditions. They flourish on their own, without money, contracts, lawyers, stores, or advertising.

The rise of markets and the commercial mass media in the twentieth century brought with it a new ethic of ownership and control of culture. For the most part, film, television, and radio have enjoyed a benign coexistence with folk culture, even if many companies (most notably, Disney) have built valuable empires by poaching and "repurposing" public-domain material.

Now the predatory ethic is careening out of control. Not only have the commercial media largely overwhelmed vernacular culture, they seem to regard it as a form of unfair competition. How dare people create their own works from existing shards of culture without paying! How dare people *share* their "derivative creations" without obtaining permission from the "original" creator!

Folk traditions are routinely filched by commercial players, which is fine as far as it goes; the public domain *should* be available to all, even companies. What rankles is the substitution effect: some private companies expropriate folk culture, claim exclusive ownership over it, and then (because of their market power) effectively supplant it with their proprietary mass-media derivative.

As the Soviet Union in its prime showed, the supervision of acceptable expression pushes the meaning-making process underground, warping it in the bargain. A similar process is at work today as overly broad intellectual property rights suppress the free imagination and the free flow of culture. When people cannot gain access to prior creative works, it should not be surprising that the sorts of creativity that do result tend to be more artistically safe, homogeneous, and sterile. Artists who wish to make bold, daring, and idiosyncratic works find it easier to flee to subterranean venues than to risk crippling encounters with the law.

"A culture could not exist if all free riding were prohibited," writes legal scholar Wendy Gordon. "Culture *is* interdependence, and requiring each act of dependency to render an accounting would destroy the synergy on which cultural life rests." Part of the problem is that copyright and trademark law, as a matter of principle, declares that *individuals* are solely responsible for the value associated with creative works. Members of the public are cast as passive consumers who have nothing creative of their own to contribute. Only media businesses create valuable (read profit-making) culture, an ethos reflected in a now-retired tagline for Disney: "The company that taught you how to laugh."

My friend the comedian-philosopher Emily Levine deftly deflates the conceit of romantic authorship when she tells her audiences: "If you liked the show, give yourself a hand. Your response helps me shape and refine it. Although, if the show becomes a big hit, I'm not paying you a penny." The law gives creators the right to control and monetize all the value that flows from their works—even if the works themselves derive from prior works. The public's role in giving works cultural meaning and economic value goes uncredited.

The cultural theorist Rosemary J. Coombe makes the point that a trademark can become valuable only if there is widespread word of mouth and a social acceptance of its meaning, often known in the law as "goodwill." Yet the law in effect grants all legal control over a trademark's goodwill to its private owner. It presumes that the "secondary meanings" associated with a trademark were caused only by the owner's marketing investment. The public's role in creating and sustaining a trademark's cultural meaning is deemed negligible, and people have few clear rights to use trademarked characters or symbols, even for noncommercial purposes.

A war over the control of culture is being waged here. Companies increasingly assert a private monopoly over public meanings. Yet people in a free society have their own ideas of what needs to be said and in what manner. Shall cultural symbols (and meanings) be strictly controlled by those with property-like rights in them, or shall they circulate more freely, as befits an open society? As the stories below show, a crush of expansive property claims in knowledge and creativity is crowding out the public interest.

Vaudeville Comedy: Appropriation Is the Seed of Originality

Groucho Marx hurled some memorable zingers at Warner Bros. attorneys when they objected to the title of a planned Marx Brothers film, *A Night in Casablanca* (see page 111). Too bad that the later owners of Groucho's copyrights did not take the same approach to the producers of a Broadway play that parodied Hollywood films, using the Marx Brothers as characters. The play, whose title was *A Day in Hollywood, A Night in the Ukraine*, spoofed Hollywood movie musicals of the 1930s and hilariously imagined how the Marx Brothers might have interpreted Chekhov's short play *The Bear*.

The owners of the copyrights and publicity rights for the work of Groucho, Chico, and Harpo Marx (all of whom had died by this time) were not happy with the new production; it used the Marx Brothers' names and likenesses without permission or compensation. They sued the producers of *A Day in Hollywood, A Night in the Ukraine* in federal district court, and prevailed in a 1981 ruling. The court declared the play to be an imitative work lacking in "significant value as pure entertainment" and therefore not protected by the First Amendment.

An editorial writer for *Fortune* magazine, no critic of property rights, scoffed at the idea that the highly original play could be legally considered an "imitation." He pointed out that the court itself had made "the self-undermining qualification that the imitation comes 'in a new situation with new lines.' In the immortal words of Rufus T. Firefly, the Groucho character in *Duck Soup*: 'A four-year-old child could understand this. ... Run out and find me a four-year-old child.'"

A court of appeals was summoned instead. It declared that, under California law at the time, rights of publicity do not descend after death. (The copyright issues were not addressed.) After great expense, the court got it right, but only by showing that the real problem is not variable adjudication of the law, but the law itself. The legal standards for publicity rights are vague or simply tautological. "In a sense, the value of this property [*A Day in Hollywood, A Night in the Ukraine*] stems from the fact that the law recognizes it and protects it," the Duke law professor David Lange wrote in his landmark law review article, "Recognizing the Public Domain."

Why should the law be so stubbornly ignorant about the imperatives of parody? Groucho himself admitted that the Marx Brothers were a derivative creation incubated on the vaudeville circuit through exposure to dozens of other zany acts:

The average [comedy] team would consist of a straight man and a comic. The straight man would sing, dance or possibly do both. And the comedian would steal a few jokes from other acts and find a few in the newspapers and comic magazines. They would then proceed to play small-time vaudeville theaters, burlesque shows, night clubs and beer gardens. If the comic was inventive, he would gradually discard the stolen jokes and the ones that died and try out some of his own. In time, if he was any good, he would emerge from the routine character he had started with and evolve into a distinct personality of his own. This has been my experience and also that of my brothers, and I believe this has been true of most of the other comedians.

Professor David Lange astutely noted that "what Groucho is saying in this passage is that although he and his brothers began as borrowers they ended as inventors. . . . It is a central failing in the contemporary intellectual property literature and case law that that lesson, so widely acknowledged, is so imperfectly understood." Lange, quoting from a book by J. DiMeglio, *Vaudeville, U.S.A.*, goes on to exhume the history of vaudeville comedy and the rampant "piracy" that was at its core:

Ben Blue was once accosted by W. C. Fields, himself notorious for lifting lines, and was accused of stealing a routine. Blue called Fields a liar and other performers finally convinced Fields that he had originally stolen the material from Blue. In an open letter in *Variety*, Bert Lahr accused Joe E. Brown of having stolen the Lahr character. Though Brown never replied, Sam Sidman, an old-time Dutch comedian, did, angrily. He claimed Lahr had stolen the character from him and not only that, but Sidman had stolen it from Sam Bernard. "I admit it, why don't you?" demanded Sidman of Lahr.

The lifting of material from other comics was a way of life in vaudeville, writes DiMeglio: "As Benny Rubin related, 'Mel Klee did Al Herman, Marty May did Jack Benny . . . Sid Marion did Jack Pearl [and] there were more.' "

Copyright law nurtures the fiction that authorship is solely a matter of individual originality. In truth, as the history of virtually any artistic movement confirms, originality is nearly always wrapped up in a larger creative and social community. Every artist "borrows," if only to get started and learn to experiment. The borrowing can be blatant and intentional; subtle and unconscious; credited or uncredited; or seemingly similar because it uses the conventions of the genre. Arguably, this is an inevitable, recurring process for any artist seeking to enter a creative community. Once an artist becomes established, however, strict and absolute copyright protection suddenly seems like a very attractive deal—even if it means "pulling up the ladder" that newcomers need to develop themselves.

This more or less describes the United States' shifting stance toward copyright law over time. In the eighteenth century, the nation brazenly allowed American printers to publish popular British authors without obtaining their consent or paying them. But once the United States became an economic powerhouse in its own right, based in no small part on its free access to others' work, it became a zealous champion of a full-scale copyright lockdown. *Plus ça change . . .*

Shakespeare the Imitator

Even though Mark Twain was a strong advocate of broad copyright protection, he admitted that "substantially all ideas are second-hand, consciously or unconsciously drawn from millions of sources . . . ; whereas there is not a rag of originality about them." While Twain obviously brought considerable creativity to the writing of *Huckleberry Finn*, literary critics have long compared the story to Homer's *Odyssey*, which itself is but a single version of multiple versions that circulated in oral tradition. Homer's tale was more recently the inspiration for the movie *O Brother, Where Art Thou?* (just as the soundtrack album from that movie drew upon public-domain mountain music, hobo tunes, gospel, and bluegrass).

Few if any works of art spring full-blown, wholly original and without antecedents, like Athena from the head of Zeus. The Greek legend of Pygmalion was the basis for a George Bernard Shaw play of the same name and later for the musical *My Fair Lady*. The great copyright scholar Melville Nimmer has said that *West Side Story* would infringe *Romeo and Juliet* had Shakespeare been able to copyright it. But then, *Julius Caesar* was a derivation of Sir Thomas North's 1579 translation of *Lives of Noble Grecians and Romans*, by Plutarch. The chain of creative appropriation is tangled and long.

If no work of art could draw upon prior material with impunity, then Shakespeare would be quickly adjudged a thief. Writes Judge Richard Posner:

> *Measure for Measure* would infringe *Promos and Cassandra*, *Ragtime* would infringe *Michael Kohlhaas*, and *Romeo and Juliet* itself would have infringed Arthur Brooke's *The Tragicall Historye of Romeo and*

Juliet, published in 1562, which in turn would have infringed several earlier *Romeo and Juliets*, all of which probably would have infringed Ovid's story of Pyramus and Thisbe—which in *A Midsummer Night's Dream* Shakespeare staged as a play within the play. If the Old Testament had been copyrighted, *Paradise Lost* would have infringed it, not to mention *Joseph and His Brothers*.

The Supreme Court justice Antonin Scalia has echoed this sentiment in a 2003 dispute over whether a television series based on General Eisenhower's book about the Allied campaign in Europe during World War II infringed the copyright of a previous television series. Justice Scalia acknowledged, "Without a copyrighted work as the basepoint, the word 'origin' has no discernible limits. A video of the MGM film *Carmen Jones*, after its copyright has expired, would presumably require attribution not just to MGM, but to Oscar Hammerstein II (who wrote the musical on which the film was based), to Georges Bizet (who wrote the opera on which the musical was based), and to Prosper Mérimée (who wrote the novel on which the opera was based). In many cases, figuring out who is in the line of 'origin' would be no simple task. Indeed, in the present case, it is far from clear that respondents have that status."

A few centuries ago, Voltaire got it mostly right when he wrote, "Originality is nothing but judicious imitation. The most original writers borrowed from one another. The instruction we find in books is like fire. We fetch it from our neighbor's, kindle it at home, communicate it to others, and it becomes the property of all."

Who Owns Folk Quilts and Needlepoint Patterns?

The Shaker community believed that its creative arts mysteriously came as gifts from the spiritual world. As Lewis Hyde writes, "Persons who strove to become receptive of songs, dances, paintings, and so forth, were said to be 'laboring for a gift,' and the works that they created circulated as gifts within the community. Shaker artists were known as 'instruments'; we know only a few of their names, for in general it was forbidden that they be known to any but the Church elders."

The vitality of folk art stems from the "gift economy" of the folk community; creativity is seen as a gift that must be allowed to freely circulate among members of the community. Once a work becomes proprietary, the creative spirit begins to diminish or even stop.

In this sense, folk arts are products of a cultural commons shared by everyone; there are no individual owners. Stunning creativity can arise even though there are no "property incentives" from copyright law to encourage it. Indeed, it is precisely the weakness of property rights that facilitates creative recombinations and innovations, and the flowering of a folk culture. Woody Guthrie recognized this fact. When his songs lost their association with him and merged into the great mass of living folk tradition, he considered it his ultimate achievement. It meant that his creativity had reached its widest acceptance.

Flash forward to the 1980s. Antiques dealer Judi Boisson had been selling antique American quilts, especially Amish quilts, for twenty years. But because the supply was getting so scarce, she decided to design and manufacture her own quilts and sell them to stores selling linens, gifts, antiques, and children's wear. In 1991, Boisson designed and produced two alphabet quilts, "School Days I" and "School Days II," each consisting of square blocks with capital letters of the alphabet displayed in order. The letters and blocks were made up of different colors and set off by a white border and colored edging.

Alphabet quilt samplers are stock Americana, of course. But the quilts that Boisson had designed were "original," at least in the eyes of copyright law. So when Vijay Rao, an electrical engineer turned quilt entrepreneur, began selling three quilt designs of his own that looked remarkably similar to Boisson's "School Days" quilts, the courts were summoned to decide a question that folk artists would consider absurd: *Who is the lawful owner of this folk quilt design?*

The point here may be that Boisson's quilt design was really a faux folk quilt. The district court found that the letters of the alphabet, its formation in six rows of five blocks, and the colors, were in the public domain and thus unprotectable. But that hardly exhausts the issue of what was "original" about the Boisson quilts. The Second Circuit Court of Appeals declared that while color cannot be protected by copyright, the *specific combination or arrangement* of colors may. Thus, in this case, the choice of colors and the specific formation of the blocks of letters may be considered "original" and defended against imitators.

The court said, furthermore, that the originality of the two sets of quilts must be determined by assessing their "total concept and feel." The defendant's work may be found to infringe Boisson's copyrights if "the ordinary observer, unless he set out to detect the disparities, would be disposed to overlook them, and regard their aesthetic appeal as the same." After conducting such an analysis of its own, the Second Circuit ruled that two versions of Rao's quilts were illegal copies of Boisson's "School Days I" quilt. The question of remedies was remanded to the district court.

The case raises a worthwhile question: Is there any place in today's world for folk art—works that no one owns and that can be freely used and modified as one wishes? Or must everything be propertized and assigned to individuals, based on the premise that sufficient individual "originality" can be discerned in nearly every "new" work? The latter model of creativity implicitly favors larger commercial vendors who can appropriate folk motifs with impunity, while small-time folk art/crafts artists have few resources to retain lawyers to defend their works.

This dilemma is currently roiling the world of needlepoint design as well. One of the leading designers in the field, Darla Fanton, told MSNBC: "Copyright infringement has always impacted the needlework pattern field because people would illegally photocopy the books and give the copies to friends." But now low-priced scanners and the Internet are making it feasible for needlepoint patterns to be shared freely among thousands of aficionados.

Copyright owners consider this piracy, and they have a point. But in other respects, the new networking technologies are simply enabling the folk culture of old to reassert itself. Needlepoint design, after all, was originally a vernacular household art before pattern companies arose to transform it into a privately owned, market-based art form. So why should there be a problem if "the folk" step in to reclaim their art form? In the short term, of course, this development comes at the expense of proprietary design makers (who decades earlier had built their businesses on the foundation of folk designs). Over the long term, however, the technologies are resurrecting a folk art ecology that once existed, and are giving it a broader foundation than ever before.

In response, the needlepoint pattern industry has shown the same hostility toward its customers that the record industry shows toward music fans. Needlepoint companies are trying to shut down online clubs that illegally distribute their designs, while championing "copyright education" so that people will stop their "illegal sharing."

Some needlework fans admit that sharing copyrighted designs is wrong, but others persist in it anyway and defend it as inevitable. After being hit with a lawsuit for copyright infringement, one needlepoint fan complained on a Web site: "You know what this feels like? It feels like I walked into a grocery store, grabbed a peanut out of the bin, ate it and all of a sudden cops jump out of nowhere and haul me off to jail."

While the copyright mentality tends to depict sharing among a community of interest as shameful and even illegal, sharing and collaboration are not necessarily rip-offs of someone else's work. Software developers discovered this in the 1980s when a hardy band of computer programmers decided to create free software—computer programs that were not protected by copyright, but by a "copyleft" license that allowed programmers to freely share their code without fear that someone else would "take it private" through copyright law. This special license, the General Public License, or GPL, provided the legal foundation for the GNU/Linux operating system and other open source software that now compete with Microsoft software.

One wonders if the needlepoint pattern community could develop a license analogous to the GPL to protect its collective creativity in the future. The nonprofit group the Creative Commons has crafted a number of licenses that are expressly intended to allow creators to retain some rights (such as commercial sales) while authorizing noncommercial copying and reuse, for example.

Copyright maximalists often discount the importance of a commons in creative output. The controversies over folk quilts and needlepoint designs suggest that what is really needed is a new equilibrium between the proprietary and the commons. The fashion industry long ago reached such a rapprochement by accepting the fact that creativity in clothing design is too large and fugitive to be owned outright as property. Its commercial vitality relies heavily on the public domain.

To be sure, the fashion industry aggressively protects its brand names and logos, utilizing trademarks and licensing agreements, among other legal regimes. In most cases, however, the actual creative design of garments is not owned by anyone. The couture dress worn by a Hollywood starlet on the red carpet can be immediately knocked off and legally appear days later on department store racks. In fashion—as in folk art—ideas arise, evolve through collaboration, gain currency through exposure, mutate in new directions, and diffuse through imitation. The constant borrowing, repurposing, and transformation of prior works are as integral to creativity in music and film as they are to fashion.

Yet despite minimal legal protections for its creative design, fashion remains a massive industry that thrives in a competitive global environment. Virtually all players in fashion recognize and accept that derivation, recombination, imitation, revivals of old styles, and outright knockoffs are part of what makes the industry robust. Few denounce, let alone sue, the appropriator for "creative theft." They are too busy trying to stay ahead of the competition through the sheer power of their design and marketing prowess.

Even quilt and needlepoint patterns need a cultural commons for their creativity to remain fresh. The legendary designer Coco Chanel understood this fact when she said: "Fashion is not something that exists in dresses only; fashion is something in the air. It's the wind that blows in the new fashion; you feel it coming, you smell it . . . in the sky, in the street; fashion has to do with ideas, the way we live, what is happening."

If it is to be fresh, passionate, and transformative, creativity must have the room to breathe and grow, unfettered and alive. It is a lesson that folk artists learned a long time ago.

Squabbling over the Ownership of Gettysburg Ghost Stories

For most of human history, people have told stories to each other and then passed them along—to children, to families sitting around the hearth, to the next generation. While there have always been singular storytellers, their originality has generally consisted of the *telling* of the story, not the story itself. After all, the stories and myths that a culture tells to its members have survived only because everyone participates in passing them along.

It is a peculiar myth of modern industrial society that an *individual* can actually "own" a story, as if he or she invented it from scratch in splendid isolation. The presumption is well illustrated by Mark Nesbitt's claim that he owns the copyright on ten ghost stories dealing with the spooky aftermath of the Civil War in Gettysburg, Pennsylvania.

Nesbitt is a former park ranger and author of a number of history books. He published a book of ghost stories in 1991, and a few years later began the "Ghosts of Gettysburg Candlelight Walking Tour." Visitors were taken to haunted spots and told tales of severed limbs, footfalls when no one was there, and other supernatural spookiness.

Shortly thereafter, the Farnsworth House, a local bed-and-breakfast, started its own evening walking tours of haunted spots. When Nesbitt learned that the stories contained striking similarities to the ones he had published in 1991, he sued for copyright infringement. Farnsworth House argued that the stories were in the public domain and could not be copyrighted.

A lawsuit ensued, and in October 2001, a federal district court dismissed nine of the ten infringement claims, ruling that Nesbitt's works were "derivative works" of existing works. Judge Sylvia Rambo said that Nesbitt's creative elaborations could be copyrighted, but not the plotlines or general themes. Despite the ruling, Nesbitt was happy because it pressured Farnsworth House to stop reading most of his stories in their ghost tour. The case was eventually settled.

The paradox of the case is that ghost stories have credibility only if they have some wider provenance and belief among a local community. If they are wholly original creations, as Nesbitt claimed, who will believe them?

Disney Privatizes the Classics and Folktales

When it comes to the aggressive defense of copyrights and trademarks, few corporations rival the Walt Disney Company. One of the company's more astonishing legal threats, for example, was directed at Florida daycare centers for putting Disney characters on their walls without authorization. There is a withering irony to Disney's hardball defense of "its property": much of the Disney empire was built upon the open plunder of materials from the public domain. Disney has always been a "rapacious strip-miner" in the "goldmine of legend and myth," said journalist Gilbert Seldes. The company has appropriated dozens of folk stories and literary classics, scrubbed them up with the perky Disney touch, and then claimed the entire franchise as its own.

The strategy made shrewd commercial sense. What could be more lucrative than capitalizing on the considerable "brand awareness" of beloved children's stories that had been around for generations? The list of folktales commandeered by Disney is long and multicultural. It includes *Aladdin, Beauty and the Beast, Cinderella, Hercules, The Hunchback of Notre Dame, Robin Hood, Snow White*, and *Sleeping Beauty*. Among the American folk legends that were morphed into Disney properties are *The Legend of Sleepy Hollow, Pocahontas, Song of the South* (the Uncle Remus tales), and *Davy Crockett*.

The treasury of classic children's literature has also been a favored source of productions. Prominent Disneyfications include *The Jungle Book* (Rudyard Kipling), *Alice's Adventures in Wonderland* (Lewis Carroll), *Oliver Twist* (Charles Dickens), *Treasure Island* (Robert Louis Stevenson), *The Wind in the Willows* (Kenneth Grahame), *The Three Musketeers* (Alexandre Dumas), and *Pinocchio* (Carlo Collodi). While Disney has paid for the rights to some children's stories—*Peter Pan* (J. M. Barrie), *Bambi* (Felix Salten), and *Winnie-the-Pooh* (A. A. Milne)—the company has a habit of going to court to dispute arcane technicalities of copyright law in order to gain control over a work. (A thirteen-year litigation battle with A. A. Milne's heirs over merchandising royalties for *Winnie-the-Pooh* ended with a Disney victory in March 2004; a separate copyright lawsuit is still pending.)

Time magazine's cultural critic Richard Schickel scoffed at the philistine transformations that Disney made of *Peter Pan* and *Alice in Wonderland*: "There was something arrogant about the way the studio took over these works. Grist for a mighty mill, they were, in the ineffable Hollywood term, 'properties' to do with as the proprietor of the machine would. You could throw jarring popular songs into the brew, you could gag them up, you could sentimentalize them. You had, in short, no obligation to the originals or to the cultural tradition they represented."

But of course, anyone, even the great Disney colossus, is entitled to use the public domain as one sees fit. Culture is enriched by the sorts of creative adaptations that Disney has made, even if some people object to the new versions on aesthetic, social, or political grounds. But Disney was not just plucking the low-hanging fruit from the public domain. As one of the biggest entertainment conglomerates in the world, the company has the market dominance—and legal firepower—to substitute its proprietary version of a story for the folk version, effectively eradicating the latter from public memory.

When the Fox Network planned a *Peter Pan* half-hour cartoon series based on J. M. Barrie's public-domain work, the Disney Company said that Tinkerbell could be presented only as a single point of light because Disney animators had come up with the idea of portraying her as a young woman. Fox retorted that J. M. Barrie himself had described Tinkerbell as a slightly plump girl "gowned in a skeleton leaf, through which her figure could be seen to best advantage."

Disney has also claimed the folktale of *Snow White* as its own. In 1989, when the Academy of Motion Pictures Arts and Sciences opened the annual Oscar awards ceremony with a song-and-dance number spoofing *Snow White*, Disney demanded an apology. It felt that the sketch besmirched the innocent, wholesome image of Snow White, one of Disney's most valuable intellectual properties.

When the academy refused to apologize for its parody, Disney threatened a lawsuit, prompting the *New York Times* to jest that Disney should be given the "Can't Take a Joke" award. Cartoonist Garry Trudeau drew a fanciful strip in which a furtive Snow White secretly meets with a journalist to talk about her ill treatment by Disney. In the last panel of the strip, a Disney lawyer materializes to take Snow White away, whistling, "Hi ho, hi ho, it's off to court we go!" On another occasion, the mere threat of litigation by Disney was enough to stop a French AIDS awareness campaign that featured Snow White in garters and fishnet stockings and Cinderella striking a seductive pose.

Would Disney have prevailed in court against these send-ups? Probably not. Disney does not own any rights in the name "Snow White," because it came from the public domain. Still, the company could invoke Section 43 of the Lanham Act, which is supposed to prevent companies from using someone else's trademark to "confuse" consumers in the marketplace.

It is an eminently fair standard, that people should not be duped by a specious trademark into buying a counterfeit good. Over the past several decades, however, this standard has expanded in all sorts of dubious ways. Courts have ruled that the law prohibits trademark uses that might result in "initial interest confusion, reverse confusion, non-purchaser confusion, after-market confusion, subliminal or unconscious confusion and dilution." (I am grateful to Professor Jessica Litman for this inventory.) Taken together, these legal standards empower owners to assert even stricter control over how trademarked characters and logos can be used in the general culture.

No public allusions to Disney characters, no matter how remote or friendly, seem to escape the censorious gaze of Disney attorneys. When the leaders of White River, Ontario, wanted to honor a bear cub named Winnipeg that had been born in the town in 1914 (it was later sent to the London Zoo, where it reportedly inspired A. A. Milne to write the Winnie-the-Pooh books), Disney formally objected. Erecting a public statue of the bear cub, Disney said, would violate "contractual commitments and present and future plans for this character." (The town eventually reached a settlement allowing it to erect a Pooh statue at its train station.)

Disney has even gone after an antipornography group for quoting a single line of Walt Disney's—"Our greatest natural resource is the minds of our children"—in one of its brochures. A court would almost certainly regard the quotation as fair use, but not many small nonprofits can afford to go up against the Disney legal machine to vindicate their rights.

There is something sad and unseemly about a company that built its fortunes on a foundation of public-domain Americana acting like a proprietary bully. "The man who expropriated so much from others," write cultural critics Dorfman and Mattelart, "will not countenance any kind of petty theft against himself." The frightening part is that Disney's voraciousness only feeds on itself, emboldening it to demand more and more.

It was not enough for Disney to pluck the juiciest morsels from the public domain; it wanted to shut down the public domain, or at least tame it. As described on pages 148–152, the company in the 1990s persuaded Congress to privatize a huge chunk of the public domain by extending copyright terms for twenty additional years. In order to keep Mickey, Goofy, and all the others under Disney control, the public is now denied access to its own cultural heritage and must pay billions of unnecessary dollars for work that rightfully belongs to it.

Fan Fiction: You Are Not Allowed to Imagine Batman and Robin as Gay

"Picard had always thought he preferred women on the slender side, but how the gentle give of Deanna's soft flesh thrilled him as his hands roamed over her. She held him tightly between her legs and he seemed to be completely enveloped in her cushy breasts and thighs . . ."

Captain Jean-Luc Picard of *Star Trek: The Next Generation* is only one of dozens of fictional characters of mass culture to be recast by their fans in imaginary, unauthorized stories. "Fan fiction" (sometimes called "Fan-Fic"), a somewhat underground genre of creativity, is an obsession for untold thousands of people, especially Internet users.

According to Henry Jenkins, author of the classic *Textual Poachers: Television Fans and Participatory Culture*, fan fiction is "a subculture that exists in the 'borderlands' between mass culture and everyday life and that constructs its own identity and artifacts from resources borrowed from already circulating texts." Instead of drawing upon folk traditions, FanFic communities draw upon plotlines, characters, and alternative universes of mass culture, including such offbeat TV shows of the 1960s and 1970s as *Starsky and Hutch*, *Batman*, *The Avengers*, *Beauty and the Beast*, *Blake's 7*, and *Scarecrow and Mrs. King*, as well as more recent shows such as *The X-Files*. "Trekkies," the devotees of *Star Trek*, constitute the largest and best-known fan community.

It is easy to dismiss fan fiction as a goofy oddity in American culture. Yet fan communities are not so different from many other social communities. Rebecca Tushnet, the author of a major law review article on the topic, writes that fan culture resembles traditional folk culture: "It constructs a group identity, articulates the community's ideals and defines its relationship to the outside world. Fan culture, like traditional folk culture, is transmitted informally and does not define a sharp boundary between artists and audiences. . . . Fan texts, like many folk texts, often do not achieve a standard version but exist only in process, always open to revision and reappropriation."

The genre has a special appeal for women, minorities, and gays and lesbians, writes Henry Jenkins, who notes that the practice of appropriating or "recoding" mainstream cultural forms is a standard political strategy for socially marginalized groups. For its participants, the thrill of fan fiction comes in creating new characters and inventing new stories to fill in gaps in the official plot. Writers also enjoy giving free rein to their fantasies, especially sexual fantasies, about what might occur between two characters.

One remarkably durable subgenre involves homoerotic romances between male characters, a genre known as "slash" fiction because the two characters who are imagined having sex are referred to by a slash, as in "Kirk/Spock." Slash stories are generally written by women for other women, and frequently involve first-time sexual encounters between the characters.

Not surprisingly, fan fiction raises some provocative questions for copyright and trademark law. Is this sort of creativity protected by the fair use doctrine, or does it represent the organized destruction of valuable intellectual property?

There is no easy, general answer, but as a matter of law, fans are in a vulnerable position. Copyright and trademark law protects fictional characters that are "distinctly delineated," a standard that would apply in most FanFic cases. According to an online FAQ (frequently asked questions) maintained by the Stanford Center for Internet and Society, "If a FanFic author creates a new story about Darth Vader, the author will have infringed both the derivative right and the right to reproduce that character." A fan story could also violate the doctrine of "trademark dilution," which prohibits uses of famous trademarks if they harm their distinctive quality. Disney has used trademark dilution to stop pornographers from using the Snow White and Sleeping Beauty characters.

Skeptics might wonder if Disney really has the right to claim ownership in those characters. After all, they existed as folk stories well before Disney appropriated them. To the law, however, this fact is not necessarily relevant at all. For example, the Tolkien estate once threatened to sue a children's entertainer whose stage name was "Gandalf the Wizard Clown." In response, the entertainer insisted that the Gandalf character comes from ancient Scandinavian literature and so belongs to the public domain—a point that Tolkien attorneys said was irrelevant. What matters in a trademark claim is how the public now *perceives* the trademark. (The Tolkien estate and the Wizard Clown eventually worked out a settlement.)

On the other hand, the fair use doctrine seems to protect the kind of "secondary creativity" that fan fiction represents. Fan stories are not simply rip-offs of existing works, after all. They are transformative creations. Moreover, since fan fiction is generally for noncommercial purposes and does not harm the market for a work (it may well expand the market!), fan stories would also seem to pass muster as fair use. All the more so if the fan fiction is using "scènes a faire"—the general milieu of a fictional world—which cannot be copyrighted or trademarked.

As a practical matter, the issue is not necessarily about who has the law on his side. It is who has the economic resources to prevail. Large media companies are accustomed to sending out nasty cease-and-desist letters that intimidate individuals into submission, no matter the actual language of the law. Viacom and Paramount are among the most aggressive studios; Fox is said to be more accommodating to fan-created works, or at least selectively willing to recognize the valuable role that fans play in bolstering the market for shows.

While fans freely acknowledge the "authorship" of Hollywood studios, they resent the legal bullying over how their characters may be used. A *Star Trek* fan told one reporter, "Viacom owns the right to produce *Star Trek*. But the real people who 'own' *Star Trek*, in my opinion, are the fans. Without us, it would have died twenty-seven years ago." Another fan told Henry Jenkins: "The text already belongs to us; we are not taking anything other than our own fantasies, so therefore we are not stealing anything at all." Still another fan ridiculed the studios' claims: "*The X-Files* is the creation and exclusive property of Chris Carter et al. Yeah, right. The way a pearl is the exclusive property of an oyster!"

Fans generally recognize that they don't have clear legal rights, and even go so far as to explicitly admit this fact when publishing their stories. Yet it irks them that the law regards them as illegitimate pests even though they have a deeper personal commitment to the characters and stories than the copyright owners themselves. As Rebecca Tushnet explains, fans see themselves as "guardians of the texts they love, purer than the owners in some ways because they seek no profit. They believe that their emotional and financial investment in the characters gives them moral rights to create with these characters."

The "owners" of the fictional characters of mass culture want to have it both ways. They want to exploit the economic value that comes when large numbers of people develop a personal bond with fictional characters and stories, yet they want to retain strict legal control at the same time. Writes Jane M. Gaines: "The owners of popular forms, which constitute our most widely shared culture . . . are in the contradictory position of encouraging the widespread uses of Batman, Superman and Snow White. But when those forms are used spontaneously . . . the owners want to take them back."

Tushnet proposes a more generous-minded rapprochement between copyright holders and fan fiction writers. Fans should not be able to assert any copyrights in their own (derivative) works, she argues, especially if the derivative uses might inhibit the original copyright holder from drawing upon the fan fiction. Yet there is no reason the law should consider fan fiction itself as a copyright infringement. Why not let fans use the popular characters yet give the copyright holder "a unique privilege or implied license" to use fan writings? Such a license would clarify and thereby strengthen fans' rights, an improvement over the vagaries of the fair use doctrine. "There is no reason fan authors should receive all or nothing when intellectual property law is replete with partial rights," argues Tushnet.

It is not widely appreciated that fan Web sites were a flourishing niche of Internet culture in the 1990s. *Salon.com* detailed the excitement generated by www.fandom.com, a site that aggregated dozens of independent fan sites and provided legal protection against the studios. The site touted itself as "by the fans, for the fans." But soon the corporate desire to control fan postings took over, and the site's freewheeling discussions were neutered.

Carol Burrell, the founder of a number of fan sites, told *Salon*: "I hope that the Web, with its marvelous potential to give voice to individuals, won't turn into the private playground of companies. . . . The Internet has made people aware that they are, in fact, part of something called fandom. It has given the individual the power to shout out loud." The real question is whether copyright and trademark law will be used to suppress this vernacular culture.

Who Owns Video-Game Characters?

Can fandom exact its own vengeance on corporations who invoke trademark and copyright law to overly restrict people's "folk rights"? One arena in which this question is being tested is online gaming. In a number of "massive multiplayer online games" (MMOGs), such as *EverQuest* and *Asheron's Call*, hundreds of thousands of players interact in an online fantasy world using characters of their own making, virtual money, and invented weapons and props. In a sense, these gaming communities are alternative cultures that happen to be hosted by software companies.

With increasing frequency, controversies are arising over who owns the fictional personas and artifacts of these virtual cultures. T. L. Taylor of North Carolina State University explores this question with great insight in a recent essay (which is the primary source for much that follows).

It helps to understand how MMOGs work. Players come together online to create their own fictional characters in fantasy universes devised by an online software/entertainment company. Literally thousands of characters can interact in distinct geographical spaces and rooms. They carry on conversations, learn from each other, barter and buy goods in a virtual economy, create languages and traditions for their online cultures, engage in combat, and make friendships and alliances. In a very real sense, the users, acting collectively over time, are *creating* the game and its culture. For a monthly subscription fee, the software company provides an online architecture that enables a highly complex virtual culture to evolve.

If individual users have spent a great deal of time and creativity building their online avatar—their fictional alter ego—then shouldn't they have some control over their work? If some truly inspired player creates a fantastic new artifact or geographical space, then should not that be considered "property" in a traditional copyright or trademark sense?

Well, no. Or more accurately, it is property, but the gaming companies insist that the virtual culture belongs to them—all of it, even the players' considerable creative contributions. *EverQuest's* tagline—"You're in our world now"—is a double entendre worth pondering.

One of the more dramatic confrontations with this issue erupted in 2000, reports Taylor, when an *EverQuest* player, "Mystere," posted a piece of fan fiction detailing the graphic rape of a character. Even though the story was published on a third-party Web site, Sony/Verant Online terminated the player's *EverQuest* account. The fictional rape account was also pulled from the independent Web site, presumably after pressure from Sony/Verant Online. A corporate representative explained: "We make determinations based on information at hand regarding who is or is not having a positive effect on *EverQuest's* community."

The general counsel for Sony Online Entertainment claimed that the law authorizes such control: "Fortunately, the body of intellectual property law that has developed over the past 225 years—the laws governing the use of copyrighted material, derivative works, trademarks and trade dress—gives us the exclusive right to permit or disallow the outside use of our intellectual property so that we can properly manage our business and nurture the *EverQuest* brand."

Of course, other legal scholars dispute the idea that copyright is meant to protect a company's market share, brand image, or the subsequent cultural life of a character. The depiction of a fictional rape may understandably upset some people and cause them to sympathize with the game's hosts. Yet such expansive copyright and trademark control may also be used in more authoritarian ways to control online users' behavior, personal creativity, and expression.

Should companies be allowed to own online identities created by users? The very premises of copyright law suggest that such rights ought to belong to individual authors, not to the corporate host of an "expressive space" such as an MMOG. Yet the corporate hosts have asserted the right as the price of admission (using contract law), much as record labels require artists to surrender their copyrights as the price for reaching mainstream audiences.

What is especially interesting in the MMOG world is how users are starting to monetize their interests in their creative output—just as corporations have routinely done. To this, the corporations cry foul. Some *EverQuest* players have used eBay to try to liquidate their interests in their online identities, earned skill levels (entitling them to play on certain levels of the game), online weapons, and virtual money. Individual players are asking why they shouldn't be able to "cash out" on their creative output, much as Disney or Sony appropriates folk stories and public-domain characters and then claims property rights in this derivative output in order to earn real money.

By selling virtual products on eBay, Taylor reports, "You could in fact buy your way around quite a few hours of developing that character, gaining levels and perfecting game skills. Indeed, many in the *EQ* community itself find this one of the most loathsome aspects of what are now commonly termed 'eBayers' (users who have bought loaded accounts/ characters but have no real game skill and have not 'paid any dues')."

Of course, the gaming companies regard eBay sales of avatars and other gaming artifacts as a threat to their business model. If a player can use eBay to "arbitrage" around the long, difficult process of earning skills and game powers, it essentially shrinks corporate revenues from the game. It seems another question entirely, however, whether copyright law should protect such "losses," especially when the artifacts have been created by the players themselves.

Within the *EverQuest* environment, players are allowed to trade items and virtual money in online auctions hosted by the game itself. So what is the problem with doing the same thing via an outside channel such as eBay? "Is it that users are obtaining items outside of a definition of appropriate gameplay or that some are profiting from it?" asks Taylor.

"And that indeed that profit is not simply in 'virtual money' (as any long-time player is likely to have acquired through normal buying and selling over the course of gameplay) but *actual* money?"

The beauty of these philosophical and legal quandaries is that they highlight some basic problems of copyright and trademark law today. "If indeed companies want to retain all the privileges of being primary owners of these worlds," asks Taylor, "do they then have corresponding sets of responsibilities to their userbase? . . . Should users have meaningful rights to shape the nature of representation in the world? Or the development of its culture and structure? Should game companies be meaningfully accountable to their users?"

As a practical matter, companies can usually get around such issues and assert control over a user community through contract law (the terms of service that users "agree to"). Copyright owners end up having it both ways: they have strict control of a culture that they have played only a partial role in creating, and they have no obligations to the creative needs and property interests of people. Online citizens have become virtual serfs. Is this a portent of the future?

PART TWO

Trademarking
Public Life

It is hard to overestimate the competitive advantages of monopolizing culture. One of the most vivid accounts comes from Scott McNealy, the CEO of Sun Microsystems, who described what it means for Microsoft to own the operating system for personal computers: "The only thing I'd rather own than Windows," said McNealy, "is English or Spanish or Chinese because then I could charge you $249 to speak English and I could charge you an upgrade fee when I add new letters like 'n' or 't.'"

Something approximating this situation actually exists in the "operating system" of our culture. The very names of companies, products, and celebrities that constitute our cultural firmament are often monopolized and withheld from us, much as if Microsoft owned letters of the alphabet and could charge us to use them. Two of the leading tools for this enclosure of the cultural commons are trademark law and publicity rights law, which have evolved in recent years to give companies extraordinary private rights over the words, images, and symbols that constitute our society.

If the justifications used by trademark law make sense in the context of the marketplace, they make much less sense now that the marketplace has *become* our culture. As Rochelle Cooper Dreyfuss explains:

[I]deograms that once functioned solely as signals denoting the source, origin and quality of goods, have become products in their own right, valued as indicators of the status, preferences and aspirations of those who use them. Some trademarks have worked their way into the English language; others provide bases for vibrant, evocative metaphors. In a sense, trademarks are the emerging lingua franca: with a sufficient command of these terms, one can make oneself understood the world over, and in the process, enjoy the comforts of home.

There are advantages, to be sure, in everyone having common points of reference, whether those points of reference are *Simpsons* cartoon characters or classic works of music. Taken as a whole, such symbols comprise a cultural currency; they help us communicate in succinct, widely understood ways.

While it is certainly legitimate for companies to prevent their product names from being used to confuse or defraud consumers—the traditional function of trademark—it is another matter entirely when trademark law becomes a means for absolute control over the flow of symbols in our society. Trademark law has become, in the words of Rosemary Coombe, "the ruse by which corporations protect themselves from competition and from uncompensated circulation of their cultural indicators."

A companion body of law governing publicity rights is used in an equally ludicrous way by celebrities to control how people may talk about and depict them. All sorts of strange things happen when celebrity personas are considered property rights. Dead people—via their estates—actually have legal rights to their image and reputation. Below, some of the more egregious (claimed) private monopolies over our public life.

CHAPTER 4

Trademark Owners Whine, "No Making Fun of Me!"

We are symbols and inhabit symbols. So should we be paying rent?

—Professor Rochelle Cooper Dreyfuss

Trademark law has historically sought to prevent consumer fraud, counterfeiting, and confusion in the marketplace. Its basic goal is consumer protection: consumers should be able to associate certain qualities with a trademarked name or logo, without risk of being confused or deceived by competing products.

But something new is happening: companies are trying to use trademark law to claim nearly absolute control over culture, overriding people's free speech rights and their ability to use common images and phrases. One impetus for this trend is the Trademark Dilution Act of 1995, which gives owners of "famous" trademarks new powers to silence any uses that might conceivably "blur" or "dilute" their trademarks even if there is no likelihood of fraud or confusion. The Anti-Cybersquatting Consumer Protection Act of 1999 has also contributed to this trend. This law gives trademark holders new powers to force Internet domain-name holders to surrender domain names.

The perverse result is that the more power and influence a company acquires, the more able it is to stifle robust public discussion about it and its products—even where no consumer would be confused. As if from the sky, well-heeled trademark holders can figuratively deploy a gigantic Monty Python foot to squash unauthorized uses of a trademarked name or image, no matter how innocent, noncommercial, or trivial. All that matters is whether the offending reference to the trademark "dilutes" or "tarnishes" it.

Often, the legal merits of an offending usage may be irrelevant because the hapless defendant cannot begin to consider litigation against the likes of McDonald's or Microsoft. This imbalance of power enables large trademark holders to make threats they know to be legally dubious or erroneous. Very few of the bullied victims can afford to ascertain their rights, let alone fight back in court.

Trademark law, then, often serves as a blunt instrument of cultural intimidation and censorship. The actual risk of market fraud or confusion may be remote. But that is frequently not the real concern of many trademark holders, who care only about squelching ridicule or criticism. Unflattering social criticism can do nasty things to a valuable brand. Even when there might be a plausible threat that a third-party use of a trademark could cause commercial harm—critics mocking a company, artists parodying a corporate logo—there is no reason that trademark protection should trump all other interests in our society, especially free speech and artistic commentary.

The Legal Lockdown of Barbie

Barbie, the impossibly statuesque and buxom doll made by Mattel, is much more than an eleven-and-a-half-inch piece of pink plastic. She is an American icon. Barbie has come to embody an ideal of feminine beauty that is loved and reviled, but in either case represents a potent symbol of Western consumer culture. Every year, millions of Barbies are sold in 150 countries—Malibu Barbie, Army Barbie, President Barbie, and dozens of others—bringing in approximately $1.5 billion in revenues to Mattel.

To judge from its aggressive litigation, Mattel seems to believe that it has the legal right to maintain Barbie dolls in a cultural bubble. Invoking both copyright and trademark law, Mattel has waged dozens of legal campaigns over the years against anyone who dares to depict or invoke Barbie without the company's permission. Songs, photographs, book titles, and anything else that uses Barbie's image or name is considered a form of cultural contraband.

For the legions of artists and critics who invoke Barbie in unauthorized works, most are likely to hear from Mattel's lawyers. Few can survive the formidable legal gauntlet that the company has erected to frighten Barbie critics. One notable exception involved a Danish band, Aqua, which included a song called "Barbie Girl" on its 1997 album *Aquarium*. The song featured lines such as, "I'm a blonde bimbo girl, in a fantasy world / Dress me up, make it tight, I'm your dolly," and the memorable chorus, "I'm a Barbie girl, in my Barbie world / Life is plastic, it's fantastic." The song also had a few naughty lyrics such as, "You can brush my hair, undress me everywhere," and "Kiss me here, touch me there, hanky panky." Within weeks of its release on August 19, 1997, "Barbie Girl" shot to No. 7 on the *Billboard* magazine pop singles chart.

Mattel quickly filed a lawsuit against Aqua's record label, MCA, claiming that the song constituted an unauthorized use of the Barbie trademark. The company argued that the song leads consumers to believe that Mattel is affiliated with the song, and that the song "dilutes" the Barbie trademark. Anticipating such complaints, MCA had included a disclaimer on the group's album saying that the song was a "social commentary [that was] not created or approved by the makers of the doll." Mattel scoffed: "That's unacceptable. . . . It's akin to a bank robber handing a note of apology to a teller during a heist. It neither diminishes the severity of the crime, nor does it make it legal."

A federal court found no legal basis for a trial. Mattel then appealed the case to the Ninth Circuit Court of Appeals, but to no avail. Aqua's right to mock Barbie was upheld. A bemused Judge Kozinski opened his opinion, "If this were a sci-fi melodrama, it might be called Speech-Zilla meets Trademark Kong."

Kozinski tipped his hat to the traditional argument that trademarks must be protected so that consumers are not deceived about the source of a product. But he concluded that the Aqua song did not mislead people into thinking Mattel released the song any more than consumers would think that Janis Joplin had entered into a joint venture with the luxury carmaker when she sang, "Oh Lord, won't you buy me a Mercedes-Benz?" His ruling pointed out:

> Trademarks often fill in gaps in our vocabulary and add a contemporary flavor to our expressions. Once imbued with such expressive value, the trademark becomes a word in our language and assumes a role outside the bounds of trademark law. . . . Simply put, the trademark owner does not have the right to control public discourse

whenever the public imbues his mark with a meaning beyond its source-identifying function.

As for the dilution claim made by Mattel, the court held that "the song Barbie Girl is not purely commercial speech, and is therefore fully protected."

Not one to take a lawsuit lying down, MCA had filed its own counterclaim against Mattel, charging that Mattel's accusations that MCA had committed a "heist," "crime," and "theft" constituted defamation. In his ruling, Kozinski tartly replied, "No one hearing this accusation understands intellectual property owners to be saying that infringers are nautical cutthroats with eyepatches and peg legs who board galleons to plunder cargo. In context, all these terms are nonactionable 'rhetorical hyperbole.' The parties are advised to chill."

A number of photographers and artists have found Barbie to be an irresistible symbol for commenting upon Western ideals about beauty and consumerism. In 1997, Web artist Mark Napier used the Photoshop software program to develop "Alternative Barbies," which he billed as a "behind-the-scenes look at the seamy underbelly of Barbie's world." Two of the imaginary images included *Fat and Ugly Barbie* and *Mentally Challenged Barbie*.

"I created this site to explore the phenomenon of Barbie," wrote Napier on his Web site. "Not Barbie as a toy or collectible, but Barbie as a symbol that a culture has created, absorbed, shaped and been shaped by. The site is a visual exploration. Just as children mutilate their dolls to create new stories and meanings, so I too mutilated Barbie, created new faces for her, changed her weight, her expression, added emotion or removed that tiny shred of emotion that she normally has. Through this I dissected the meaning that Barbie carries." Napier counted at least seven other artists whose Barbie-related works had been squelched by Mattel.

Mattel, of course, has little interest in allowing *any* cultural commentary about Barbie unless it promotes sales. Company attorneys insisted that Napier and his Internet service provider remove the *Distorted Barbie* photos from the Web. In an attempt to comply, Napier performed some extreme distortions of his Barbie images so that the doll would not be recognizable as Barbie. But even this was not good enough for Mattel, which asserted the new images ran afoul of the 1995 Trademark Dilution Act. Napier's Photoshop morphings of Barbie are now gone from the Web.

In the aftermath, Napier wrote that Mattel's attack on the *Distorted Barbie* "is grounded less in profit than on preserving the fiction of Barbie. Like any great symbol, her meaning must be preserved. If her meaning is distorted, she will cease to exist."

The same rationale was at work when Mattel went after Susanne Pitt, a British doll maker who transformed Barbie dolls into an adult "Dungeon Doll" clothed in a "lederhosen-style Bavarian bondage dress and helmet in rubber with PVC-mask." But the court found that the doll was not "a market substitute for Barbie dolls" and therefore not likely to cause economic harm to Mattel. Judge Laura Taylor Swain declared, "To the court's knowledge, there is no Mattel line of S&M Barbie."

Mattel is combative even toward its best customers. In 1997, the company filed a lawsuit against Barbara and Dan Miller, the publishers of *Miller's*, a magazine that caters to adult collectors of Barbie, who buy an estimated 750,000 dolls a year. At the time, *Miller's* had a staff of five and a circulation of more than 30,000, reaching Barbie fans in all fifty states and twenty-eight foreign countries. Even though the magazine featured many flattering photos of Barbie, it had also published some negative product reviews and even satire. Mattel accused the Millers of trading upon images of Barbie without permission, and demanded that they sign a licensing agreement that would let Mattel review any Barbie-oriented periodicals before they are published.

Mattel was not about to take no for an answer. "We want the Millers's house," a Mattel lawyer told Chris Lynch, the Millers's attorney, during a 1997 meeting, according to the *Spokane Spokesman-Review*. (Mattel's law firm, Quinn Emanuel Urquhart Oliver & Hedges, has denied making the threat.) The *Spokesman-Review* reporter speculated, "What probably tweaks Mattel most is that the Millers on occasion explore the dark side of sexy Austrian Barbies. Or how Mattel sometimes rips off collectors by offering supposed 'exclusive' dolls and then mass-marketing them at lower prices later."

When Barbie collectors heard about Mattel's lawsuit against *Miller's* magazine, they went nuts. Online chat groups vowed a boycott; others slammed Mattel for revoking the Bill of Rights. The self-styled rebels stopped using the "b" in Barbie in their Internet postings and demanded meetings with Mattel executives. Dubbed the "Pink Anger" rebellion, a protest Web site materialized and quickly was translated into Japanese and German.

Mattel is legendary for fighting unauthorized depictions of Barbie. So it comes as a surprise to learn that Barbie can trace direct lineage to "Lilli," a German adult novelty doll from the 1950s (pictured here) that Mattel took the liberties to adapt.

Mattel's aggressive control over its icon, oddly enough, has provoked contempt among both lovers and haters of Barbie. Critics of the Barbie ideal in 1989 formed the Barbie Liberation Organization, a project of the "culture-jamming" ®™ARK group ("artmark"), to stage cultural events that mock the doll. In one of its more famous gambits, the group in 1993 furtively switched the voiceboxes on three hundred talking versions of Barbie and G.I. Joe dolls sitting on store shelves. The goal was to have unwitting consumers buy Barbies who would then yell, "Vengeance is mine!" and G.I. Joes who would sigh, "Let's plan our dream wedding." Stickers on the packages advised consumers to call their local media to report the subterfuge.

Mattel's protests about unsavory depictions of Barbie are hilariously ironic given the doll's close resemblance to a German "streetwalker" doll, "Lilli," an adult novelty gift from the 1950s and a collector's item, which itself was inspired by a cartoon character in the newspaper *Bild*. Ruth Handler, the creator of Barbie, adapted the German doll (dare anyone say "stole"?) and transformed it into the all-American doll we all know today.

Like Disney, Mattel thinks it is fine to borrow liberally from the public domain or competing products, but no one is allowed to mess with "its" product.

The intimidation can go to ridiculous extremes. When Ophira Edut edited a 1998 book of essays, *Adios, Barbie: Young Women Write about Body Image and Identity*, Mattel pressured Seattle-based Seal Press into changing the cover art of the book, which was then reissued with a new title as well. Edut toyed with renaming the book, *Kiss My Azz, Babs*, but eventually settled on *Body Outlaws* as the new title.

Artists and companies who receive cease-and-desist notices from Mattel are likely to believe that resistance to Trademark Kong is futile. After all, even if the law supports a fair use of Barbie's image or name, who can afford to fight a mega-corporation with bottomless legal resources?

Remarkably, one brave, independent art photographer, Tom Forsythe of Kanab, Utah, recently managed to prevail in a major court battle against Mattel. In 1999, Forsythe began preparing a series of seventy-eight photographs that he named *Food Chain Barbie*. The photos featured naked Barbie dolls posed inside a food blender (*Oster Dive*), beneath an eggbeater (*Missionary Barbie*), inside party glasses (*Champagne Barbie*), and wrapped up in a tortilla (*Enchilada Barbie*), among other scenes with kitchen appliances and food. In an "Artsurdist Statement," Forsythe explained, "I use absurdity in the kitchen motif to illuminate how when we try to find nourishment through a chunk of plastic, all we're going to get is a bad case of indigestion."

Forsythe set about selling the photos at community fairs, art galleries, and art shows. He launched a Web site to sell thirty-nine of the Barbie photos, and printed up postcards with *Enchilada Barbie* to promote the photo series. Shortly after Mattel learned of the photos, a local sheriff showed up at Forsythe's door to serve him papers charging him with violating Mattel's copyrights and trademarks. The timing was ironic because only two weeks earlier Forsythe had resolved to stop selling the photos. "While the work made people laugh," he recalled, "it didn't make enough of them want to put it on their walls."

Still, despite the dismal sales, Forsythe was adamant about fighting back: "I wasn't going to let a corporation known for selling an impossible beauty myth to so many generations of children get away with censoring my work." Forsythe spent five months looking for legal counsel, but the idea

Mattel brought suit against photographer Tom Forsythe for his *Food Chain Barbie* exhibit, which contained this image, *Enchilada Barbie,* among several dozen others. Forsythe's landmark appeals court victory in 2003 may signal a new day for Barbie-related art and commentary.

of locking horns with Mattel was apparently a big deterrent to attorneys. Finally, the ACLU of Southern California agreed to take up the case. It soon realized that the case required greater expertise in intellectual property law than it had, so it handed the case over to the law firm Howard Rice Nemerovski Canady Falk & Rabkin, of San Francisco, which represented Forsythe on a pro bono basis.

Douglas Winthrop, one of the attorneys who managed Forsythe's case, said the ferocity of the litigation with Mattel was "like nothing I'd seen before" in ten years of legal practice. In an effort to impeach expert witnesses from the San Francisco Museum of Modern Art and the Guggenheim Museum in New York (who were to testify about how Forsythe's photos exemplified certain traditions of twentieth-century art), Mattel demanded documents relating to each museum's licensing and copyright enforcement practices. By forcing the witnesses to disclose institutional policies that had nothing to do with the litigation, Mattel's subpoenas, said the court, "were served for the purpose of getting the museums to exert pressure on the witnesses not to testify." They were "served for the purpose of annoying and harassment and not really for the purpose of getting information."

For the trial, Mattel had commissioned a survey of 200 Internet users in eight different cities to see how many thought Mattel was affiliated with the photos ("at least 21%"). It commissioned another survey of 606 respondents in six cities around the country to try to establish that the photos did not constitute a parody of Mattel or Barbie ("only 1–3%" of respondents supposedly recognized the parody).

Frustrated by his excruciating passage through the legal meat-grinder, Forsythe, in a fit of inspired whimsy, staged a private "execution" of the Barbie dolls. He dressed up in combat fatigues and an NRA hat, fired over a hundred rounds of bullets into his Barbie collection, and video-taped the whole thing. Mattel accused him of "spoliation of evidence," even though the dolls had already been produced to counsel for Mattel and later lodged with the court. Trying to capitalize on the episode, Mattel requested that an armed United States marshal attend Forsythe's deposition and sought to have a "threat assessment expert" testify to the "threat" posed by him.

Against this onslaught, Forsythe's attorneys argued that "the legal question of parody is not an opinion poll, nor a popularity contest"; that no evidence had been presented showing that *Food Chain Barbie* had caused economic harm to Mattel; and that the "sculptural copyright" claimed for Barbie's head was invalid because the only unique feature of Barbie's head, according to Mattel's own witness, was "an overbite" and a "ski nose."

"We knew [this case] would be a real fight," said Winthrop. "I didn't appreciate that Mattel would engage in such extreme litigation tactics to run up the costs." But Winthrop said such tactics simply made him "that much more outraged and determined to prevail." In a declaration about the case cited in *California Lawyer* magazine, Winthrop said, "[A]t virtually every turn, counsel for Mattel has engaged in unprofessional, abusive and manipulative tactics the likes of which no one of Defendant's attorneys has ever before witnessed. . . . [T]he last time counsel for Defendant called to make a request of counsel for Mattel, she wrote back and called Defendant's counsel liars." The Howard Rice team that handled this case also wrote that Mattel "is known in the legal community for writing a blank check to lawyers whose motto is 'litigation is war,' namely the Quinn Emanuel firm."

Mattel has claimed that its enforcement efforts do not distinguish "between social commentary and commercial exploitation." To honor this principle, the company was willing to spend huge sums and years in court to shut down a photo series that, according to court documents, generated gross revenues of only $3,659 for Tom Forsythe and cost $5,088 to produce.

Mattel suffered a serious defeat in federal district court, which declared that Mattel did not have a sufficient legal complaint to proceed to trial. Mattel appealed the summary judgment ruling to the Ninth Circuit Court, and finally, on December 29, 2003, the court handed down a sweeping victory for Forsythe. After reviewing four statutory criteria for assessing fair use, the court declared, "It is not in the public's interest to allow Mattel complete control over the kinds of artistic works that use Barbie as a reference for criticism and comment. . . . Allowing Forsythe's use serves the aims of the Copyright Act by encouraging the very creativity and criticism that the Act protects."

Winthrop estimated that his firm incurred at least $1.6 million in litigation expenses. Forsythe said he personally incurred $200,000 in expenses. If that is not enough to deter future claimants from asserting their fair use rights, the district court refused to award attorneys' fees to Forsythe's law firm. Courts often award legal fees to defendants victimized by frivolous or unreasonable lawsuits, or in cases where deterring abusive behavior is valuable. Fortunately, the appeals court later ordered the district court to reconsider its denial of awarding attorneys' fees. Forsythe was then awarded nearly $1.6 million in attorneys' fees and $242,000 in costs.

The court also had some stinging words of rebuke for Mattel: "Plaintiff had access to sophisticated counsel who could have determined that such a suit was objectively unreasonable and frivolous. Instead it appears plaintiff forced defendant into costly litigation to discourage him from using Barbie's image in his artwork." By awarding attorneys' fees, the court sought to deter the type of "groundless and unreasonable" trademark dilution claim that Mattel had brought against Forsythe.

For Mattel, which earns billions from Barbie-related sales, the court award to Forsythe would seem like chump change. After all, spending a few million dollars out of a $1.5 billion franchise is surely a cost-efficient business expense if it can prevent alternative images of Barbie from gaining a foothold in the culture. In this case, however, unlike most of its previous ones, Mattel lost. A company representative did not respond to a request for comment on the verdict

Forsythe was ecstatic at his victory: "The more ubiquitous brands become the more important it is for artists to be able to use recognizable brands in their socially critical work. The brands keep getting bigger and bigger. It's up to artists to blow holes in the fatuous world view of these corporate panderers." While Forsythe is heartened that his litigation "sent a loud and clear message to Mattel," he also worries that "the legal system is little more than a boxing ring for the rich, with the common people not even invited to experience the proceedings on pay-per-view. We may be free to express ourselves, but if that expression involves offending a rapacious corporation, they're equally free to sue; and unless we have the wherewithal to fight off high-powered attorneys, that's where our free speech ends."

Straight Eye for Queer Trademark Intimidation

Cultural observers frequently note the gay community's use and transformation of pop culture images to express themselves and their cultural identity. From drag queens who imitate Marilyn Monroe and Judy Garland to playful parodies of cartoon characters, gay performers and artists love to be interactive with the artifacts of pop culture. Inevitably, problems arise because parodies and creative imitations use trademarked characters or images. And since the Trademark Dilution Act authorizes trademark holders to silence the unauthorized use of trade names that might conceivably "blur" or "dilute" their marks, the gay community has had its share of run-ins with trademark bullies.

Seizing upon the fantasy that UPS deliverymen are attractive hunks, Totem International, a doll manufacturer, and BeProud.com, an online retailer, developed a "Billy" doll that parodied the image of UPS deliverymen. The doll was clothed in a brown uniform that bore the words "Billy Parcel Service" and a "bps" logo.

UPS was not amused. In 2002, it threatened legal action against the manufacturer and retailer of the gay-oriented novelty doll for violating its trademark. UPS said that the doll created an "undesirable, unwholesome and unsavory" image of UPS because it was anatomically correct, "grotesquely so." While defending the legality of their parody, Totem and

BeProud.com were apparently intimidated by the potential legal costs and complied with the UPS cease-and-desist demand.

Another trademark holder, MGM-Pathé Communications, owner of the rights to the Pink Panther movies, took offense when a group of gay men in the West Village of Manhattan organized themselves into a civilian patrol group that they dubbed the Pink Panthers. It was 1991 and attacks on homosexuals in New York City were soaring. The patrol and its dashing name were seen as a way to combat hate crimes against homosexuals.

MGM-Pathé did not like the idea of the jaunty Pink Panther being associated with gays. It sued in federal court complaining, "The Pink Panther movies were created and promoted in the spirit of lighthearted, noncontroversial family fun and entertainment, a purpose and history not in keeping with the issues the Pink Panther Patrol faces."

Leaders of the Pink Panther patrol replied that the company was homophobic. Matt Foreman, the head of a group fighting violence against gays and lesbians, told the *New York Times*: "Given what spawned the Pink Panthers last year—this enormous wave of hate-motivated violence—for the group to be attacked by a major corporation is just unbelievable. It's part of this pattern we see all the time which feeds anti-gay violence, and that is that one must disassociate oneself from anything that has any hint of being gay or lesbian."

A federal judge agreed that the group's use of "pink panther" could "seriously impair the value and continued usefulness of the trademark" and do damage to "the character's carefree, comedic, non-political fun."

Like so many trademark controversies—think Barbie or Mickey Mouse—trademark owners want their icons to become a part of American culture yet never acquire any unofficial, unauthorized meanings. That may account for the ultimate sterility of so many freeze-dried corporate characters—and the vitality of the social reinterpretations made by the gay community.

Bully-Boy Fruit of the Loom Doesn't Think Underwear Is Funny

John Halcyon Styn wasn't going to let any *underwear company* intimidate him into yanking his lowbrow parodies from the Web. Styn, the creator of the irreverent Web site Prehensile Tales (www.prehensile.com), created a

Web parody in 1998 about the marketing of Fruit of the Loom underwear. His commentary featured a modified Fruit of the Loom logo with the words "Meat of the Loom," followed by his musings:

> How did the advertising wizards at Fruit of the Loom convince the homophobic consumers of our nation to cradle their manly organs in a binding piece of clothing with the word "Fruit" on it? I would have thought "Meat of the Loom" would be better targeted at the average American male.
>
> The actual marketing strategy was so bizarre it bordered on science fiction. They dressed up grown men in fruit costumes. What were these stoners thinking? . . . This is *proof* that use of psychedelics was much higher in this country than experts thought.

Styn's parody then went on to suggest alternative names for the underwear that the company's marketers might have rejected, such as "Fruit of the Loins," "Banana in my Briefs," "Looming Fruit (In my Undies)," and "Fruity Panties," among others. (The original mock ad and the legal aftermath are available on the Web at http://www.prehensile.com/does/fruitloom.htm.)

Styn's commentary elicited a stern, threatening letter from Fruit of the Loom's corporate counsel, Ross W. Blair, accusing Styn of infringing the company's trademark. "Our trademarks, such as FRUIT OF THE LOOM, are among our company's most valuable assets and we must protect these assets from diminution in value," wrote Blair on March 2, 1998. "To the extent that persons or entities not affiliated with our company begin using marks which are the same as or similar to our marks, this can result in a likelihood of confusion for consumers and the public, and can dilute the value of and/or tarnish our marks."

Blair gave Styn five days to remove his ads before commencing legal action, including a vague threat to "discontinue" Styn's use of his domain name.

Styn was unmoved. "You'd think a company that used grown men in fruit costumes in their TV ads would have a better sense of humor," he complained. "They should have gone after the guy in the marketing department who approved those ads. He did far more to tarnish their trademark than I ever could."

Styn made two follow-up queries to Fruit of the Loom asking for clarification in how he was supposedly breaking the law. The company's answer—in corporate legalese but paraphrased here by Styn—was, "Just take it down and there won't be any trouble. You can't afford to fight us. We're corporate America."

Rather than capitulate to Fruit of the Loom's intimidation, Styn fought back. Within forty-eight hours he had contacted more than a hundred independent Web publishers who pledged to support his cause. Banner ads reading "Freedom of speech doesn't end at an elastic waistband—Support your right to be funny" and "Rotten Fruit" images appeared on hundreds of Web sites, along with links to the Prehensile Tales site.

Styn estimates that fewer than 1,500 people had seen the "Meat of the Loom" parody in the eight months it had been posted online. But within two weeks after he launched his Web crusade against Fruit of the Loom, more than 250,000 visitors had checked out www.prehensile.com.

That Web-facilitated show of public support and anger proved to be decisive. Fruit of the Loom quickly sought peace. Or as Styn put it, "The wedgier quickly became the wedgied."

On March 17, 1998, fifteen days after sending a cease-and-desist letter, Fruit of the Loom sent a new, more conciliatory letter with weak, ingratiating attempts at humor: "We do want you to know that, while this subject has generated some excellent, often funny e-mail discourse, we have received some hate-filled, threatening e-mail messages that cause us concern. We will file them under 'Fruits' or 'Nuts,' and let's all hope the First Amendment withstands their support. . . . To those in cyber-land who might be listening, we want to make it clear that no un-fair use of our trademarks will be tolerated."

Styn's victory was celebrated by a flood of giddy commentary from his Web supporters, including a mock cease-and-desist letter signed by John Cardinal O'Connor to Fruit of the Loom: "It has come to our attention that your company is in violation of our famous Catholic prayer: 'Blessed be Mary, Mother of God, and the fruit of thy womb, Jesus.' Your company has taken these holy words in vain by naming your product, 'Fruit of the Loom.' Taking this phrase about Our Savior and using it to sell undergarments is both blasphemous and a trademark violation."

Styn's triumph illustrates the power of public exposure in pushing back on trademark bullies. It also suggests a larger avenue of strategic counterattack against a body of trademark law that is profoundly hostile to free speech and cultural expression. Styn's final word on the controversy: "Prehensile Tales prefers boxers." A Fruit of the Loom spokeswoman in 2004 declined to comment on the whole episode.

Superspy Shakedown:
James Bond Roughs Up Austin Powers

It should not be surprising, perhaps, that the companies that control the James Bond film franchise have their own private means of "persuading" evil adversaries. If James Bond can vanquish maniacal villains out to destroy the world, surely he should be able to prevent Austin Powers from making fun of him.

New Line Films in January 2002 announced that it would release a third Austin Powers movie, to be named *Goldmember*—an obvious takeoff on the 1964 James Bond movie *Goldfinger.* Jealous about any commercial harm to the Bond series, MGM and Danjac Productions, owner of the Bond films, complained that the title was "inadmissible" because it infringed upon MGM's copyright. MGM issued a statement saying it had "a zero-tolerance policy towards anyone who tries to trade in on the James Bond franchise without authorization."

One might think that the First Amendment would protect anyone who wanted to do a film parody. And in fact, New Line had produced *The Spy Who Shagged Me* in 1997, an obvious send-up of the 1977 007 adventure, *The Spy Who Loved Me.* But film studios that belong to the Motion Picture Association of America are obliged to clear their film titles through an MPAA-run title registration service. This voluntary process allows studios to proceed with script and film titles with the confidence that no one else will have an identical or similar title. Opting out of the system and settling issues through the court system would expose film studios to far greater risk and expense than voluntarily participating in a title-clearance commons.

But that means abiding by the rules of that regime. Although New Line followed official procedures for registering *The Spy Who Shagged Me,* it apparently failed to do so for *Goldmember.* This gave MGM enough of a reason to object to the film's title and press a claim for something in return. After an MPAA arbitration panel barred the *Goldmember* title, New Line was forced to shut down the *Goldmember* Web site and withdraw

11,000 movie trailers within a day. By April 2002, after negotiations between New Line and MGM, Austin Powers had found his mojo again and was able to proceed with the *Goldmember* title.

"Specific details were not released," according to the *Hollywood Reporter*, "but all future titles that may be construed as parodies of James Bond titles will be subject to MGM's approval." According to industry sources quoted by the *Reporter*, New Line agreed to attach a trailer for MGM's new Bond film, *Die Another Day*, to *Goldmember* prints in exchange for use of the title.

So it is that film studios can game the title-clearance process to prevent parody titles, or at least to extract concessions from wise guys.

The Grave Threat of Goofy T-Shirts

Parody is a classic genre of human societies and one of the most effective forms of political expression. But can it survive copyright and trademark law of the twenty-first century? A survey of court rulings over the past several decades shows that it can be dangerous to tweak the powerful. On countless occasions, the courts have banned naughty parodies and T-shirts that lampoon company logos because they allegedly violated trademark and copyright law.

What is maddening about these cases is their philosophical incoherence. Even when the factual patterns are remarkably similar, some spoofs are adjudged fair use while others are not. "Almost four decades of copyright cases in which parodists have been charged with infringement have not resulted in any consistent, predictable and coherent application of the fair use doctrine, at least until the Supreme Court's attempt in *Campbell v. Acuff-Rose Music, Inc.*," writes the Valparaiso University law scholar Geri J. Yonover. As if to betray their own incompetence at judging parodies, the courts make excruciatingly abstract critiques and highly contrived distinctions whose real purpose, it would appear, is to disguise the sheer subjectivity of the rulings.

Some legal scholars have noted that there is, in fact, no principled limit to the scope of trademark protection when the tests are as vague as "trademark dilution" or "tarnishment." Add in the variable cultural tastes of judges, and it is no surprise that courts apply highly inconsistent standards for parodies. Each case is something of a crapshoot for the defendant jokester.

Parody is particularly vulnerable to accusations of copyright and trademark infringement because it necessarily must quote from the original work, sometimes at great length or in total. How can you mock a song or a cartoon character without depicting it in some fashion? Conceding this point, courts have devised the "conjuring up" test: Does the parody conjure up enough—*but only enough*—of the original work to achieve its comedic effects? Any superfluous uses are prohibited.

Obviously, this standard of judgment may be asking a bit much of comedians. It virtually requires them to consult lawyers to ensure that their ridicule is properly calibrated so it will pass muster with copyright law. It also asks comedians to assume that their audiences are morons who will confuse a subtle parody with the trademarked work.

In 1983, for example, Franklyn Novak, to protest the nuclear arms race, produced and sold T-shirts bearing the words "Mutant of Omaha." The shirts also featured a side view of an emaciated human head wearing a feather bonnet that conjured up the Mutual of Omaha trademark, an Indian head. Alongside the design Novak had put the words "Nuclear Holocaust Insurance."

Naturally, Mutual of Omaha, the insurance company, did not like its trademarked logo being used for political commentary. To show that the T-shirt design would trigger a "likelihood of confusion" with its Indian head logo, the company surveyed four hundred people. One in ten people said they believed that Mutual had "gone along" with the T-shirts "in order to help make people aware of the nuclear war problem." Both the district and circuit courts found this compelling evidence of a trademark violation.

The clear message: if 10 percent of your audience doesn't get the parody, it may be illegal. Circuit court judge Heaney, in dissent, pointed out the truth: "The t-shirts simply expressed a political message which irritated the officers of Mutual, who decided to swat this pesky fly buzzing around in their backyard with a sledge hammer (a federal court injunction). We should not be a party to this effort."

Sometimes the courts don't wield a sledgehammer; they simply stand aside and let the corporate bullies act as the heavies. Take the T-shirts that a Houston nonprofit group, Doctors Ought to Care, produced to protest what it regarded as the irresponsible marketing of beer. Miller Brewing Company had just sponsored a splashy marketing campaign proclaiming,

"We're having a party" in Texas, which included Labor Day bashes open to the public in several cities. Meanwhile, Miller Lite touted its support of a health charity, the Texas Special Olympics.

Doctors Ought to Care came up with a protest T-shirt featuring a spoof on Miller Lite, "Killer Lite," with the mock slogan, "We're pushing a drug." The back of the shirt featured a man throwing up into a toilet, with the caption, "We're grabbing a potty." In September 1989, Miller Brewing sued the group, charging that the parody infringed on its trademark "in a manner calculated to slander plaintiffs' business reputation and dilute its goodwill." Miller also asked for an injunction to stop the sale of the shirts and unspecified damages.

The founder of the physicians' group, Dr. Alan Blum, defended its First Amendment right to spoof advertising. Most small-time parodists immediately fold when a large company accuses them of a trademark violation. Who can afford the legal fees? In this case, the physicians fought to a stalemate. Both sides settled and walked away from the litigation, citing its expense, with neither side acknowledging that the other party was right.

Typically, the inequality of economic power between corporation and parodist tends to determine who prevails in trademark infringement lawsuits. Because it takes a lot of money to win a serious debate on the legal merits, the weaker party—the parodist—is effectively censored and denied due process.

An unlikely victor against a trademark bully was Michael Berard, who in 1987 was a student at the University of North Carolina at Chapel Hill. Berard had designed a T-shirt that he planned to sell as a souvenir of Myrtle Beach, South Carolina. It depicted a beer can with a red, white, and blue label—think Budweiser—but instead of grandiose references to the great hops and barley of Bud, Berard substituted references to Myrtle Beach: Berard's T-shirt said, "Myrtle Beach contains the Choicest Surf, Sun, and Sand." Instead of "This Bud's for You," the T-shirt read, "This Beach is for You."

Get it? On appeal, the judges found no likelihood that consumers would falsely believe Bud had sanctioned the T-shirts, even though Bud also produced a line of Bud apparel. Anheuser-Busch, the maker of Budweiser, lost. But if Berard had known about the "Mutant of Omaha" ruling, he might never have dared to produce his innocuous T-shirt.

It is risky business trying to second-guess the federal bench's funny bone. For example, a federal court took a dim view of a parodist who sold novelty underwear that bore the script monogram for General Electric, but was altered to read, "Genital Electric." The court granted an injunction to stop sales of the goofy underwear.

By contrast, both district and circuit court judges looked more kindly upon a lighthearted spoof of Jordache Jeans. In 1984, two New Mexican entrepreneurs, Marsha Stafford and Susan Duran, formed a company, Hogg Wyld, Ltd., later Oink, Inc., to sell blue jeans to "larger women." They considered a variety of funny names—"Thunder Thighs," "Buffalo Buns," "Seambusters," "Rino Asirus," "Hippo Hoggers," "Vidal Sowsoon," and "Calvin Swine"—before settling on "Lardashe." Their logo, sewn into the seat of the pants, consisted of a smiling pig and the words, "You can't make a silk purse out of a sow's ear." They ultimately sold a thousand pairs.

Jordache, then the fourth largest maker of jeans in the country, charged Lardashe with trademark infringement. On appeal, the judges agreed that there was enough difference in the logo designs and script, despite the similarity of names, that there was no infringement. Go figure.

In general, parodies that put wholesome cartoon characters into off-color or obscene circumstances don't seem to go over too well in the federal courts. One of the landmark cases in this area is *Coca-Cola Co. v. Gemini Rising*, in which a marketing company created a poster that adapted the famous Coca-Cola script. Instead of reading "Enjoy Coca-Cola"—the drink's marketing slogan at the time—the parodist substituted, "Enjoy Cocaine." The court found a likelihood of confusion and business injury, and banned it: "[To] associate such a noxious substance as cocaine with [Coca-Cola's] wholesome beverage as symbolized by its 'Coca-Cola' trademark and format would clearly have a tendency to impugn that product and injure plaintiff's business reputation."

Free expression, anyone? The irony is that Coca-Cola's original formula actually contained cocaine. Mark Pendergrast explains in his history of Coca-Cola, "For over seventy years, the fact that the name clearly stemmed from its ingredients would inspire harried Coca-Cola lawyers to write tortured legal briefs arguing just the opposite."

If a court could hold that Coca-Cola would be tarnished by a spoof associating it with cocaine, it would seem that the Girl Scouts should enjoy similar protection against a scurrilous poster. Anyone who grew up in the sixties will remember a ubiquitous poster of the times—a smiling girl dressed in a Girl Scout uniform, holding her hands above her clearly pregnant abdomen—below which were the words, "Be Prepared." The Girl Scouts, like most parody victims, were offended.

While the court bemoaned the poster's bad taste, decrying that the defendant's name appeared in "regrettably small type" on the poster, it ruled that there was no likelihood that the public would believe the poster was sanctioned by the Girl Scouts. "Those who may be amused at the poster," wrote the court, "presumably never viewed the reputation of the plaintiff as being inviolable. Those who are indignant obviously continue to respect it. Perhaps it is because the reputation of the plaintiff is so secure against the wry assault of the defendant that no such damage has been demonstrated."

While the Girl Scouts could not prevail against a parody that questioned its sexual virtue, the makers of the immensely popular "Cabbage Patch Kids" dolls were able to stop sales of a series of novelty stickers for children known as the "Garbage Pail Kids." The Cabbage Patch Kids were a huge craze in the early 1980s. Parents stampeded toy stores to buy the dolls for their children at Christmastime, and shortages were common. More than forty million of the soft-sculptured dolls were sold.

Ever attuned to merchandising trends in the children's market, Topps Chewing Gum decided to launch its spoof stickers, the Garbage Pail Kids. While the Garbage Pail Kids had the same general appearance as the Cabbage Patch Kids and were aimed at the same demographic, seven- to ten-year-olds, the characters on the stickers were depicted in "rude, violent and frequently noxious settings," in the words of the court. Among the early cards: "Heavin' Steve" (a character vomiting) and "Potty Scott" (a character falling into the toilet). Kids loved them. The Garbage Pail Kids became so popular, especially in 1986, that Topps sold more than 800 million of the stickers, and licensed the images for T-shirts, school notebooks, balloons, and more.

The makers of the Cabbage Patch dolls sued. They argued that Topps' sales of the stickers were "unfair and infringing acts and that such acts will result in irreparable injury and damage to plaintiff for which there is no adequate remedy at law." The Garbage Pail Kids were no parody, said the doll maker, but simple piracy—a commercial exploitation of the Cabbage Patch Kids craze. The court agreed, and granted an injunction to stop sales of the cards.

The likelihood that someone might make money off a parody has historically been a big hurdle for spoofers. When a singing telegram service in Atlanta, Georgia, used two characters, "Super Stud" and "Wonder Wench," to sing "Happy Birthday" to guests, DC Comics, the trademark owner of Superman and Wonder Woman, sued. In 1984, the court ruled in favor of DC Comics, holding that "Defendants do not engage in critical comment that constitutes part of the 'free flow of ideas' underlying the doctrine of fair use. Instead, they seek to augment the commercial value of their own property by creating new, and detrimental, associations with plaintiff's property."

Campbell v. Acuff-Rose Music—the "Pretty Woman" parody discussed on pages 21–22—is clearly a landmark in the legalization of parody, especially for striking down the presumption that a commercial use is illegal and for clarifying and expanding the judicial standards that will apply. Still, pranksters should not rest easy. Send-ups that are too subtle are still likely to be regarded as theft. And there are still plenty of other legal doctrines— trademark dilution, state publicity laws, business disparagement, etc.—that aggrieved targets of parodies can invoke to silence the mockery.

Another Dangerous Art Form: Bawdy Spoofs

If naughtiness is occasionally given a pass by the parody police, bawdy spoofs seem to face a much higher hurdle. Or at least, judges show a chilly disdain when dealing with raunchy parodies, unwittingly adding to the humor with their prim legal analyses of smutty songs and cartoons. Such amusement aside, bawdy spoofs play an instructive role in showing us just how much cultural freedom we actually enjoy. Sometimes it takes a provocative parodist to demonstrate just how far the First Amendment has been whittled away.

Many judges do not seem to appreciate that sometimes the only effective way of communicating a point is by quoting a prior work. Just because that work is copyrighted or trademarked does not mean that the quotation should be considered "theft." But when so much of culture is reflexively regarded as property, that is precisely what happens.

In the early 1980s, the disc jockey Rick Dees did a tame spoof of the 1950s standard "When Sunny Gets Blue." He asked Marvin Fisher, a co-composer of the song with Jack Segal, if he could have their permission to use the tune. Fisher refused. Several months later, Dees cut an album that included a song called "When Sunny Sniffs Glue." Instead of the lines, "When Sunny gets blue, her eyes get gray and cloudy, then the rain begins to fall," Dees substituted, "When Sunny sniffs glue, her eyes get red and bulgy, then her hair begins to fall." The parody copied the first six bars of music in the song's thirty-eight bars, and ran for twenty-nine seconds of the forty minutes of Dees's album.

In this case, the court broad-mindedly upheld the parody as fair use. But the fact that it took a federal case to decide the legality of the parody is itself a powerful deterrent to would-be humorists. It is asking rather much for someone who wants to dash off a silly ditty that he be prepared to litigate all the way to the Ninth Circuit Court of Appeals, as Dees did (thanks to his corporate codefendants, Atlantic Recording Corporation and Warner Communications).

The era of Lenny Bruce may have passed, but parodists must still beware of the legal fragging they might have to endure to make an audience laugh. Copyright owners like to invoke the law to send a stern threat to anyone who mocks them. A classic case of this was the lawsuit that occurred when *Saturday Night Live* did a takeoff on the ubiquitous "I Love New York" advertising jingle created by Elsmere Music, Inc., for the New York State Department of Commerce.

The 1978 comedy sketch featured the cast of *SNL* portraying the mayor and members of the chamber of commerce of the biblical city of Sodom. They were discussing how the town's seamy image was hurting tourism and how they might showcase the more attractive aspects of Sodom's nightlife. The Sodom city fathers end up breaking into an a cappella chorus of "I Love Sodom," sung to the same four notes as "I Love New York"—D, C, D, and E, in that sequence.

The copyright owners of the jingle, Elsmere Music, Inc., sued NBC for copyright infringement, unfair competition, and defamation. To adjudicate such claims, the federal courts have become hairsplitting music critics. The judges needed to answer: Did "I Love Sodom" actually parody the original work, or was it simply exploiting the jingle for its renown? Did "I Love Sodom" appropriate more of the plaintiff's work than was necessary to "conjure up" the original? In this case, the court found "I Love Sodom" to be fair use.

Perhaps because his humor was a bit raunchier, Earl Wilson Jr. did not fare as well with the musical parody in his play *Let My People Come*, performed at the Village Gate in New York from 1974 to 1976. Wilson wrote a takeoff of the song made famous by the Andrews Sisters, "The Boogie Woogie Bugle Boy of Company B," which he renamed the "Cunnilingus Champion of Company C."

Wilson claimed he chose the song because it was "immediately identifiable as something happy and joyous and it brought back a certain period in our history when we felt that way." The juxtaposition of an unspoken sexual practice with a chirpy popular song evoking the 1940s was, of course, part of the joke. With dour disdain, however, the court sneered at Wilson's aesthetic. It could not resist noting that, contrary to Wilson's associations of "joy" with "The Boogie Woogie Bugle Boy," the song had "achieved its greater popularity during the tragic and unhappy years of World War II, in which 292,131 Americans lost their lives."

The problem with Wilson's parody, said both the district court and appeals court, was that it was not really a parody or burlesque, or even a comment on 1940s music; it had merely exploited the original song to enhance its own commercial appeal. "If the copyrighted song is not at least in part an object of the parody, there is no need to conjure it up. . . . We are not prepared to hold that a commercial composer can plagiarize a competitor's copyrighted song, substitute dirty lyrics of his own, perform it for commercial gain, and then escape liability by calling the end result a parody or satire on the mores of society. Such a holding would be an open-ended invitation to musical plagiarism." This sort of legal hairsplitting leads lawyers to distinguish between parodies (sometimes acceptable) and satires (not acceptable). Can you tell the difference?

The First Amendment seems to protect most instances of pornography, but that protection seems to end abruptly if trademarked characters are involved. One of the landmarks in this area is a parody published by *Screw* magazine in 1977. The magazine's publisher, Al Goldstein, commissioned an artist to sculpt three-dimensional plaster-of-paris replicas of the Pillsbury Company's trade characters "Poppin' Fresh" and "Poppie Fresh." The artist used the label from a can of Pillsbury cinnamon rolls to make her rendition of the Pillsbury doughboy and doughgirl.

The resulting parody, published in the December 19, 1977, issue of *Screw*, showed the two dough characters engaged in sexual intercourse and fellatio. Pillsbury sued for copyright and trademark infringement, violation of a state antidilution statute, and several counts of "tortuous tarnishment" of its trademarks and trade characters. Four years later, an

appeals court concluded that while Pillsbury failed to prove an infringement of its trademark, it did demonstrate "a likelihood that the defendants' presentation could injure the business reputation of the plaintiff
[Pillsbury] or dilute the distinctive quality of its trademarks."

The First Amendment was also nowhere to be seen when the courts
ruled that the producers of a famous 1970s porn movie, *Debbie Does Dallas*, could not depict a character wearing the same uniform worn by the
cheerleaders of the Dallas Cowboys football team ("white vinyl boots,
white shorts, a white belt decorated with blue stars, a blue bolero blouse,
and a white vest decorated with three blue stars on each side of the front
and a white fringe around the bottom").

The court noted, "In the movie's final scene Debbie dons a uniform
strikingly similar to that worn by the Dallas Cowboys Cheerleaders and
for approximately twelve minutes of film footage engages in various sex
acts while clad or partially clad in the uniform." Fair use? No, said the
court, because there was no parody involved—just a simple appropriation—and because "there are numerous ways in which defendants may
comment on 'sexuality in athletics' without infringing plaintiff's trademark." The preliminary injunction against the film was upheld.

It is a stretch for many people to invite pornographers under the
canopy of First Amendment protection. But if the court is serious about
free expression for "sexuality in athletics," one wonders why it should be
so objectionable for a film (of any sort) to evoke the uniforms of the
Dallas Cowboys cheerleaders. Prohibiting visual references to the trademarks of professional sports teams would make *any* speech about them far
less effective. Perhaps that is the real point. Fortunately, the Second Circuit, in a case brought by Ginger Rogers against the film *Ginger and Fred*
(see pages 134–135), retreated from its *Dallas Cowboys* opinion.

Still, if one were to believe the narratives told by federal court opinions, the bawdy parody cases are simple cases of piracy or pornography
that should not be given the time of day. The judicial accounts typically do
not understand, or choose not to recognize, that many parodies are cultural or political protests fully deserving of First Amendment protection.

One of the most stunning examples of this point can be found in
the "Air Pirates" spoofs of Disney characters published by a scruffy, talented band of underground cartoonists in the 1970s. The unreconstructed
hippie-cartoonists who comprised the Air Pirates lived communally in a
rented warehouse space in San Francisco and were led by Dan O'Neill,

who once drew the *Odd Bodkins* syndicated cartoon strip. Living in the countercultural hothouse of San Francisco of the late 1960s, the Air Pirates decided to go after Disney because of its "corporate seizure of the American narrative." They named themselves after a group of villains who fought with Mickey Mouse in some of his cartoons in the 1930s.

The Air Pirates considered themselves not just cartoonists in a traditional sense, but defiant political players determined to use their wicked caricatures of the Disney ethos in the cause of cultural liberation. Some cartoons depicted Mickey and Minnie Mouse having sex; others showed Disney-style animals on drugs or cursing. Still other cartoons—the ones that gained the most attention in the court opinion—showed Mickey masturbating. If the Disney characters were drawn with remarkable verisimilitude, the plotlines and dialogue were decidedly original.

Some 20,000 copies of two issues of *Air Pirates Funnies* were sold for 50 cents apiece in the summer of 1971. Both were billed as publications of Hell Comics—"If you're looking for laughs, go to Hell"—a goof on Dell Comics. When the comics initially failed to provoke a reaction from the Disney Company, the Air Pirates arranged to have some comics smuggled into a Disney board meeting.

In no time at all, Disney sought a preliminary injunction against the Air Pirates, claiming that their use of seventeen Disney characters constituted copyright infringement, trademark infringement, unfair competition, intentional interference with business, and trade disparagement. Disney sought damages of $5,000 per copyright infringement; treble damages for trademark infringement; compensatory damanges for unfair competition; and punitive damages of $100,000 per defendant.

The renegade cartoonists had virtually no assets to speak of; scraping together $1,000 to print the copies of *Air Pirates Funnies* had been challenge enough. Still, they did manage to find sympathetic San Francisco attorneys to take their case and argue that their comics should be protected under the fair use doctrine and the First Amendment.

In a hilarious and well-written book about the case, *The Pirates and the Mouse: Disney's War Against the Counterculture*, Bob Levin pointed out that the Air Pirates had some compelling legal arguments on their side:

> The parodists had created an original work, distinct in plot, dialogue, setting, themes and character personalities from anything Disney had ever done. Moreover, the Pirates were not trying to pass

their comics off as a Disney product. They aimed at a different market: adult hippies, not children. They sold through different outlets: head shops, not newsstands. They were not competing with any past, current—or probable—future Disney creation.

Since Disney's proprietary interests were not being hurt, argued the Air Pirates, Disney should not be allowed to squelch parodists who seek to comment on "an internationally known symbol of American culture and power."

At the time, there was some question whether a copyright owner could own a fictional character. The prevailing court precedent stemmed from a 1930s controversy over the ownership of Dashiell Hammett's detective character Sam Spade. Hammett had sold his *Maltese Falcon* story to Warner Bros. and then, years later, wrote a series of radio broadcasts for CBS, *The Adventures of Sam Spade*. This prompted Warner Bros. to sue CBS for using "its" fictional character. But the court sided with CBS, saying that "if the character is only the chessman in the game of telling the story he is not within the area of protection afforded by the copyright." By the reckoning of the Sam Spade ruling, Mickey Mouse should have been considered fair game. As a bland corporate spokesman, Mickey is remarkably dissociated from any particular story line.

In August 1975, a district court judge granted Disney's motion for summary judgment, essentially ruling that the Air Pirates had no fair use or First Amendment rights to use Disney's copyrighted characters. Three years later, in September 1978, a court of appeals affirmed this ruling. In the kind of legal parsing that is standard in parody cases, the Ninth Circuit held that the Air Pirates were entitled to make a "recognizable caricature" of Disney characters, but that "excessive copying precludes fair use." In a sense, because the Air Pirates were *too good* in their caricatures of Mickey et al., they had exceeded the bounds of fair use! The Ninth Circuit ingeniously wriggled out of its own Sam Spade precedent by declaring that that legal test applied only to literary characters, not to cartoon characters, because the latter have "physical as well as conceptual qualities" while the former do not.

If the legal reasoning for banning the Air Pirates' cartoons seems contrived and contorted, well, that's because it is. In his amusing account of the case, author Bob Levin offered this irreverent coda: "'The Ninth Cir-

This trash-talking Mickey Mouse appeared in an *Air Pirates Special Pirate Edition* produced by the New Mouse Liberation Front, a self-described "renegade operation in no way affiliated with the original Air Pirates Studio or its members." Still, one wonders . . .

cuit Court of Appeals ruled . . .' sounds infinitely more impressive than 'Three guys named Moe said . . .'; but, really, isn't that what it comes down to? Three men—lots of degrees—*mucho* eminence—seriousness up the gee-gee; but how do they put their pants on? Three Moes."

The cartoonists lost, but the sting of their parodies remains. An anonymous cartoonist of great skill, operating under the alias Mouse Liberation Front, later reprised the Air Pirates Comics. He cast Mickey Mouse as a hard-boiled corporate executive, who in one strip is talking on the phone to Disney CEO Michael Eisner: "That's right, Eisner. We've got to bury those fourth quarter earnings before the fucking Democrats change the tax code!" Another panel shows a defiant Mickey Mouse proclaiming: "I am Mickey Mouse and I am the American Dream!! It's simple. . . . I got mine. . . . Fuck you!"

And so the alternative imagining of Mickey Mouse, declared illegal under copyright law, returns with vulgar majesty.

CHAPTER 5

The Corporate
Privatization of Words

Polo Ralph Lauren products became famous by basking in the reflected glow of an elegant sport. Polo Ralph Lauren now asserts that it, not the sport, is the source of the glow.

—Judge Edith Jones, Fifth Circuit Court of Appeals

For marketers trying to insinuate their products into people's everyday lives, there is nothing like the appropriation of a common word. Owning a word is like owning the corner store at a busy intersection; its cultural visibility is unbeatable. If a company can own a trademark in a common word—say, "windows," "polo," "priceless," or "fair and balanced"—it can edge out a lot of would-be competitors.

But can words seized for use in the market be utterly sequestered from cultural use? Should the law allow only one acceptable meaning and set of associations for a word—the ones designated by the trademark owner? Or should a trademarked word be allowed to circulate freely so long as it is not used to perpetrate consumer confusion or fraud? This chapter looks at some of the absurd controversies that occur when property rights in words expand to ridiculous extremes.

Who Owns "Casablanca"?
Groucho Takes On the Studio Lawyers

Groucho Marx was not one to let copyright lawyers or studios get the better of him. In 1944, he got his opportunity to use his devastating power of ridicule to demolish both. Warner Bros. was fearful that the new

Marx Brothers film, *A Night in Casablanca*, might encroach upon the rights of their 1942 film *Casablanca*. The studio's legal department wrote Groucho warning him of a possible copyright problem.

As the copyright scholar Siva Vaidhyanathan tells the story in his book *Copyrights and Copywrongs*:

> First, Marx expressed surprise that the Warner Brothers could own something called "Casablanca" when the name had for centuries been firmly attached to the Moroccan city. Marx declared that he had recently discovered that in 1471 Ferdinand Balboa Warner, the great-grandfather of the Warners, had stumbled upon the North African city while searching for a shortcut to Burbank. . . .
>
>   Then Marx turned the issue of name ownership on the Warners. He conceded that they could claim control of "Warner," but certainly not "brothers." Marx claimed, "Professionally, we were brothers long before you were." Marx pointed out that even before the Marx Brothers, there were the Smith Brothers, the Brothers Karamazov, Detroit Tigers outfielder Dan Brothers and "Brother, can you spare a dime?" which Marx asserted was originally plural, "but this was spreading a dime pretty thin, so they threw out one brother." Marx asked Jack Warner if he was the first "Jack," citing Jack the Ripper as a possible precursor. Marx told Harry Warner that he had known several Harrys in his life, so Harry Warner might have to relinquish his title as well.

The dogged studio attorneys were no match for Groucho. When they tried to get him to disclose the film's plot to check for similarities with their film, Groucho made up an outlandish story involving his brother Chico living in a small Grecian urn on the outskirts of Casablanca, and then another one about a character named Bordello, the sweetheart of Humphrey Bogart, and Chico running an ostrich farm. And so on.

Eventually, Warner Bros. gave up. It is safe to say that no one would mistake *A Night in Casablanca* for *Casablanca*.

McDonald's "Ownership" of 131 Words and Phrases

Each day, millions of Americans show brazen contempt for property rights by daring to use dozens of words and phrases that McDonald's *owns*. It is not clear how many scofflaws have received nasty letters from McDonald's legal department, but chances are that anyone who publicly uses the words "Changing the Face of the World" or "Fun Always" may be trampling on McDonald's registered trademarks.

They own at least 131 of them. McDonald's also owns such phrases as "We Feed the Community in More Ways than One" (#74667812), "Play and Fun for Everyone" (#74618461), "Nothing But Net" (#78019374), and "Monster Snack" (#74421293). The company's trademark rights extend to dozens of other phrases that are now off-limits to the rest of us. Don't even think about treading on such phrases as "Healing through Happiness," and "Immunize for Healthy Lives," and "Black History Makers of Tomorrow." (For more on McDonald's fierce campaign to eradicate the use of the prefix "Mc" by any food-related enterprise, see page 212.)

It's not enough that McDonald's has remade large sectors of the American economy, including the meat and potato industries, in order to deliver predictable, standardized burgers and french fries. The company has a cultural agenda, too—to homogenize and privatize the cultural commons. Perhaps you don't think that a storm-trooping Ronald McDonald might pay you a visit for using his trademarked phrases. "Hey, it could happen." Oops! McDonald's claims a trademark—#74568193—for that phrase too!

You Must Be Socially Acceptable to Use the Word "Olympics"

In the early 1980s, the nonprofit San Francisco Arts & Athletics organization initiated plans to convene a "Gay Olympic Games" in San Francisco. The event sought to emulate the traditional Olympic Games with its ceremony, competition, and international goodwill, with the notable difference that it would feature gay athletes. A relay of over 2,000 runners would carry a torch from New York City to San Francisco; 1,300 athletes from twelve countries would compete in eighteen different events; and gold, silver, and bronze medals would be awarded. Merchandise promoting the Gay Olympic Games would be sold to finance the event.

A few months into the planning of the games, the organizers received a shock. The United States Olympic Committee informed them that it was illegal for them to use the word "Olympic" to describe or market their games. Since 1950, it had been a criminal act for anyone to use the words "Olympic," "Olympiad," "Citius Altius Fortius," or any combination of these words. The law had proven unworkable because it required proof of criminal intent, so in 1978, Congress made the unauthorized use of "Olympic" words a civil offense under Section 110 of the Amateur Sports Act. It also broadened the offense to include "any simulation or confusingly similar derivation . . . that falsely suggests a connection with the United States Olympic Committee or any Olympic activity."

Remarkably, the law gave the USOC exclusive control over the word "Olympic" without regard to whether an unauthorized use would actually cause confusion in the public mind. Simply using the word would be illegal. None of the customary defenses to the use of a trademark, as enumerated under the Lanham Act, could protect a defendant from liability for trademark infringement. The USOC was entitled to exclusive control over the word "Olympic," Congress concluded, because the USOC had distinguished the word through its own efforts. Along with the International Olympic Committee, the USOC had used the word since at least 1896 and had developed the format for the games that San Francisco Arts & Athletics was now imitating.

The USOC's stewardship of the word "Olympic" was hardly evenhanded, however. While prohibiting gays from using the word "Olympic," it allowed disabled children to use it for their "Special Olympics." Meanwhile, hundreds of listings of the word "Olympic" can be found in the telephone books of major cities, yet those uses of the word are not prohibited by the USOC. (One must wonder why the USOC finds any associations between the Olympics and homosexuals so distasteful given the sexual mores of the ancient Greeks who originated the games.)

In the USOC's lawsuit against San Francisco Arts & Athletics, a federal district court upheld Congress's authority to grant the USOC exclusive use of the word "Olympic" without having to prove that unauthorized uses were confusing. It also found no violation of the First Amendment. These rulings were upheld by the Ninth Circuit, and then appealed to the U.S. Supreme Court. In 1986, the Supreme Court reaffirmed by a 7-to-2 margin the lower court's ruling in *San Francisco Arts & Athletics, Inc. v. United States Olympic Committee*. The USOC's monopoly over words, the court held, amounted to "incidental restrictions on First Amendment freedoms" when balanced against the "substantial governmental interest" of giving the USOC "an incentive to continue produc[ing] a 'quality product.'"

The gay athletes had also claimed that the USOC's enforcement of its rights was discriminatory in violation of the equal protection component of the Due Process Clause of the Fifth Amendment. The USOC—a congressionally chartered organization exercising its congressionally granted power (over usage of the word "Olympic")—had approved use of the "Special Olympics" but rejected the "Gay Olympic Games." In a dissent at the circuit court level, Judge Alex Kozinski had noted this very point: "It seems that the [United States Olympic] Committee is using its control over the term Olympic to promote the very image of homosexuals that the [Athletics Group] seeks to combat: handicapped, juniors, police, Explorers, even *dogs* are allowed to carry the Olympic torch, but homosexuals are not." But the Supreme Court rejected this argument, saying that the USOC was not sufficiently a government agent for the equal protection component to apply.

The court's ruling has reached far beyond a ban on "Gay Olympic Games." At the Winter Olympics in 2002, the Salt Lake Organizing Committee vetoed all sorts of promotional language that alluded to the games. A Christian group that wanted to conduct religious outreach to visitors at the games were told that they could not use the phrase "2002 Games: A Window of Opportunity" or the words "More Than Gold" and "Salt Lake City 2002." An SLOC spokeswoman told a reporter, "The words 'Utah' and 'Games' and even '2002' are all fine, but when you connect Salt Lake City and 2002, there's a concern." When the Brighton Ski Resort in Utah took out the Internet domain www.brightonupthegames.com, the USOC filed a federal lawsuit claiming it was an unfair association with the Olympic Games.

Even Salt Lake City, the host city, was castigated by the SLOC brand police for its unauthorized references to the games. The city's economic development department naïvely thought it could refer to the "Olympics" in a marketing brochure. When the SLOC discovered the transgression, it ordered the brochure reprinted. A cowed city official later apologized: "We certainly meant no disrespect to the SLOC by saying the Olympics are coming to Salt Lake City."

Only Fox News Can Claim to Be "Fair and Balanced"

Disputes over ownership of words are often surrogates for other conflicts. Take the feud between Bill O'Reilly, the Fox commentator/host, and Al

Franken, the comedian and political progressive, over who can legally use the words "fair and balanced."

"Fair and balanced" has long been a clichéd objective of journalism. In 1998, Fox registered the phrase as a trademark and proceeded to spend $61 million promoting it. But because many TV viewers and even journalists consider the network's news coverage to be anything but fair and balanced, the tagline was ripe for a spoof. Al Franken was ready to oblige.

In August 2003, Franken was readying himself for a promotional campaign for his new book, *Lies and the Lying Liars Who Tell Them: A Fair and Balanced Look at the Right*. The book offers some scorching ridicule of Bill O'Reilly, author Ann Coulter, President George W. Bush, and other leading right-wing politicians and pundits.

By a number of accounts, O'Reilly went ballistic over the book. He reportedly prevailed upon the management of Fox News to sue Franken for trademark infringement in order to teach his critics a lesson: "You have a movement among the ultraleft to discredit me and Fox News Channel any way they can. They can't win the debate. They can't win the ratings war. So let's turn to defamation and we'll hide behind the satirist's label to defame. We don't have to be honest and accurate. It's a charade—people see it for what it is. It had to be exposed, and that's what that lawsuit did."

In their formal complaint, Fox lawyers said that "since Franken's reputation as a political commentator is not of the same caliber as the stellar reputations of FNC [Fox News Channel's] on-air talent, any association between Franken and Fox News is likely to blur or tarnish Fox News' distinctive mark." Even though the word "Lies" appears in large red letters on the book cover next to Bill O'Reilly's face, Fox News alleged that the Franken book was likely "to cause confusion among the public about whether Fox News has authorized or endorsed the Book, and about whether Franken is affiliated with FNC."

The complaint alleged, "Franken is commonly perceived as having to trade off the name recognition of others in order to make money." In a style more suited to a Fox commentary than a trademark complaint, the legal papers also called him a "C-level political commentator" with a "sophomoric approach to political commentary" who "appears to be shrill and unstable."

The federal court in Manhattan considered the lawsuit and its claims over the top. "There are hard cases and there are easy cases," said the U.S.

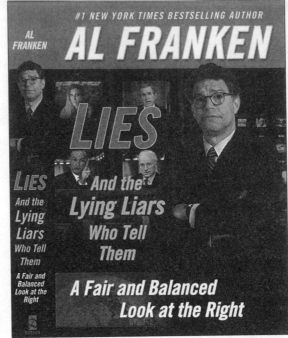

Does this book cover mislead you into thinking that Fox News authorized or endorsed the book? Fox News thought so.

district court judge Denny Chin. "This is an easy case. The case is wholly without merit both factually and legally. . . . It is ironic that a media company that should seek to protect the First Amendment is instead seeking to undermine it."

Judge Chin had pointed out during the proceedings that one of O'Reilly's own books—*The O'Reilly Factor: The Good, the Bad and the Completely Ridiculous in American Life*—trades upon a movie title, *The Good, the Bad and the Ugly*. Chin also suggested that a challenge to the Fox News trademark might well succeed because common words typically have weak protection. "It's highly unlikely that the phrase 'Fair and Balanced' is a valid trademark," he said.

"If Fox's intention was to break a large, undercooked ostrich egg on its corporate face while pouring streams of golden ducats into Franken's pockets," wrote a *Salon.com* reporter, "it carried out its plan to perfection." As a tool for intimidation, the lawsuit was an utter bust. Moreover, it handed Franken an astonishing publicity bonanza and a federal judge virtually invited a legal challenge to the Fox News trademark.

A Fox spokesman struck a bravura pose: "We don't care if it's Al Franken or Al Lewis or Weird Al Yankovic. We're here to protect our trademark and our talent." Floyd Abrams, the renowed First Amendment attorney who had represented Franken and his publisher, Penguin/Dutton, said: "Fox's lack of grace in ending its suit is of the same nature as its name-calling and silly efforts to deal with criticism of it in the first place."

Ultimately, as a matter of law, the Franken versus Fox dispute over "fair and balanced" is a sideshow of little significance. Fox News had no case. But as a case study of how trademark law is invoked as an attempt to intimidate defendants and settle scores, the controversy is a classic. What was rare in this case was its outcome: the defendant-parodist swiftly and decisively bested his attacker. Franken was lucky. He is a well-known author and had a publisher willing to shoulder the considerable legal expenses of pursuing the case. For every Franken, however, there are a thousand cease-and-desist letters that find their mark, silencing the critics of big companies and famous people without bothersome publicity.

Who Came First—Ralph Lauren or the Equestrians?

You would think that a clothing company that rips off the image and upper-crust associations of polo, the equestrian game, would have a little humility in what it seeks to own. But for trademark bullies, taking a little is an invitation to take still more. Over the past twenty years, Polo Ralph Lauren, the fashion company, has engaged in numerous squabbles with the U.S. Polo Association over who may use the word "polo" and in what ways.

Even though polo, the game, has been around for centuries, it was Polo Ralph Lauren that first trademarked the term "Polo" for its clothing, in the late 1960s. This proved to be a setup for a series of legal skirmishes that continue to this day. In 1984, a federal judge ruled that Lauren was entitled to the trademarks and logos that the U.S. Polo Association (USPA) argued were generic to the sport. The court held that Ralph Lauren had the exclusive right to use the word "polo" in its clothing and fragrance product lines, while the USPA could only use the word in connection with its name. The Polo Association was allowed to use a logo featuring a mounted horseman polo player so long as it differed from Ralph Lauren's logo.

But in 1999, Ralph Lauren initiated another set of trademark infringement complaints. It charged that a "re-launched" version of *Polo* magazine was aimed not just at polo enthusiasts but at affluent general readers—the very people whom Ralph Lauren considered to be *its* franchise. It forced the USPA to change the name of its magazine, *Polo* (it is now *Polo Players' Edition*); the clothing company now publishes "the Ralph Lauren online lifestyle magazine," *Polo.com*. When the association decided to sell its own polo-related clothing through a licensing deal with Jordache, Ralph Lauren sued again—and notified retailers such as J.C. Penney and TJ Maxx of the litigation. The association charged that Lauren "wrongfully intimidated" retailers into discontinuing sales of clothing and accessories bearing the association's name or logo. In a 2004 filing with the Securities and Exchange Commission, Polo Ralph Lauren said that it had simply "informed these retailers of our position in the original trademark action [the 1999 lawsuit]."

Polo Ralph Lauren would not comment further on its pending litigation, but a U.S. Polo Association attorney told me that it had reached a "partial settlement" with PRL. USPA may use the word "polo" so long as it is part of its name and is not emphasized with a larger font or different color, for example. For its part, PRL will continue to have rights over "polo" as a stand-alone word, when used in connection with sports apparel.

A separate controversy, still unresolved, is over the respective "horseman" logos for the two organizations. PRL's logo shows a polo player on horseback; USPA's logo features a "double horseman" with the polo mallet in a different position. If no agreement over the logo can be reached, arbitration may follow.

There is a certain irony, of course, that a clothing maker has usurped the elite image that originated with the sport of polo. As an appeals court in the dispute over *Polo* magazine stated, "PRL [Polo Ralph Lauren] products became famous by basking in the reflected glow of an elegant sport. PRL now asserts that it, not the sport, is the source of the glow. In a sense, PRL is biting the hand that fed it." Nevertheless, the court sided with the clothing company, finding a trademark infringement even as it worried about the First Amendment implications. There is a long tradition in corporate America (think Disney, Mattel, and record companies) of poaching the public domain and then claiming exclusive rights in the proprietary knockoff. Polo Ralph Lauren's innovation was to apply this strategy to an entire sport, and to do it in the 1960s, well before anyone else had discovered the marketability of the elite sport.

Patrolling the Boundaries of Mental Association

Like most owners of famous trademarks, V. Secret, Inc., the company that operates the Victoria's Secret catalog, does not want anyone messing with the mental associations that hover around the words "Victoria's Secret." The "goodwill" associated with that trademark consists of images of scantily clad models in suggestive poses, as well as its famous titillation webcast and television "shows" featuring pouty models parading down a fashion catwalk.

Enter Victor and Cathy Moseley, an Elizabethtown, Kentucky, couple who started a mom-and-pop store selling lingerie and adult sex toys. In a business that thrives on the coy come-on, Victor Moseley came up with an arresting title for his strip-mall store—"Victor's Secret." Its motto: "Everything for romantic encounters."

The rise of a sex toys retailer with a name that evoked Victoria's Secret did not sit too well with V. Secret, the company that had registered "Victoria's Secret" as a trademark in 1981. V. Secret felt that "Victor's Secret" would elicit unauthorized, unattractive associations with its trademark and thereby cause economic harm. At the time, the company claimed it was sending more than 3.5 million copies of its catalogs to Kentucky residents, and 39,000 a year to residents of Elizabethtown alone. (This claim raised some eyebrows in court since the town has only 20,000 residents.) In 1998, claiming trademark dilution and tarnishment, V. Secret sued the Moseleys.

The Moseleys tried to mollify V. Secret by adding the word "Little" to their store's name, making it "Victor's Little Secret." But V. Secret was not placated. The case rolled on through the courts until it reached the U.S. Supreme Court in 2002. The case represented the first time that the high court had interpreted the scope and meaning of the federal trademark dilution law. Because the case might have sweeping implications for the meaning of trademark dilution, a number of public-interest organizations, including Public Knowledge and the Electronic Frontier Foundation, submitted friend-of-the-court briefs supporting the Moseleys.

The crux of the case was to determine what legal standard should be used in establishing trademark dilution. If trademark *infringement* can be demonstrated by consumer confusion—a fairly clear standard for which empirical tests are possible—trademark *dilution* has been notoriously difficult to define in real-life cases. "We know what it is to be confused, but as a cognitive event we don't know exactly what it is to experience a diminution of good will," Jonathan Moskin, a New York City intellectual property attorney, told the *New York Times.*

The nation's largest corporations understandably sided with V. Secret; they wanted dilution to be defined as any alteration of consumers' mental associations with a trademark. But in its 2003 ruling, the Supreme Court rejected that standard as too vague and speculative, insisting that trademark owners must demonstrate some current harm from the use of a similar mark: "[The statute] unambiguously requires a showing of actual dilution, rather than just a likelihood of dilution," wrote Justice John Paul Stevens for the unanimous court.

Unfortunately, the court declined to give any specific guidance on how a victim of trademark dilution must demonstrate that she suffered harm. The court sent the case of "Victor's Little Secret" back to the district court to assess whether the Moseleys inflicted any discernible harm on "Victoria's Secret." However the case comes out, the meaning of trademark dilution is not likely to be resolved anytime soon.

The Value of Godzilla? Priceless!

In their obsession to prevent the hoi polloi from using proprietary words without permission, brand-name bullies seem to instigate new controversies every few weeks. Over time, after a very public and nasty controversy, these common words acquire a kind of stigma, an aura that sets them apart as contestable words that are likely to trigger litigation. Consider the claimed ownership of "priceless," "Godzilla," "entrepreneur," and a handful of other prosaic terms.

One of the more memorable word grabs was MasterCard's claimed monopoly over "Priceless." In the midst of his 2000 run for the presidency, Green Party candidate Ralph Nader aired a series of television advertisements that used the word "priceless," mimicking MasterCard's well-known series of ads. The MasterCard ads typically recited the monetary costs of some experience—dinner out or a baseball game—then named a sentimental moment associated with the event as "priceless." The ads ended with the tagline, "There are some things money can't buy. For everything else there's MasterCard."

In Nader's ad, an announcer reads, "Grilled tenderloin for fund-raiser: $1,000 a plate. Campaign ads filled with half-truths: $10 million. Promises to special interest groups: over $10 billion. Finding out the truth: price-less. There are some things money can't buy. Without Ralph Nader in the presidential debates, the truth will come in last."

Claiming its trademark had been violated, MasterCard sued Nader for $15 million. A spokesman said, "This is clearly not a spoof; it's a misap-propriation of our valuable property in an ad intended for promotional use." Nader's ads, she said, "could create the confusing impression that we support Ralph Nader."

In response, Nader reportedly quipped, "I guess MasterCard doesn't think the word 'priceless' is really priceless." Nader said his spots were clearly parodies, and thus protected, expressive speech. "Let me assure MasterCard's executives that the last thing I want consumers to believe is that my campaign is in the business of selling credit cards," he told CNN.

In characteristic fashion, Nader seized upon MasterCard's attack as an opportunity to counterattack: "It is certainly time for everybody in the country to focus on the enormous gouging that millions of Americans are exposed to, the deceptive practices of credit card providers," he said. "MasterCard is taking itself a little too seriously and, in typical corporate style, is trying not only to dominate the credit card industry . . . but also wishes to control the arena of free speech and the free flow of creative ideas in the political arena."

To defend his ads in court, Nader enlisted the UC Berkeley law pro-fessor Mark Lemley, who said that the case was the first time that anyone had tried to enjoin a campaign ad in the middle of a campaign. He added, "It would be a bad precedent to be enjoining political ads on the basis of trademark claims." The court brief filed for Nader insisted that the ads were a spoof: "It seems quite clear that everyone except MasterCard 'gets' the joke. Virtually all the news commentary on the ad comments on the ironic juxtaposition of Nader's 2000 ad with MasterCard's campaign."

On September 12, 2000, a federal judge dismissed MasterCard's request for an injunction, saying the company had failed to prove irreparable harm to itself. But the lawsuit was still pending in 2004.

When a company trademarks a term, the law grants greater protection to distinctive words that have acquired a "secondary meaning" associated only with the company or product. For example, made-up words like "Xerox" and "XyWrite" are clearly more distinctive and therefore more protected than common words. Yet this general principle did not help California entrepreneur Scott Smith. A court told him he could not name his public relations firm "EntrepreneurPR" or name an annual publication *Entrepreneur Illustrated*.

A company called Entrepreneur Media Inc. already claimed a trademark in "Enterpreneur," the title of its magazine. In 2000, a federal judge stopped Smith from using the word "entrepreneur" and ordered him to pay $337,280 in damages. Smith subsequently changed his company's name to "BizStarz." On appeal, the Ninth Circuit upheld the claim of infringement with respect to *Entrepreneur Illustrated* because the word "Illustrated" was in much smaller type, making it more likely that consumers would confuse it with *Enterpreneur* magazine. But it ordered that a jury assess whether the other uses of "entrepreneur"—EntrepreneurPR and the Web site address "entrepreneurpr.com"—constituted a trademark infringement.

Entrepreneur Media Inc.'s campaign against other uses of "entrepreneur" did not stop there. It informed *Female Entrepreneur*, a new magazine, of its displeasure with its name, persuading its publisher to change the name to *Fempreneur*. The company's affiliated radio program, membership organization, and regional publications, each of which also used the term "female entrepreneur," also changed their names. Another magazine that felt the heat from Entrepreneur Media and changed its name was *Young Entrepreneur*.

One wonders if other publications using the word "entrepreneur"— *Entrepreneur's Journal*, *Entrepreneurs' Chronicle*, *Dental Entrepreneur*, and *Extreme Entrepreneur*—will soon be sporting new names.

No word is apparently too common to fight about. In September 2003, the Fédération Internationale de Football Association threatened legal action against Nike, the sportswear maker, for using the words "USA 2003." The association claimed that using these symbols on apparel would constitute unfair competition and false advertising. The association said that it had successfully defended trademarks in "France 98," "Korea/Japan 2002," and "Germany 2006" on shirts, hats, and other merchandise. "USA 2003" was just another example of unauthorized use of a trademarked term, the association said. Nike responded that the term was not even trademarked and won a court ruling that the association had failed to establish a "secondary meaning" for the term.

There are plenty of newspapers named *Times* and *Gazette*. So why should the *Village Voice* be able to claim a monopoly on newspapers named *Voice*? In 1998, Fran Reichenbach started a community newspaper in Hollywood and named it the *Beachwood Voice.* She used the same blue-and-white rectangular design as the *Village Voice.*

Even though the newspaper was published only four times a year for only 5,000 readers, attorneys for the *Village Voice* in 2003 accused her of "a calculated attempt to confuse" readers about its affiliation with the New York City paper. Reichenbach obligingly redesigned the logo for the newspaper so that it looked completely different. But even this was not enough for the *Village Voice's* law firm, Kay & Boose, which informed the *Beachwood Voice* that unless it changed its name, it would proceed "at its peril."

This was not an isolated case. As Alexander Zaitchik reported in the *New York Press,* Stern Publishing, then the owners of the *Village Voice,* was bullying all sorts of newspapers with "Voice" in their names to change their names. In the face of legal threats, The *Bloomington Voice* became the *Bloomington Independent,* the *Tacoma Voice* became the *Tacoma Reporter,* and the *Dayton Voice* became the *Dayton Impact Weekly* and later the *Dayton City Paper.*

When the *Village Voice* tried to use this track record of intimidation to force the *Cape Cod Voice* into surrendering its name, the Cape Cod paper hired a Boston law firm and took the issue public. Soon Norman Mailer, a resident of Provincetown, was writing that the *Village Voice's* tactics were "enough to make one retch. It's monstrous. It violates everything *The Village Voice* stood for over the decades." The *Village Voice* columnist and civil libertarian Nat Hentoff also denounced the action, calling it "ridiculous" and "embarrassing."

The *Cape Cod Voice* ultimately prevailed and still holds its name today. Fran Reichenbach, editor of the *Beachwood Voice,* said that, following publication of an article in the *New York Press* describing the episode, she never heard from the *Village Voice* attorneys again.

The revenues to be reaped from owning a popular word are sometimes astonishing. In 1989, then–Lakers coach Pat Riley was sitting beside a pool in Hawaii trying to think up a way to motivate his basketball team to try to win a third consecutive championship. Lakers guard Byron Scott came up with the word "three-peat" to describe such an achievement, and Riley soon launched the word into public usage through interviews with the press. Although the Lakers did not win a three-peat, Riley and a group of investors proceeded to register it as a trademark.

When the Chicago Bulls won the first three-peat in 1993, Riley et al. reaped a bonanza by licensing the word to merchandisers, who plastered it over countless T-shirts, hats, pennants, and other items. Although their actual take is not known, when the Lakers in 2002 had the chance to win a three-peat, merchandising experts predicted that Riley would "earn" 5 percent of $3 million in anticipated sales of three-peat merchandise, or $150,000.

The presumption of owning a popularly used term is not only ridiculous, it can stifle legitimate popular uses. Take "Godzilla." The term is commonly used as a synonym for a giant monster. So should its trademark owner, Toho Co. Ltd. of Japan, be able to shut down derivations that use "zilla"?

That's what happened to Dave Linabury, the owner of an online humor Web site, Davezilla.com. In August 2002, Toho sent Linabury a "nasty-gram" letter claiming that the domain name and its use of a "'reptile-like' character as well as a 'monster-like' character . . . constitutes a trademark infringement and confuses consumers and the public into believing that your 'Godzilla' character originates from Toho, which it does not."

The idea that anything that is "reptile-like" or "monster-like" and associated with the phoneme "zilla" belongs to the trademark holder of God-zilla is daffy, of course. "The silly thing is," said Linabury on his Web site, "[Toho's cease-and-desist letter] reads like a form letter and it's quite obvious they've never visited my site. I have no mentions [until posting their letter] or images of Godzilla anywhere on my site. Google has 29,000 links to my site but no Godzilla on there."

Toho has ignored many other derivations using "zilla." It has not apparently gone after Mozilla, the open source version of the Netscape browser; Issuzilla, a software bug-reporting system; Go!zilla, a software download program; or Budgiezilla, a mock movie advertisement on the Web about giant birds that destroy a city. Paul Alan Levy, an attorney with the Public Citizen Litigation Group, noted that the Patent and Trademark Office's electronic database features a number of trademarks ending in "zilla," including "bosszilla, bootzilla, dogzilla, webzilla and bockzilla."

One wag captured the real significance of the Davezilla legal quarrel: "Coming soon: 'Lawyerzilla: The Monster That Ate the World!' "

The Internet and the Rise of Super-Trademarks

In their zeal to control a trade name in the Internet age, many companies are asserting ownership of common words or phrases even though the risks of consumer fraud or confusion are nil. Because the Internet has expanded the scope of business activity, some trademark holders seem to believe that they should be able to control all uses of their trade name, whether on the Internet or in local advertising.

Trademark disputes over Internet domain names occur frequently. Such Internet domain names as airport.biz., brands.biz., paint.biz, and taxman.biz have been forcibly transferred from domain-name registrants to trademark holders who claimed an overriding legal right to the word. Kalmar Industries USA Inc., a Texas company that owns a trademark in the word "Ottawa" as it relates to truck tractors, forced the owner of the Internet domain name "ottawa.biz" to surrender the name even though Ottawa, the Canadian city, obviously came first. The singer Madonna succeeded in shutting down a site using the word "madonna." An online U.S. retailer, eToys (at etoys.com), once tried to shut down an avant-garde group of prankster/artists who go by the name etoy (at etoy.com).

One reason that trademark holders have acquired preferential rights in words and phrases is policies adopted by ICANN, the Internet Corporation for Assigned Names and Numbers. This private body, acting under powers ostensibly delegated to it by the U.S. Department of Commerce, acts as a quasi-governmental policymaker in resolving domain-name disputes, among other things. ICANN developed a system for resolving domain-name disputes through mandatory arbitration known as the Uniform Dispute Resolution Policy, or UDRP, but losers in this process can still resort to the courts.

A great many domain-name disputes involve trademarked words and phrases, and studies have shown that trademark holders tend to prevail. The UDRP allows trade- or service mark holders to acquire an existing domain name if three conditions exist: the name is "identical or confusingly similar," the registrant has "no rights or legitimate interests" in the domain name, or the domain name was registered "in bad faith." In practice, writes Professor Michael A. Geist, these standards give "trademark holders far greater rights online than offline and in the process effectively created a new super-trademark."

Sometimes the trademark holder may not actually have greater legal rights, but simply the resources to intimidate individuals and small businesses. In 2000, the Ford Motor Company decided that anyone who held domain names with the words "Ford," "Jaguar," or "Volvo" was a cybersquatter who should be legally stripped of the domain names. (Ford owns the companies that make the latter two lines of cars.) Ford sent letters to

a club of Jaguar automobile fans (www.jaguarenthusiasticsclub.com), a Volvo
repair shop in Santa Cruz, California (www.volvoguy.com), and a children's Web site about endangered wildcats (www.jaguarcenter.com), threatening legal action unless they surrendered their domain names.

The Electronic Frontier Foundation agreed to defend the owners of
six domain names, at which point Ford's enthusiasm for pursuing the cases
cooled. An EFF attorney had to prod the cases along in court, which suggested that Ford was simply hoping to wear down its adversaries through
attrition. That is exactly what happened. Despite free legal representation
and little likelihood of paying damages, four of the EFF clients found the
litigation too stressful and surrendered their domain names to Ford.

Microsoft Corporation, which enjoys a veritable monopoly on computer operating systems, seems to think that it should own the word "windows" as well. The company sued Lindows.com, Inc., a company that
markets a version of the GNU/Linux operating system with a Windows-
like interface and compatibility with Windows programs. Linux, of course,
is one of the most potent competitive threats still facing Microsoft, so
naturally Microsoft has every interest in seeing Linux fail. But it is a bit of
a stretch to argue that any consumer would believe that "Lindows" is a
Microsoft product.

Fortunately, a federal district court rejected Microsoft's claims in February 2004. It held that once a word is generic, no amount of marketing
can make it proprietary. "Essentially, the court's ruling confirms that a
company, no matter how much money it spends, cannot buy a word out
of the English language," said the lead trial counsel for Lindows.com.

Although the court prevented Microsoft from taking a generic English
word private, the company shrewdly saw the value of pursuing lawsuits
against the "Lindows" trademark in foreign nations. Since the market for
computers is global, foreign litigation had the effect of making retailers
wary of doing business with Lindows, especially after Microsoft announced
plans to appeal the U.S. district court ruling. Unable to weather the market uncertainties, the Lindows company in April 2004 decided to change
the name of its operating system to "Linspire" while retaining its company name for U.S. operations. It will continue to battle in the U.S.
courts for the right to use the word "Lindows."

If your name is Ray and you want to name your neighborhood pizza
joint after yourself, there's a good chance that trademark law will interfere

with your plans. Ever since U.S.A. Famous Original Ray's Licensing Corp. acquired the trademarks for Ray's Pizza, Famous Ray's Pizza, Famous Original Ray's Pizza, and The Original Ray's Pizza, its lawyers have been going after local pizzerias that use the name Ray.

No matter that your corner Ray's Pizza may have come first. A lawyer for U.S.A. Famous Original Ray's told the *Wall Street Journal*, "People crop up all the time trying to copy a successful trademark, and we intend to continue stopping them. They are infringers."

The idea that trademark law allows an absolute national monopoly on a given word or phrase is a new one. "Trademark law is designed to allow multiple, concurrent use of the same name by different people in the same business in different places or by substantially different businesses in the same place," explains the University of Miami law professor A. Michael Froomkin. Even though trademark is a federal body of law, it allows local and regional variations to coexist with national names. In addition, companies in different lines of trade, such as Apple Computer and Apple Records, or Delta Airlines and Delta plumbing fixtures, can share the same word.

But this principle of mutual coexistence in sharing words or phrases has come under siege now that the Internet has made the entire globe a single, unified arena of public consciousness. The desire among trademark owners to control the fate of a word and its use on a global scale becomes irresistible.

Earl Farmer, who sells and repairs vacuum cleaners, was sued by the maker of Kirby vacuums for naming "Kirby" in his Yellow Pages ads as one of the brands he services. The Kirby Co. claimed that its trademark had been used without authorization. Robin C. Mueller, a psychic from Armonk, New York, was told by the Intel Corporation, maker of computer chips, that she could not name her company "SpiritInside" because it supposedly infringed upon Intel's trademark, "Intel Inside."

When Warner Bros. released its first Harry Potter film, it claimed that unauthorized use of the Harry Potter name and characters, even for noncommercial purposes, "was likely to cause consumer confusion or dilution of intellectual property rights." This inescapably meant that Warner Bros. had to threaten its core audience, children, with legal action.

Fifteen-year-old Claire Field of Great Britain received a letter from Warner Bros.' legal department in August 2000 claiming that her Web site, www.harrypotterisawizard.co.uk, would have to be surrendered. It offered £9.99. The girl alerted the British press about the threat and unleashed a firestorm of public outrage.

"Warner Brothers seems to be operating under the proviso that *anything* with the words 'harry potter' in it are its property," wrote the *Register.* "What the hell is wrong with a young fan having a fan site? Nothing, WB will say. Then what the hell are they supposed to call it?" The editorialist continued, "What we have here is a vast, ugly corporation which makes most of its money from entertaining children, firing out legal letters and bullying those very kids without any thought given to the facts or the receiver."

Perhaps this sort of publicity had a chastening effect on Warner Bros., or perhaps the value of "viral marketing" was discovered. In any case, the studio by 2004 was inviting fans to join the AOL Hometown service and create their own Harry Potter Web site.

The Forbidden Words: "This Corporation Sucks!"

Should trademark holders be able to shut down domain names that in some way use their trade name? Trademark owners often succeed in bullying small businesses and individuals into forfeiting Internet domain names that they legitimately acquired, even if the legal claims are dubious and the disputed name has a common or generic meaning.

A classic case involved a dispute between Nissan Motor Co., the Japanese automaker, and Nissan Computer Corp., a North Carolina–based corporation. Uzi Nissan, an Israeli American, owns the latter business, and on its behalf he registered the domain name Nissan.com in June 1994, and Nissan.net in March 1996. His last name, he points out, happens to mean the month of April in Arabic and is the seventh month in the Hebrew calendar.

In 2000, Nissan Motor Co. sued Nissan Computer Corp., seeking $10 million in damages and an order to prevent Uzi Nissan from using his family name for business purposes on the Internet. Although the court dismissed the automaker's cybersquatting complaint against Uzi Nissan, it held that Mr. Nissan had diluted the automaker's trademark by posting criticisms of Nissan and advertising for rival auto companies on www.nissan.com and www.nissan.net. Mr. Nissan appealed the case to the Ninth

Circuit Court of Appeals, which reversed the lower court in August 2004, clearing the way for a possible trial. Public Citizen, a group that has often defended free speech rights on the Internet, has argued to the court that Uzi Nissan's free speech interests in the domain name should be protected so long as he disclaims any connection with the automaker.

In similar disputes, Caterpillar, the industrial machines company, succeeded in forcing domain-name holders to relinquish sites named "caterpillar.com" and "catmachines.com." The Tata Group India, a multi-billion-dollar industrial company, brought an action against an Internet domain-name holder that used the term "bodacious tatas." A Uniform Dispute Resolution Policy/World Intellectual Property Organization panel ruled that the Tata trademark "deserve[s] wide protection" due to its "aura of high repute," and that because the term means "large female breasts" in some parts of the United States, the domain name was confusingly similar to the Tata trademark and must be relinquished.

Should the clothing maker J. Crew have the right to bar domain-name holders from the word "crew"? The ICANN domain-name dispute resolution board thought so. But a dissenter on that panel objected, "the majority seems to assume that a trademark owner has some sort of God given right to use the trademark to the exclusion of others. As Justice Holmes observed, 'A trademark does not confer a right to prohibit the use of the word or words. A trademark only gives the right to prohibit the use of it so far as to protect the owner's goodwill against the sale of another's product as his.' *Prestonettes, Inc. v. Coty*, 264 U.S. 359 (1924). In short, the Complainant does not own all rights to the generic word CREW by virtue of its trademark registration."

This legal principle does not inhibit law firms from sending nasty letters trying to force the owners of domain names to surrender them. Most of these letters are more bark than bite in terms of their legal force, since trademark law only protects against consumer confusion. But most people do not understand that they have rights that can be asserted against trademark owners whose lawyers misstate the law. Nor can most individuals afford a legal opinion to learn their rights, let alone wage protracted litigation. So they acquiesce, forfeit their rights, and turn over the domain name.

The result is not only a basic inequity, but an assault on cultural expression and free speech. Many such cases involve humor or parody.

CNNfn, the Cable News Network's financial network, sought to shut down CNNdn, a spoof site that billed itself as "the financial crash network," dedicated to commenting on the state of the economy. A critic who legitimately acquired the domain name "jerryfalwell.com" was sued by the Rev. Jerry Falwell. (Falwell lost an arbitration ruling and a procedural issue in federal court before the critic surrendered the domain name rather than risk further lawsuits.) And the Republican Party of Texas sent a cease-and-desist letter to the owners of www.EnronOwnstheGop.com, which featured a logo that mimicked the party's official logo. (The GOP apparently dropped its lawsuit; the site is still up.)

A great many other disputes revolve around whether the word "sucks" can be added to a trade name and used as an Internet domain name. A notable recent example was a ruling by the U.S. Court of Appeals for the Sixth Circuit holding that a critic of the Taubman Company, which builds shopping malls, cannot be forced to remove its "taubmansucks .com" Web site. But an international domain-name dispute involving "vivendiuniversalsucks.com" was decided in favor of the company by the World Intellectual Property Organization on the grounds that "non-English-speaking Internet users would be likely to attach no significance to the appended word 'sucks' and would therefore regard the disputed domain name as conveying an association with the Complainant [Vivendi/ Universal]."

The real point, of course, is that large corporations don't like to be criticized on a public stage as big as the Web. Trademark law provides a handy shield. In the meantime, many major corporations are preemptively acquiring derisive domain names for themselves. The Volvo automobile company controls Volvosucks.com. Charles Schwab & Co. has bought up Screwschwab.com and Schwabsucks.com. Chase Manhattan Bank has gone so far as to buy up IhateChase.com, ChaseStinks.com, ChaseSucks.com, and ChaseBlows.com.

So many critics have availed themselves of "sucks" domain names that the Nader-founded Consumer Project on Technology once proposed to ICANN that ".sucks" be added as a top-level domain similar to .com or .org. (The idea was rejected.) Critics of corporations are therefore forced to fend for themselves while trademark owners stomp across the cultural landscape like marauding Godzillas.

CHAPTER 6

Property Rights in Public Image

Only that audience out there makes a star. It's up to them. You can't do anything about it. . . . Stars would be Louis B. Mayer's cousins if you could make 'em up.

—Jack Nicholson

It is well-known that the Founding Fathers of the United States loathed the idea of an aristocracy and wanted to establish an active and engaged democratic culture. To that end, Madison, Franklin, Jefferson, and the others not only framed the Constitution and the Bill of Rights, they also treated their own fame as an "open access" resource in the forging of a national culture. In the spirit of the First Amendment, anyone could depict the Founders on everything from fine art and sculpture to mass-marketed plates and medallions. The record shows that they didn't charge licensing fees or gripe about unauthorized reproductions of their images.

To the early American leaders, fame was considered its own reward—the highest republican virtue. When Franklin discovered that his picture was being used on chamber pots, the great patriot—who was no slouch at exploiting moneymaking opportunities—laughed it off with a joke.

Nowadays, of course, fame is associated with wealth, as in "rich and famous." This has a lot to do with the granting of property rights in personality and public image. It may seem utterly normal today for fame to be treated as a species of capital—a scarce asset to be leveraged for cold, hard cash. Yet for most of American history, fame was not considered an economic resource. The courts did not recognize a property right in fame until 1953, when one enterprising company published baseball cards with the photos of players who had appeared in another set of baseball cards.

An appeals court ruled that the players had a legal interest in the commercial value of their photographs.

A year later, the copyright scholar Melville Nimmer wrote an influential law review article urging the courts to recognize a right of publicity—"the right of each person to control and profit from the publicity values which he has created or purchased." In short order, the race was on to commodify the intangibles that the mass media consider the raw material for their business—celebrity images, fictional characters, merchandising, publicity, and more.

Far from a benign evolution of law, the growth of publicity and persona rights inaugurated a new sort of culture war. It instigated new conflicts over who would be able to determine the public meanings of famous personalities or symbols. With the creation of property rights in publicity and personas, control over famous images and symbols would flow to corporations and the wealthy, and the general public would be prohibited from using them. The free circulation of celebrity images and public commentary upon them would be choked off.

There is a broad consensus that falsely invoking famous people as endorsers of a product should be prohibited. This ethic is codified in the Lanham Act, which bans any "false description or representation" of a good or service. Suggesting that a celebrity is associated with a product or company when they are not, or fostering a "likelihood of confusion" about that fact, is illegal under the Lanham Act.

But does this standard mean that celebrities should be entitled to prohibit depictions and even references to their identities that they find unattractive? This outcome is virtually inevitable now that publicity rights are considered broad legal entitlements. Or as Elizabeth Taylor once remarked, "I am my own commodity. I am my own industry."

In a landmark 1993 article questioning the growth of publicity rights, legal scholar Michael Madow described how "the law has moved more and more of our culture's basic semiotic and symbolic resources out of the public domain and into private hands." This transfer of cultural power is part of an ongoing contest, he writes, "in which dominant groups try to naturalize the meanings that best serve their interests into the 'common sense' and 'taste' of society as a whole, while subordinate and marginalized groups resist this process with varying degrees of effort and success." A fundamental hypocrisy is at work when celebrities promote their image while also claiming strict control, writes Madow:

When a quintessentially "postmodern" (that is, openly and unabashedly derivative) performer like Madonna complains of unauthorized appropriation of her image, she is seeking to have it both ways. Having drawn freely and shamelessly on our culture's image bank, she is trying to halt the free circulation of signs and meanings at just the point that suits her. She is seeking to enforce against others a moral norm that her own self-consciously appropriationist practice openly repudiates. The law need not be party to such contradiction.

And yet, as publicity rights have expanded, this branch of law has become a powerful new vehicle for the private censorship of culture. The law has proceeded so far that it can be illegal even to *evoke* a celebrity's identity without permission. The judge Alex Kozinski has written: "It's now a tort [an injury that can be litigated] for advertisers to remind the public of a celebrity. Not to use a celebrity's name, voice, signature or likeness; not to imply the celebrity endorses a product; but simply to evoke the celebrity's image in the public mind. This Orwellian notion withdraws far more from the public domain than prudence or common sense allows."

The invocation of Orwell is not far-fetched. As Madow writes, "The 'right of publicity' issue requires us to make a fundamental choice . . . about the allocation of cultural (meaning-making) power in contemporary society. Framed in its most general terms, that choice is between centralized, top-down management of popular culture on the one hand, and a more decentralized, open, 'democratic' cultural practice on the other."

For Madow, the answer to this choice is easy: "As a general matter, the law ought to align itself with cultural pluralism and popular cultural production." Yet even with the rise of powerful new instruments of cultural pluralism—the Internet and other digital technologies—the leviathans of mass culture continue to insist upon controlling the circulation of "authorized" meanings. What follow are some of the stories of this ongoing struggle.

Evoking Celebrity Personalities Is Prohibited

If fame can be totally unearned—and indeed, talented, hardworking actors concede they have only modest control over whether they can make it big—then what is the moral justification for sweeping property rights in fame? To be sure, some celebrities have a genuine talent for acting, singing, or politics. But countless other people, even untalented ones, have become famous through dumb luck.

Historically, the courts have assumed that if there is any financial value to fame, then *of course* it should be recognized as the exclusive property right of the famous person. But doesn't the public have its own interests in being able to invoke a celebrity's persona and assert its own sense of what that persona should mean? After all, the public plays no small role in affirming who shall be famous.

Yet the public is largely disempowered. Once celebrities are sufficiently famous nowadays, they are legally able to ban not just unauthorized depictions of themselves, but any unwanted "cultural extensions" of their identity, broadly construed. Elroy "Crazylegs" Hirsch, a famous football player, successfully asserted this prerogative when S.C. Johnson & Son started marketing a women's shaving gel product called "Crazylegs." The bandleader Guy Lombardo once sued a car dealer who aired a television commercial depicting a New Year's Eve party with a bandleader and an orchestra playing "Auld Lang Syne" while several cars rotated in the foreground. A court found that the ad unfairly traded upon Lombardo's "public personality as Mr. New Year's Eve" and unfairly imitated his "likeness and representation."

To be sure, the courts sometimes reject some cultural extensions of a famous identity. When the media conglomerate Viacom decided to revamp its TNN network into a male-oriented network and call it "Spike TV," the filmmaker Spike Lee took it personally. He asserted that Viacom was trying to trade on his reputation of irreverence and aggressiveness, and that viewers would falsely think he was associated with the channel. There have been other "Spikes" in American culture—Spike Jones, the bandleader, is perhaps the most famous, and his name was actually imitated by the film director Spike Jonze (Richard Coufey). Despite the existence of other Spikes, Spike Lee did succeed in getting a preliminary injunction stopping Viacom from moving forward. Before settling the case for undisclosed terms, Viacom said the suit cost it at least $17 million in wasted advertising and promotional losses.

Big stars seem to believe that they ought to control the evocations of their names, no matter the context. Federico Fellini's 1986 film *Ginger and Fred* provoked Ginger Rogers, the famed dance partner of Fred Astaire's, to sue for violating her publicity rights and misleading consumers that she was associated with the film. It took two years of legal discovery, a district court trial, and an appeals court ruling to establish that *Ginger and Fred* was a legally acceptable title for the film.

The actor Paul Newman lampooned such proprietary control of names in the wake of the Fox News Channel's litigation against Al Franken over use of the words "fair and balanced." In a *New York Times* op-ed article, Newman deadpanned: "In a 1963 film, *HUD*, for which Mr. Newman was nominated for an Academy Award, the ad campaign was based on the slogan, 'Paul Newman is HUD.' Mr. Newman claims that the Department of Housing and Urban Development, called HUD, is a fair and balanced institution and that some of its decency and respectability has unfairly rubbed off on his movie character, diluting the rotten, self-important, free-trade, corrupt conservative image that Mr. Newman worked so hard to project in his film. He claims that this 'innocence by association' has hurt his feelings plus residuals."

Even satire cannot catch up with reality these days, however. An attorney for former Rolling Stones bassist Bill Wyman sent a cease-and-desist letter to Bill Wyman, a music critic for the *Atlanta Journal-Constitution*, demanding that he cease using his name unless he adds a disclaimer "clearly indicating that [you are] not the same Bill Wyman who was a member of the Rolling Stones." It turns out that the real name of Bill Wyman of the Stones is William George Perks, who adopted the stage name Bill Wyman out of admiration for a Lee Whyman. (Bill Wyman the music critic continues to use his name, without a disclaimer.)

Granting property rights in fame is a dangerous proposition in no small part because celebrities tend to be control freaks. Most have boundless ambitions to "manage" their image and reputation. As their egos expand, so do their publicity rights. They conceive of their rights as granting them permission to ban any cultural expressions that tread on their alleged identity.

One of the more scary-funny instances of this involved a lawsuit that comedian Johnny Carson brought against a portable toilet maker who named his enterprise "Here's Johnny," the phrase that Carson's sidekick, Ed McMahon, always used to introduce Carson's nightly monologue. The portable toilet maker advertised his product as "The World's Foremost Commodian." The King of Comedy wasn't laughing. Carson claimed that his men's clothing company used the phrase "Here's Johnny" on its labels and marketing; the use of "Here's Johnny" by another company, he said, represented unfair competition and an infringement of his publicity rights.

A federal appeals court ruled for Carson, finding that there was a "like-lihood of confusion" that consumers would falsely associate the toilet company with him. It declared that because the public tends to associate the words "Here's Johnny" with "Johnny Carson," the toilet company had unfairly evoked Carson's identity without his permission!

The aftermath of this 1983 case leads one to wonder: Will Judy Garland's estate be able to sue anyone who tries to exploit the image of ruby slippers, which are forever associated with Garland's legendary performance as Dorothy in *The Wizard of Oz*? Will Frank Sinatra's publicity rights be violated when a corporate executive also claims to be the "Chairman of the Board"?

The Carson case was not an aberration. The scope of a protectable public identity is shockingly broad, as the 1992 case of *Vanna White v. Samsung Electronics America, Inc.* illustrates. Nostalgia buffs will remember Vanna White as the attractive assistant to Pat Sajak on the popular television game show *Wheel of Fortune*. Her role consisted almost entirely of wearing stylish clothes, turning oversized letter tiles, and clapping giddily when a contestant won.

In 1989, Samsung Electronics ran a series of print advertisements in national publications, each depicting a current object of popular culture and then matching it with a futuristic Samsung product. The idea was to showcase the company's technological innovation in a humorous way. For example, one ad featured a raw steak with the caption, "Revealed to be a health food. 2010 A.D." Another ad showed the then-popular talk show host Morton Downey Jr. in front of an American flag, with the caption, "Presidential candidate. 2008 A.D."

The ad that incited Vanna White to sue, all the way to the Ninth Circuit Court of Appeals, featured a female robot dressed in a wig, gown, and jewelry. The fanciful robot stood next to a game board that clearly resembled the *Wheel of Fortune* set. The caption of the ad read, "Longest-running game show. 2012 A.D." In her lawsuit, White claimed that Samsung had appropriated her identity in the ads by *referring* to her in an unmistakable way, albeit through a robotic spoof. As in the "Here's Johnny" case, neither White's name nor likeness was used.

In a judgment that shows the court's dim respect for the intelligence of the average consumer, the Ninth Circuit Court of Appeals found that there *was* a sufficient likelihood that the public would confuse the robot for Vanna White and that therefore a jury should consider the matter. The court also rejected Samsung's defense that the ad was a parody, saying that the robot was part of a commercial message, not a noncommercial bit of fun, and was therefore unprotected.

The only sane voice in this decision came from Judge Alarcon, who, in partial dissent, bluntly declared, "No reasonable juror could confuse a metal robot with Vanna White." He also pointed out that there is a difference between Vanna White the person and Vanna White as hostess of *Wheel of Fortune*. "The fact that an actor or actress became famous for playing a particular role has, until now, never been sufficient to give the performer a proprietary interest in it," wrote Judge Alarcon. Under the legal tests that have evolved, the judge wrote:

> Gene Autry could have brought an action for damages against all other singing cowboys. Clint Eastwood would be able to sue anyone who plays a tall, soft-spoken cowboy, unless, of course, Jimmy Stewart had not previously enjoined Clint Eastwood. Johnny Weismuller would have been able to sue each actor who played the role of Tarzan. Sylvester Stallone could sue actors who play blue-collar boxers. Chuck Norris could sue all karate experts who display their skills in motion pictures. Arnold Schwarzenegger could sue body builders who are compensated for appearing in public.

When a request was made for the full court of appeals to rehear the case, Judge Alex Kozinski submitted one of the most forceful and memorable opinions in intellectual property jurisprudence. "Intellectual property rights aren't free," he wrote. "They're imposed at the expense of future creators and of the public at large. Where would we be if Charles Lindbergh had an exclusive right in the concept of a heroic solo aviator? If Arthur Conan Doyle had gotten a copyright in the idea of the detective story, or Albert Einstein had patented the theory of relativity? If every author and celebrity had been given the right to keep people from mocking them or their work? Surely this would have made the world poorer, not richer, culturally as well as economically."

Judge Kozinski offered an impressive inventory of cases in which world leaders, companies, and celebrities invoked trademark, copyright, or publicity rights law to try to squelch unauthorized allusions to their public identity. Saddam Hussein wanted to keep advertisers from using his picture in unflattering contexts. George Lucas sought to prevent the Reagan administration's "Strategic Defense Initiative" from being called "Star Wars." Uri Geller wanted to be paid for a Timex ad showing psychics using telekinesis to bend spoons. Paul Prudhomme wanted payment for ads featuring corpulent bearded chefs. After reviewing an extensive list of such property claims in names and images, Judge Kozinski concluded, "Something very dangerous is going on here."

In the end, however, the protests by Judges Alarcon and Kozinski were to no avail. Vanna White's proprietary interests in her celebrity identity as a letter-turner were upheld. The grievous damage that Samsung had inflicted on White was ultimately deemed to be worth $403,000.

The law has actually encouraged these sorts of silly results by making publicity and persona rights "descendible." This means that a celebrity image can be inherited as property. Through descendibility, a corpse with no discernible interest in its fame or identity can be reconstituted as a capital asset. A famous image or personality exists as a disembodied cultural artifact, no longer associated with a living person. It becomes the alienable "intellectual property" of heirs or "assignees" (third parties who have bought or been given the rights), who usually set about finding ingenious ways to leverage the highest cash returns possible by licensing the publicity rights. If that means that the rest of the world may not depict or evoke the identity of the dead person, so much the worse for society.

The chilling effects of this doctrine can be seen in the commercial afterlife of the late actor John Wayne. His children were distraught to come upon a commercial greeting card that showed the manly Mr. Wayne wearing a cowboy outfit and bright red lipstick. "It's a bitch to be butch," said the caption. The card, obviously targeted for lesbian consumers, exemplifies a process that cultural theorists call "recoding." A subordinate community uses the most prevalent icons available to it—trademarks, entertainers, other celebrities—to fashion a subculture that reflects its own identities and worldviews. Of course, this project of borrowing commercial icons to create a subculture often conflicts with the proprietary agenda of celebrities and their estates. This latter group generally wants to assure that only the "authorized meanings" of their famous person may circulate. John Wayne must always be the manly man.

The problem with publicity rights and trademark law is that they prohibit people from expressing their natural urge to craft their own meanings about public figures. By actively assigning cultural meaning—Cary

Grant as the urbane Everyman, Clint Eastwood as the vengeful righteous man, etc.—audiences are an indispensable force in creating "value" in a celebrity identity. One reason Marilyn Monroe and Judy Garland have remained in the public consciousness, decades after their deaths, is that the gay community celebrates them. Surely it has conferred more "value" on the images of Monroe and Garland than their estates have. Similarly, the subcultures that write fan fiction have arguably done more to enhance the value of *Star Trek* and old TV series than their producers or later rights-holders. Who's doing the real "semiotic work" here, one commentator quipped—the celebrity's estate or the audience?

If anyone doubts that publicity rights have spun out of control, consider the ludicrous *Cheers* case that was heard in a federal court in 1993. Host International, a restaurant chain, licensed the rights from Paramount studios, the owner of the *Cheers* show, scripts, and characters, to operate a real-life franchise of *Cheers* restaurants. As part of that license, Host created a life-sized diorama of two animatronic robots that closely resembled the characters Norm and Cliff from the TV show. One was dressed as a mailman, and the other was an overweight beer-guzzler; they were sitting in a *Cheers*-like bar and carried on a short, gag-filled conversation.

This was too much for the actors who played Norm and Cliff, George Wendt and John Ratzenberger, respectively. They sued Paramount, claiming that the robotic portrayals violated their publicity rights even though neither of the actors' names nor likenesses was used in the scene. They demanded that the animatronic display be halted and that they be paid. The case reached the Ninth Circuit Court of Appeals, which cleared the way for the case to proceed in the lower court. The actors ended up settling the case in June 2001, reportedly for more than a million dollars.

The best commentary on this distasteful outcome may be Judge Kozinski's dissent at the appeals court. Referring to his dissent in the aforementioned Vanna White publicity rights case, Kozinski deadpanned, "Robots again."

Can the Girl from Ipanema Call Herself "The Girl from Ipanema"?

In 1962, Heloisa Pinheiro was an attractive eighteen-year-old girl sashaying down the beach in Brazil—"a golden girl, a mixture of flower and siren, full of light and grace," as one admirer put it.

That admirer, Vinicius de Moraes, and his fellow songwriter, Antonio Carlos Jobim, were so enraptured by Heloisa that they wrote a lilting jazz song that became an international sensation in 1964, "The Girl from Ipanema." The recording by Stan Getz and João Gilberto became one of the most popular versions of the tune.

The trouble came forty years later when the woman who inspired the song decided she wanted to capitalize on that role. She appeared on TV as an actress in a soap opera and as a talk show host. She secured a trademark on the song title in Portuguese, "Garota de Ipanema," and opened a clothing boutique called The Girl From Ipanema.

As reported in the *New York Times* in August 2001, the heirs of the two songwriters claimed that they had the exclusive right to commercial use of the words "the girl from Ipanema." They filed a lawsuit to force Pinheiro to rename her boutique and even wanted her to remove a photograph of herself with the two composers hanging on her boutique wall.

The heirs argued that just because Pinheiro was "inadvertently" involved in inspiring Moraes and Jobim in writing their song "does not guarantee her the right to use the images and the work . . . for commercial purposes."

The merchants' association of Ipanema, a neighborhood of Rio de Janeiro, was none too happy with the lawsuit. Its leaders feared that the songwriters' estates would try to block other uses of "Ipanema" in the future. "They have every right to control the song," said Carlos Monjardim, president of the merchants' group, "but they can't lay claim to the symbols that inspired it or the neighborhood itself."

As for Ms. Pinheiro, she said, "I never made a cent from any of that [the song], nor do I claim that I should. Yet now that I'm using a legally registered trademark, they want to prohibit me from being the girl from Ipanema, which is really going too far."

There is an ironic postscript to this story. Songwriter Antonio Carlos Jobim, during his lifetime, had always expressed reservations about the commercialization of his song.

Rosa Parks Battles Rappers for Cultural Control

Should a copyright owner be allowed to withhold a work from circulation even if it has become part of our shared cultural memory? Should copyright owners be allowed to alter our shared cultural history and transform its contemporary meaning?

Rosa Parks, a seamstress in Montgomery, Alabama, became famous when she refused to move to the back of a public bus, insisting upon sitting in the whites-only section in the front. The incident became an iconic moment in the history of the civil rights movement, and Parks has been widely lionized ever since.

Does that mean that Parks can control how her name and that incident are used by others? Parks thought so when the rap group OutKast used her name as a title in a song that featured profanity and racial slurs and a chorus, "Ah, ha, hush that fuss / Everybody move to the back of the bus." Parks argued that the use of her name in connection with the Out-Kast song violated her publicity rights under Michigan state law and constituted false advertising under Section 43 of the Lanham Act, a law intended to prevent trademark fraud.

A federal district court disagreed with Parks, allowing the rappers to refer to her in the song. (One wonders if the King family would have prevailed against a song entitled "MLK," with a refrain of "I have a dream.") The rap artist Dre had admitted that the song was not about Rosa Parks or the civil rights movement, but was simply a typical rap putdown of one's rivals, with Rosa Parks's name serving as a colorful metaphor: "The sole message is that OutKast's competitors are of a lesser quality and therefore must 'move to the back of the bus.'"

But can an artist simply invoke a famous person to increase the marketability of his work? This is essentially what the court was being asked to decide. If the song was about Rosa Parks, or had a political message, it might be legal, but if Parks's name did not have direct artistic relevance to the song, the court would likely forbid it.

In 2001, Parks appealed the case to the Sixth Circuit Court of Appeals, which in May 2003 ruled in her favor by sending the case back to the district court to be heard by a jury. The court found that "reasonable people could find that the use of Rosa Parks's name as the title to this song was not justified as being metaphorical or symbolic of anything for which Rosa Parks is famous. To the contrary, reasonable people could find that the name was appropriated solely because of the vastly increased marketing power of a product bearing the name of a national heroine of the civil rights movement."

OutKast's record company appealed to the U.S. Supreme Court, but in December 2003, it refused to hear the case. The case was sent back to the district court to make a factual evaluation of whether OutKast's use of

Rosa Parks's name in the song title was "artistically justified" or not. Now *here's* a rich scenario for postmodernist critics—a full evidentiary trial drawing upon the majestic apparatus of American law to determine whether the words "Rosa Parks" are symbolically or metaphorically relevant to the lyrics of a rap song—*Ah ha, hush that fuss / Everybody move to the back of the bus.*

The rapper Missy Elliott has the only appropriate response: *Good gawd!*

Making a Statement with Larry, Curly, and Moe

As Justice Oliver Wendell Holmes contemplated in 1903 whether circus posters ought to be afforded copyright protection, he concluded, "It would be a dangerous undertaking for persons trained only in the law to constitute themselves the final judges of the worth of pictorial illustrations. At the one extreme some works of genius would be sure to miss appreciation. At the other end, copyright would be denied to pictures which appealed to a public less educated than the judge."

Holmes's warning echoes through the decades, landing with a thud on the docket of the California Supreme Court in 2001. The artist Gary Saderup had decided to make silkscreened T-shirts and lithographs of the Three Stooges, the famous slapstick team of Larry, Curly, and Moe (and, at one point, Shemp). A graduate of the Pasadena Art Center College of Design, Saderup sold his renderings of the Stooges at shopping centers and art shows.

Saderup, who charged $250 for signed lithographs and $20 for the T-shirts ("wearable art"), told a reporter that his charcoal sketches were meant to uplift and honor the Three Stooges as they were. The point was not to satirize or caricature them in order to make a political statement, but to pay homage. From a legal point of view, that may have been Saderup's biggest mistake.

The heirs of the Three Stooges were not happy that an unauthorized artist was making money off the images of Moe Howard, Jerome (Curly) Howard, and Larry Fein. They sued to recover the $75,000 that Saderup had made from his drawings. Robert H. Benjamin, an heir and an attorney in the case, told the *Los Angeles Times*, "The First Amendment is not a license to steal."

In determining just how far the First Amendment reaches, the judges were being asked to venture into a territory that Justice Holmes had warned against—making artistic judgments. In this case, should T-shirts be considered a form of artistic expression (and thus protected by the First Amendment) or merely a commercial product, in which case the publicity rights of the heirs would prevail?

The courts have usually allowed artists to depict celebrities in unique works of art, such as Andy Warhol's painting of Marilyn Monroe, while frowning upon mass reproductions of those works for commercial sale. The one-off piece of art is generally not regarded as a significant commercial threat to the celebrity, while mass-marketed products are. In this case, Saderup not only was selling large quantities of his art, he had declined to make a parody or political statement. If he had drawn the Three Stooges as members of Congress, for example, the First Amendment would almost certainly have protected his work, even as a mass-marketed item. An expressive work does not lose its constitutional protection just because it is undertaken for profit or for entertainment, the California Supreme Court had declared.

But because Saderup's depiction of the Three Stooges was a close likeness, not a satiric interpretation, it was harder for him to make the case that the drawings were a protected form of art or expression. In the end, the California Supreme Court boldly waded into the aesthetic thicket and declared that it could "discern no significant transformative or creative contribution" in Saderup's drawings. While acknowledging his "undeniable skill," the court, playing art critic, said that that skill was "manifestly subordinated to the overall goal of creating literal, conventional depictions of The Three Stooges so as to exploit their fame."

The court ruled that literal, conventional depictions of celebrities are not protected by the First Amendment, and therefore the publicity rights of the Three Stooges' heirs must prevail over the artistic claims. Had Saderup only made his interpretation of the Stooges a bit more ironic, made a political statement, or inflected it with a little bit more nyuk-nyuk or whoop-whoop-whoop, who knows if the courts would have recognized his artistic contribution? But it would have been dicey for Saderup to rely on the court's recognizing such motives. As Justice Holmes warned, counting on the aesthetic discrimination of judges is a dangerous proposition.

Asking for consistency on these issues might be a tall order as well. While the California Supreme Court found that Gary Saderup's homage to the Three Stooges was illegal, the Sixth Circuit Court of Appeals found that a painting of the golfer Tiger Woods did not violate Woods's publicity rights or trademark rights, but was fully protected by the First Amendment. The limited-edition lithograph produced by Jireh Publishing commemorated Woods's victory at the 1997 Masters golf tournament. Woods's licensing agent claimed that it had the exclusive right to market his name, image, likeness, and signature.

But the federal district court rejected the idea that Woods could control all of the thousands of likenesses and images of him that existed: "[Woods] asks us, in effect, to constitute Woods himself as a walking, talking trademark." The court also held that Woods's publicity rights were "significantly outweighed by society's interest in freedom of artistic expression. . . . A piece of art that portrays a historic sporting event communicates and celebrates the value our culture attaches to such events." On appeal, the Sixth Circuit upheld the district court's entire ruling. Why an unauthorized commemoration of the Three Stooges should be prohibited, but one for Tiger Woods constitutes free speech, is anyone's guess.

PART THREE

The Copyright Wars against an Open Society

This cultural war is almost invisible. It is happening quietly and incrementally—in rulings by distant courts, in hearing rooms on Capitol Hill and obscure federal agencies, in the digital code that Hollywood and record labels surreptitiously implant into DVDs and CDs. Control over culture is creeping forward on cat's paws, in small, quick steps: the one-sided contracts that impose highly restrictive terms on consumers, the criminalization of exposing flaws in encryption software, the legal intimidation of ordinary consumers by large corporations.

The point is to assert as much private control over the sale and after-purchase uses of copyrighted works as possible. For those concerned about an open society, the new restrictions represent a tightening noose around the neck of creativity and free speech.

While there has always been a certain tension between copyright law and the First Amendment, in the predigital cultural environment there were meaningful "safety valves" in the law to protect the interests of an open, democratic society. The fair use doctrine sanctioned the private, noncommercial, and educational use of copyrighted works. The first-sale doctrine enabled people to resell, share, or modify the books, records, and videos that they purchased; this doctrine was notable for enabling public libraries and video rental stores to exist. And because copyright terms were limited—originally, in 1790, to only fourteen years—the public could enjoy free access to works once their copyrights had expired. (Now copyright terms for individuals last for their lifetimes plus seventy years.)

In the new digital culture that is emerging, copyright and trademark law is increasingly trumping the public's free speech interests and our traditions of open access to information. The rights of copyright holders are steadily expanding while the public's ability to access and use copyrighted works is being chipped away bit by bit.

How exactly is copyright law posing new threats to an open society? Part Three looks at the many ingenious and maddening lines of attack.

CHAPTER 7

The Theft of the Public Domain

The public domain tends to appear amorphous and vague, with little more of substance in it than is invested in patriotic or religious slogans on paper currency. It is this impression of insubstantiality that courts must dispel first.

—Professor David Lange, 1981

The public domain is often regarded as little more than an intellectual junkyard, a place where out-of-print books and antiquarian drawings languish like so many rusty cars. This wasteland (goes the thinking) consists chiefly of ancient books, music that no one really cares about, obscure government documents, and things that cannot be copyrighted such as ideas and plotlines. Essentially, copyright law regards the public domain as a form of "nonproperty."

This accounts for the indifference or contempt with which it is often treated. Copyright industries—film, music, publishing, information—routinely raid the public domain for material and, when possible, use copyright law in the classic Disney style to try to privatize it. It is no wonder that the public domain resembles "a dark star in the constellation of intellectual property," in Professor David Lange's words. Its importance to society is so dimly understood.

This chapter explores some of the more egregious attempts in recent memory to steal or shrink the public domain. Since most of the stories in this book involve some sort of misappropriation of the public domain, this chapter focuses on egregious attacks on its most basic elements—federal court decisions, state statutes, library materials, books and music whose copyright terms have expired.

Incentives to Dead Authors:
The Copyright Term Extension Act

Like most Americans, Eric Eldred, a retired Navy computer contractor, thought that the vast universe of novels, short stories, and poems that are in the public domain belongs to everyone. That was before the Disney Company and other major media corporations decided they wanted to keep large swaths of American artistry for themselves, enlisting Congress to authorize their culture grab.

The story starts in 1995, the dawn of mass usage of the Internet. Eldred's teenaged daughters had received a school assignment to read a classic of American literature, Nathaniel Hawthorne's *The Scarlet Letter.* Eldred decided to explore how the Internet might be able to make the book more interesting and accessible. After creating his own Web version of the book using a contemporary font, he added annotations to the text, a glossary of archaic words, Web links to other works by Hawthorne, and reviews of the book from the 1870s, when it was first published.

Excited by the outcome, Eldred set about expanding his project. Within a few years, he had created online versions of literature by Henry James, Oliver Wendell Holmes, Wallace Stevens, Willa Cather, and hundreds of other great American authors. Since the copyrights on all of the works had expired, Eldred could do whatever he wanted with the texts. Soon his innovative Web site was receiving 20,000 hits a day. The National Endowment for the Humanities cited it as one of the twenty best humanities sites on the Web.

In 1998, however, Congress, acting at the behest of the Disney Company, sideswiped Eldred's grand experiment. An early cartoon version of Mickey Mouse, as depicted in the 1928 cartoon short "Steamboat Willie," was due to enter the public domain in 2004. Pluto, Goofy, and Donald Duck were due to become public property in 2009. To protect its lucrative characters, Disney instigated an aggressive lobbying campaign to extend copyright terms of existing works by twenty years. It sweetened its case by giving contributions to eighteen of the twenty-five congressional sponsors of the legislation.

Besides protecting Disney characters, the bill—the Sonny Bono Copyright Term Extension Act—would also lock up an estimated 400,000 books, movies, and songs due to enter the public domain in 1998 and following years. Instead of becoming available to the public for free, as

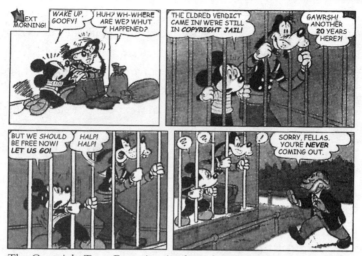

The Copyright Term Extension Act kept thousands of creative works from the 1920s and 1930s from entering the public domain. In this cartoon by Andrew Baio, Mickey and Goofy were two of the most prominent "victims."

long anticipated, these works would be owned and controlled by private parties until at least 2018.

A key rationale for copyright protection is the need to give authors a financial incentive to create new works. Unless artists have exclusive property rights in their writing, music, and films, they will not be able to sell them in the marketplace and earn a livelihood. It is a reasonable argument. Copyright scholars and content industries have long argued that copyright is a needed incentive to creative output.

But here Congress was giving a lucrative new financial incentive to *dead authors* who would never generate new creative works in return. The new monopoly rights were not going to stimulate George Gershwin, Joseph Conrad, Robert Frost, Lewis Carroll, Cole Porter, Sherwood Anderson, or F. Scott Fitzgerald to produce new masterpieces. The term extension amounted to a pure government giveaway to large media corporations and authors' estates. Critics blasted the new law as "the Mickey Mouse Protection Act" and complained that consumers would be forced to pay hundreds of millions of dollars for access to creative works that rightfully belong to them. The lockup of works was especially perverse because it was coming just as new technologies, especially the Internet, were providing the means for broader, easier public access to public-domain works.

Critics also noted the stunning inefficiency of the law. Only about 2 percent of works from the 1920s and 1930s generate any commercial revenues today. Yet the law would also restrict public access to the remaining 98 percent of works that have no apparent commercial value. Anyone wishing to use those works would find it extremely difficult to do so because of the notorious complications and expense of identifying rights-holders and negotiating licensing fees.

These arguments hardly mattered, and indeed, hardly registered. Congress enacted the Sonny Bono Copyright Term Extension Act, with virtually no debate, on October 2, 1998.

When Lawrence Lessig, then a professor at Harvard Law School, learned that the new law had forced Eric Eldred to shut down his Web site, he decided that the law was not just bad public policy, but unconstitutional. He pointed out that the Constitution, in Article I, Section 8, clearly stipulates that Congress is authorized to grant copyrights "for limited times" in order "to promote the progress of science and useful arts." The law met neither of these conditions, he argued.

While ostensibly limited, the terms of copyright protection have been extended so many times over the past two hundred years—eleven times since 1960—that the law scholar Peter Jaszi has called it "perpetual copyright on the installment plan." The first copyright law, enacted in 1790, was for a fourteen-year term, later made renewable for another fourteen years. Congress extended copyright terms so many times over the next two centuries that by 1998 copyrights for individuals lasted for the lifetime of the author plus seventy years, and for corporate copyright holders, ninety-five years. These periods of time are presumed to be necessary for authors to be sufficiently rewarded to produce what they do.

For copyright maximalists, even these generous terms were not enough. Sonny Bono's widow, Mary Bono, who succeeded her husband as a member of Congress, declared that "copyright should be forever." Jack Valenti, the film industry's top lobbyist, in shrewd deference to the Constitution's "limited times" clause, conceded he would be happy if copyright terms lasted "forever minus a day."

Determined to strike down the law as unconstitutional, Professor Lessig initiated a federal lawsuit on Eldred's behalf in January 1999. While some legal scholars considered the case a bit daffy—no one had ever questioned the constitutionality of copyright terms before—other legal experts rallied to the cause and helped Lessig frame his case. In October

1999, a federal district court upheld Congress's authority to extend copyright terms. This ruling was later upheld by the U.S. Circuit Court of Appeals, by a 2-to-1 margin.

It was something of a surprise, therefore, when the U.S. Supreme Court, in February 2002, agreed to review the case, *Eldred v. Ashcroft*. By now, the once-obscure topic of copyright terms was attracting a groundswell of public attention. The press began to explore the public's stake in copyright law. Lessig and Valenti engaged in showy debates. Eldred's brief to the Supreme Court was supported by some thirty-eight friend-of-the-court briefs submitted by such allies as Public Knowledge, the Electronic Frontier Foundation, the Free Software Foundation, Phyllis Schafly's Eagle Forum, the Intel Corporation, and a group of major economists that included Milton Friedman and Kenneth Arrow.

When the case was argued before the court in October 2002, none of the justices had positive things to say about the Copyright Term Extension Act. Justice Sandra Day O'Connor put it bluntly: "It is hard to understand, if the overall purpose of the Copyright Clause is to encourage creative work, how some retroactive extension could possibly do that." Yet the justices were wary that the court could specify an appropriate term limit for copyrights; they suggested that this is a classic legislative matter.

In January 2003, the Supreme Court upheld the constitutionality of the copyright term extension on precisely this ground. Writing for the 7-to-2 majority, Justice Ruth Bader Ginsburg said, "We are not at liberty to second-guess Congressional determinations and policy judgments of this order, however debatable or arguably unwise they may be." The court noted that Congress had, on other occasions, extended the duration of existing copyrights when extending the duration of copyrights for future works. The 1998 term extension was no different in kind, the court held.

In the wake of the decision, one copyright commentator likened it to the "Dred Scott case for culture." Justice Ginsburg had rejected the idea that copyright is a bargain with the American people, and had not even addressed how the act promoted the progress of science and the useful arts. The ruling also seemed to signal that the courts were not likely to consider the constitutional dimensions of copyright law, but to defer to Congress instead.

One bright spot in Ginsburg's ruling was her strong affirmation of the "fair use doctrine," which allows the public to use portions of copyrighted works for personal, educational, and noncommercial purposes.

But her confidence in the actual vitality of fair use—in the face of court rulings and new technologies that are nullifying those rights—seemed more rhetorical than convincing.

In a forceful dissent, Justice Stephen Breyer found no identifiable benefit to the public from the law. He also pointed out that authors will not benefit from the ruling, only "their heirs, estates or corporate successors." In short, authors and the public are getting screwed again.

In many ways, however, the *Eldred* case represented more of a beginning than an ending, and more of a rallying cry than an elegy. The day after the Supreme Court's ruling, the *New York Times* headline read, "A Corporate Victory, But One That Raises Public Consciousness." Acts of civil disobedience against the antisocial, personally intrusive claims of copyright law have only grown since the *Eldred* ruling, in part because of it.

Stealing Classical Music from the Public Domain

Dozens of small orchestras and music schools around the country rely heavily upon sheet music that is in the public domain. It is a rich repertoire of music by some of the great composers of the early twentieth century—Gershwin, Copland, Shostakovich, Sibelius, Ravel, and many others. Their sheet music is attractive to orchestras not only because of its enduring musical value, but because of its low cost. A public-domain orchestra score may cost only $15, for example, and the sheet music for individual instruments may cost $20 to $40. Moreover, orchestras do not have to rent the music; they can own it. And they do not have to pay licensing fees for performing the music; it is free.

The music world was therefore shocked when hundreds of public-domain orchestral works by foreign composers suddenly had their copyrights "restored." Like so many changes in copyright law, this one was largely propelled by the motion picture industry. It seems that some films produced in Mexico and Canada had failed to affix the proper copyright notices, as required by U.S. copyright law before 1989. The failure to follow the legal formalities meant that the films had become public-domain works, available for free to anyone. The Motion Picture Association of America was not pleased at this state of affairs.

So Congress, ever mindful of the MPAA's desires, in December 1993 "restored" the copyrights to these films. The following year, in December

1994, Congress performed a similar "copyright restoration" on thousands of books, paintings, drawings, music, films, photographs, and other artistic works created in foreign countries. The official reason for the change was to "harmonize" U.S. copyright law with that of foreign nations so that the United States could ratify the Berne Treaty.

But the means for achieving this international harmonization required an unprecedented privatization of existing public-domain works. The vehicle for this seizure was the Uruguay Round trade agreements. Section 514 of the Uruguay Round Agreements Act (URAA)—passed by Congress to implement the treaty—gave automatic, retroactive copyright protection to works that were in the public domain in the United States but were still under copyright protection in their source country.

Community orchestras that once performed Prokofiev's *Peter and the Wolf* in small venues suddenly found that they had to pay $1,000 or more to rent sheet music for a single use—a patently unaffordable rate. Music schools found that they could no longer afford to teach the music of renowned foreign composers, and small recording labels faced huge new business expenses for recording classical works that unexpectedly were copyrighted again.

With the help of Professor Lawrence Lessig, a number of conductors, music schools, and community orchestras brought a lawsuit challenging the constitutionality of the Uruguay Round Agreements Act and its privatization of foreign works already in the public domain. The lead plaintiff was Lawrence Golan, an orchestra conductor who teaches at the University of Denver's Lamont School of Music and directs the Portland Ballet Orchestra in Portland, Maine.

When the Supreme Court agreed to hear *Eldred v. Ashcroft*, the *Golan v. Ashcroft* case was put on hold until *Eldred* was resolved. When that ruling came down, the plaintiffs in *Golan* filed an amended complaint noting that the *Eldred* ruling said nothing about Congress's decision, in the URAA, to restore copyrights on works already in the public domain. *Golan* plaintiffs also asserted that Congress does not have the power to remove a work from the public domain or enact retroactive legislation that "unfairly burdens individuals and disrupts settled expectations."

In March 2004, the federal district court rejected the government's motion to dismiss the case, but several procedural hurdles remain before a trial scheduled for 2005 may begin.

Who Owns the Dewey Decimal Classification System?

Generations of librarians, scholars, and readers have built a great edifice of knowledge on the foundations of certain categories for organizing books in libraries. The categories evolved over many decades, as a kind of commons, until Melvil Dewey set forth a new and comprehensive set of categories, the Dewey Decimal Classification system, in 1876. Dewey's system soon became the standard library classification scheme, used by virtually all libraries in America. It is now a global standard used by 200,000 libraries in 135 countries.

Imagine the shock when Paul Jones, the head of an online archive called ibiblio.org, received an e-mail in September 2000 claiming that his archive at the University of North Carolina was stealing someone else's intellectual property. The letter, from the Online Computer Library Center, Inc. of Dublin, Ohio, did not use such provocative words as "theft" or "piracy." But it did suggest that Jones's online library was violating OCLC's copyrights and trademarks. Joan S. Mitchell, the executive editor and editor in chief of OCLC, explained that OCLC owns all copyrights in the Dewey Decimal Classification system, and holds trademarks in "Dewey," "DDC," and "Dewey Decimal Classification," among others.

Jones spoke by telephone with Mitchell to discuss his refusal to pay for a license to use the Dewey Decimal system. As he recalls it from his notes, the conversation went something like this:

Mitchell: "But you have our property."
Jones: "No, we have broad categories like any number of cataloging schemes."
Mitchell: "Looks like our categories to me."
Jones: "Considering that Dewey in 1876 set the standard for categories, most other schemes look somewhat like Melvil Dewey's."
Mitchell: "Do you know about OCLC?"
Jones: "Yes, OCLC makes possible the wonderful interlibrary loan system that I use and love. I respect OCLC for that. But we still don't want to license Dewey."
Mitchell: "We know our property."
Jones: "We're not interested in licensing."

After consulting with legal counsel, the ibiblio.org archive eliminated any references to the Dewey Decimal system on its Web site. In a subse-

What might happen to book publishing if the Dewey Decimal system became widely used? Cartoonist Ruben Bolling imagines the dire consequences.

quent letter to Mitchell, Jones informed OCLC that his online archive would not be licensing the Dewey system. He also noted that he does not believe that the use of broad categories "like those created by Dewey" constitutes a trademark infringement.

An attorney for OCLC, George Buzash, explained that the library co-operative acquired the rights to the classification system in the 1980s when it bought Melvil Dewey's company. To protect this investment and the costs of updating and marketing the Dewey Decimal system, OCLC wants to protect its trademark rights, he said, adding that trademark law requires trademark holders to police for violations in any case.

"We don't enforce our rights in a punitive manner," Buzash explained. "We usually notify them of our rights in the terms 'Dewey' and 'Dewey Decimal Classification,' and ask for attribution of ownership." OCLC generally allows noncommercial uses of its trademarks for free provided a user obtains a permissions letter and acknowledges OCLC's ownership of the trademarks. Usages of "Dewey Decimal Classification" or "Dewey" on posters, mugs, and T-shirts require OCLC licenses.

To its credit, OCLC has been flexible in enforcing its trademark. When the Library Hotel opened in New York City, it used "Dewey" and "Dewey Decimal Classification" in its hotel and marketing materials. But rather than litigate, OCLC and the hotel reached a settlement whereby the hotel now acknowledges OCLC's trademarks and gave a charitable contribution to a program to promote reading by children.

OCLC has not pursued a lawsuit against ibiblio.org, reports Jones. But there is a sad irony that libraries—institutions dedicated to open access to information, and which incubated the Dewey Decimal Classification system through sharing and collaboration over the course of decades—cannot freely use their own creation because it has been privatized.

West Publishing's Claim to Own Page Numbers—and the Law

One of the more creative copyright claims, made by the West Publishing Company of Eagan, Minnesota, is that the company owned copyrights on the *page numbers* of the federal court decisions it published. What might seem like a bizarre assertion of copyright protection was in fact a key legal argument by West for preserving its multibillion-dollar market monopoly in the publishing of federal court cases.

The practice of law in the United States revolves around the citation of legal cases by their page numbers. All attorneys, judges, legislators, and legal scholars must refer to the specific volume and page number of a given case, as reported in the official court reporter. "Citations fulfill an infrastructural role in legal circles which is similar to that of currency in a modern society," the law librarian Laura Gasaway has testified. "Just as the currency system allows financial transactions to occur, so the system for citing law materials facilitates information exchanges."

One company sits astride this great flow of "money," the West Publishing Company. Through its enviable data monopoly, it has been able to reap impressive profits by controlling key flows of legal information. At one time, West provided a significant service by assembling a wide variety of court decisions into a single set of published works. It was valuable to have a centralized and comprehensive compiler of court rulings. But even before the Internet became a popular medium, many critics said that

West's de facto monopoly should be replaced with a uniform citation system. Open and standardized protocols for reporting cases would allow legal opinions to be published by other publishers and be made more widely available at a cheaper cost. These arguments became even more compelling with the rise of the Internet.

Naturally, West Publishing was not eager to see its lucrative monopoly endangered by a uniform citation system or by free online access to federal cases via the Internet. Its claim to copyright protection rested on the "selection, coordination and arrangement" of its reporters, as well as a variety of editorial enhancements such as case synopses and headnotes. While West's own enhancements are surely entitled to copyright protection, the idea that the pagination reflects an "original" contribution stretches the idea of copyright to the breaking point.

Establishing the absurdity of West's claim as a matter of law was another matter entirely. The most aggressive and consistent advocate for a uniform citation system was James P. Love, then director of the Ralph Nader–affiliated Taxpayer Assets Project. (Love now heads the Consumer Project on Technology.) In 1994, Love helped convene legal publishers, librarians, lawyers, and consumer groups to explore the idea of a vendor-neutral citation system. According to Love, West tried to pack the meeting by sending dozens of people to object to the agenda; it also took out several display ads in the *Washington Post* to object to the proposal. Citation reform gained new allies in the mid-1990s as the American Association of Law Libraries, the State Bar of Wisconsin, and the American Bar Association weighed in with advocacy efforts of their own.

The public paid a dear price for West's monopoly. Based on a license that West had granted to the U.S. Justice Department, Love calculated that the cost to a single user of accessing a single year of federal court cases (approximately 15,000 cases) was $40,500. Neither West nor LexisNexis offer their online legal products to public libraries for their patrons to use; what is offered is accessible to librarians, and it costs $14 per minute to use, plus printing costs. This means that the public and pro se litigants (people who represent themselves in court) generally cannot get free or inexpensive online access to court cases even though, as taxpayers, they already finance the entire court system.

Since large companies tend to have powerful political influence, it was not surprising to see West flex its muscles. Over the years the company had settled into a cozy partnership with the federal court system. Judges and clerks enjoyed unlimited access to West's online compilation of cases, West's help in assuring the accuracy of final opinions, and even lavish West-subsidized junkets to warm destinations. The company also spread its campaign contributions around generously, and in a bipartisan manner. Everyone from Al Gore to Newt Gingrich to key congressional commit- tee chairmen enjoyed chummy relationships with West.

In 1998, the absurdity of allowing copyright law to protect the pagina- tion of federal court cases finally came to an end. The legal publisher Matthew Bender & Co. won a federal lawsuit declaring that the elements of West's case reports that other legal publishers sought to copy were not copyrightable. HyperLaw, an intervenor in the case, won a declaration that it could publish redacted versions of West's case reports without infringe- ment. Anyone may publish federal court decisions, complete with the page numbers selected by West, with impunity.

Unfortunately, the federal courts have still not adopted a public-domain, technology-neutral citation system, and West Publishing remains the dom- inant provider of court opinions. Yet the gates of competition have begun to open, and the principle has been established that no company can use copyright law to monopolize materials that are almost wholly financed by the American taxpayers.

Selling Monopoly Access to the Law

Franz Kafka, famous for his nightmarish depictions of the legal labyrinth, once warned that "the Law . . . should be accessible to every man and at all times." It is a fundamental proposition in a democracy: the people are the authors of the law and, through their government, its enforcers. So why should anyone be allowed to *own* the law?

Peter Veeck had the temerity to think that citizens should actually have the right to free, unfettered access to the law. He was in the process of rehabilitating an old building in Denison, Texas, and needed to obtain a copy of the local building code. When he couldn't obtain the regulations in the local library, he went out and bought an electronic copy for $300 (a print version cost $738). Because Veeck also happened to operate an Internet service provider, RegionalNet, he decided to do his fellow citi- zens a favor and post the town's building code online.

To the Southern Building Code Congress International (SBCCI), pub- lishing the building code amounted to a theft of its property. The nonprofit group develops and promotes a variety of model building codes for adoption as law by local governments; its technical standards cover the safe installation of plumbing, gas heating, and fire prevention measures, among others. When SBCCI learned of Veeck's Web posting, its attorney promptly notified him that it held a copyright on the technical standards and therefore owned the exclusive right to publish them or license their reproduction; Veeck's Internet posting must come down immediately.

Veeck instead went to federal district court to try to obtain a declaratory judgment that his online posting of the law did not violate the Copyright Act. SBCCI counterclaimed, asserting five counts of copyright infringement against Veeck as well as unfair competition and breach of contract (the licensing agreement that came with the software disks).

In one sense, SBCCI's claim to own the building codes seems simple and straightforward. It had spent its own private resources and labor to create the codes, after all. Why should anyone else be entitled to use them for free? The group also claimed that without copyright protection, trade groups would no longer develop model codes; local governments would then have to step into the breach and shoulder the costs and complications themselves. This is not an insignificant concern because building codes are lengthy, highly technical, and frequently changing. Legislators are not well equipped to oversee such matters directly.

Yet the idea that public law can be privately owned is troubling. Veeck insisted that once a model code is adopted as law, it enters the public domain and may no longer be considered proprietary. As one court put it, "The citizens are authors of the law, and therefore its owners, regardless of who actually drafts the provisions, because the law derives its authority from the consent of the public, expressed through the democratic process."

It is in fact a settled matter of law that judicial opinions and statutes cannot be copyrighted. Why should administrative regulations be treated any differently? Veeck considered it outrageous that even after adopting an SBCCI code as the law of the land, the Texas legislature could not reprint the code in its own statute books. The building codes might be generally available at town halls and other government offices (Veeck said he couldn't find them), but often citizens had no other choice but to buy them directly from SBCCI or bookstores.

Veeck also argued that it is a violation of a citizen's due process of law if access to the law is restricted. It seems perverse to give private, commercial vendors a monopoly over access to the law when the Internet makes it cheap and easy to make the law available to everyone for free.

In 2000, the federal district court ruled in favor of SBCCI. On appeal a three-judge panel of the Fifth Circuit Court of Appeals upheld this ruling. Peter Suber, a noted champion of open-access publishing, dryly observed, "This trend would please Caligula, who practiced at tyranny by posting the Roman laws on the top of a tall pole where no one could read them."

Given the prevalence of private standard-setting, the ruling was an ominous sign. Three private organizations have copyrights in the building codes used in forty-eight states. The National Fire Protection Association has a copyright in the electrical code used in all fifty states, and the American Medical Association has a copyright over the code for medical billing. Finally, the U.S. Office of Management and Budget has been urging all federal agencies to incorporate regulations developed by private organizations "whenever practicable and appropriate" in order to save the government money.

Fortunately, the full Fifth Circuit Court of Appeals weighed in and reversed the three-judge panel. Veeck and public ownership of the law were vindicated. The court conceded that SBCCI and other code-writers may lose revenues if copies are available online. But it astutely pointed out that copyright protection is hardly needed as an incentive for standard-setting groups to write their codes. "It is difficult to imagine an area of creative endeavor in which the copyright incentive is needed less," the court wrote, citing law scholar Paul Goldstein. "Trade organizations have powerful reasons stemming from industry standardization, quality control, and self-regulation to produce these model codes; it is unlikely that, without copyright, they will cease producing them."

Yet even in the improbable event that code-writing were to suffer a decline, there are other weighty values in the balance. Copyright law should not be allowed to interfere with core democratic principles.

Private Ownership of Sports Scores, Game Photos, and Best-Seller Lists

The rise of the Internet and alternative communications systems has triggered a new set of battles over who shall control information. One of the most contentious arenas has been professional sports. Do the play-by-play facts of a game, the statistics for a player, and the images of players during a game "belong" to the sports leagues, or are they public facts that everyone is entitled to use?

Historically, professional sports leagues have used press credentials as a "contract" to govern these issues. Reporters could cover the games, but only if they respected the proprietary terms set forth by the leagues. A team franchise would understandably try to control—and sell—the rights to as many aspects of the game as possible. This is, in fact, a recurring strategy companies use to leverage their market dominance into even stronger, more expansive property rights for their content. While this may result in a shrunken public domain and reduced market competition, that is precisely why many companies seek broad copyright protection. It can bolster their proprietary control, neutralize competition, and enable them to charge for public access.

For news photographers to gain access to NBA games, they must sign a press credential that stipulated (in 2000) that "the use of any photograph, film, tape or drawing of the game, player interviews or other arena activities taken or made by the accredited organization of the individual for whom this credential has been issued shall be limited to news coverage of the game." All baseball fans have heard the same timeless words, only slightly less famous than "The Star-Spangled Banner": "Any rebroadcast, reproduction, or retransmission of pictures, descriptions, and accounts of this game without the express written permission of Major League Baseball is strictly prohibited."

Selling broadcast rights is one thing. But should the play-by-play *facts* be subject to league ownership?

Motorola provoked the ire of the National Basketball Association in the mid-1990s when it began selling electronic pagers to die-hard sports fans so they could get real-time game information at any time. One would think that the NBA would be thrilled with the new technology because it would strengthen fan engagement with the sport. But the NBA saw only a rip-off of its proprietary rights, and sued Motorola under state misappropriation law. The court ended up siding with Motorola, allowing it to transmit scores without the NBA's authorization. But this ruling does not necessarily mean that sport scores are freely available to anyone. Other courts have held that "hot news" of great timely value can be owned. Thus, the organizers of golf tournaments and their licensees have prevailed in asserting the exclusive right to post the latest hole-by-hole news on Internet sites.

Sports leagues have also tried to assert proprietary control over the images of athletes. Many newspapers have begun to use photos of athletes to promote their sports coverage or as part of books, calendars, and posters. This practice prompted the National Basketball Association to sue the *New York Times* for selling photographs of five basketball players taken at the 1999 NBA playoffs. Individual pictures were offered for $195, and the entire collection for $900. The NBA cried foul, citing the press credentials "contract" that photographers must sign as the price of being admitted to the game.

Essentially, the sports leagues were asserting a property right in virtually anything that occurred at a game, at least on the playing floor or field. Although the claim was cast as a breach of contract violation, not as a copyright case, the effect was the same: to assert the supremacy of property rights over First Amendment rights.

George Freeman, the assistant general counsel of the *New York Times*, pointed out that "the NBA has a huge publicity machine trying to gain attention for the league all over the world. . . . Now they claim that we can't sell photographs—on the basis of a credential that photographers don't read, don't sign, and are forced to wear to do their jobs. They [the NBA] love publicity, but not so immediate that media could compete with their Web site or so historic that media could compete with the NBA's desire to monopolize all sales of products. They want to allow us a tiny sliver of coverage limited to the day after the event."

Rich Jaroslovsky, the managing editor of the *Wall Street Journal Online*, complained of the unfairness of press credential provisions: "These restrictions are being imposed on journalists as a precondition of their ability to cover the event. . . . If this is not checked, it will become pervasive."

In April 2001, the *Times* and the NBA reached a settlement and announced that they would *jointly* market NBA game photographs. The *Times* would be allowed to continue selling the photographs, and the NBA.com logo would be featured on the *Times*'s Web site and other promotional materials.

The deal represented no victory for other news organizations or sports photographers, who likely would not have the clout to negotiate their own deals for using athletes' images. The private brokering of the copyright dispute effectively ignored the public's interest in having broad, unrestricted access to sports events.

When the shoe was on the other foot, and *Times* content was being freely used by others, the *Times* was not above a power play of its own. In May 1999, the online bookseller Amazon.com began featuring the *Times*'s weekly list of best-selling books on its Web page, providing 50 percent discounts for all of the books listed. Shortly thereafter, the *Times* sent a "frosty" letter to Amazon asking it to stop posting the *Times* best-seller list.

Amazon added a disclaimer to its site, telling customers that the *Times* had not endorsed Amazon. But the *Times* called this "inadequate," and insisted that Amazon must obtain a license to use the list—just as Barnesandnoble .com had done. Amazon refused, and went to court seeking a judgment that its use of the *Times*'s list was fair use.

In the end, the court never ruled on the issue because a settlement was reached. The *Times* agreed to let Amazon continue using the list so long as it listed titles in alphabetical order (rather than by sales ranking). Amazon also agreed to post the list only after the *Times* had made it generally available and to provide its book sales information to the *Times*.

While private settlements of copyright disputes may appear to make the problem "go away," in fact they simply allow the terms of fair use to be negotiated in secret meetings on terms favorable to the large companies involved. The actual scope of fair use and the public domain thereby remains murky and vulnerable.

How Spurious Copyrights Steal the Public Domain

The director of a church choir once approached Paul J. Heald, a law professor at the University of Georgia School of Law, with a copyright question: Could some sheet music bearing a copyright symbol and published in 1954 be photocopied and distributed to her choir? The sheet music in question was a version of an anthem, "Jordan," by William Billings, who had lived from 1746 to 1800.

The original Billings version was obviously in the public domain, and should have been available for free. But it is also easy for a publisher to slap a copyright symbol on any public-domain work and start charging money for it. Heald's casual inquiry found that some of the most revered old works of Western civilization are published with copyright symbols, which tell the public that it has no right to copy or reuse them as they see fit. Heald discovered an edition of Shakespeare's *Henry IV*, a Bach cantata ("Crown Him King of Kings"), and a copy of the Declaration of Independence bearing copyright symbols.

It is conceivable, of course, that a contemporary author may add something new to a public-domain work and thereby be entitled to copyright it. But there are no statutory directives and hardly any case law on what degree of new originality is needed to copyright a public-domain work. Some publishers gamely make token changes in sheet music notation in order to "qualify" for copyright protection.

Upon investigating the whole issue of spurious copyrights, Professor Heald concluded, "Music publishers, taking advantage of this uncertainty [about what resides in the public domain], intimidate the public into buying what they already own by affixing copyright symbols to virtually all public domain music as well as trivially different arrangements of public domain music."

While the issue may seem trivial in an individual instance—a dollar here, five dollars there—the collective cost to consumers is likely quite large. While much is made of "piracy" of copyrighted works, little attention is paid to the consumer fraud of spurious copyrights.

Clearly a key reason that publishers use spurious copyrights is the absence of any sanctions. Professor Heald writes: "A publisher who falsely claims the benefits of copyright law misleads the consumer into paying a royalty or buying another work (to avoid photocopying) in a situation where no payment need be made and photocopying is entirely permissible." In the same vein, publishers have a keen interest in misrepresenting the actual fair use rights that consumers have, a deception that, taken in the aggregate, surely bilks consumers of untold millions of dollars in gratuitous purchases of books and articles.

Disturbed at the "indiscriminate and overreaching attempts to obtain compensation for any and all copying of expression," Professor Heald decided to develop some legal causes of action for suing publishers who claim spurious copyrights. His 1996 law review article focused on breach of warranty, unjust enrichment, fraud, false advertising, and class action lawsuits. It may be visionary to expect that Congress will enact statutory penalties for spurious copyrights, but it would be one small step toward affirming the public's significant stake in the public domain.

The Next Form of Private Property—Facts?

As if the commodification of the public domain had not proceeded far enough, vendors of database information systems are now seeking a new type of intellectual property so that they can legally control *facts*.

The issue arose because information vendors want to protect the commercial value of aggregated information in databases. A company that amasses a great deal of information about book prices, CD titles, real estate listings, scientific research, or statistics understandably wants to have strict proprietary control over the compilations. It would be unfair for anyone to simply download a database and then resell it with no penalty.

But if database vendors are allowed to have overly broad legal protection for their data compilations, facts can become proprietary and be removed from the public domain. This would cause serious problems for libraries, schools, science, journalism, and civic life, all of which depend upon free access to and use of facts. Facts, data, and other compilations of information are a shared resource, a public good that is enriched when everyone has access to them; they are diminished in value when they are tightly controlled.

Copyright law has never protected raw factual information, which is considered part of the public domain. But it does protect compilations of data that have been selected, coordinated, or arranged in an original way. Databases are also protected by federal laws such as the Computer Fraud and Abuse Act and state laws dealing with contracts and misappropriation.

But under the Database and Collections of Information Misappropriation Act, a bill introduced by several senators in 2004, the traditional scope of copyright protection would be radically expanded. Database vendors could have legal protection not just for their artful selection and compilation of facts, but for the facts themselves!

Public Knowledge, a leading advocacy group fighting this legislation, has pointed out that "when a Western novelist researches in the *Encyclopedia Britannica* the history of the state of Utah for a new book, nothing in his or her publication of that book will diminish the value of *Encyclopedia Britannica* in the slightest, so long as the novelist did not infringe on the copyrighted particular expression of information in the *Britannica* article." Yet under the proposed database legislation, the ordinary researcher might well encounter copyright restrictions in using "proprietary" facts.

The problem is that the law would not necessarily allow for "transformative uses" of data or facts. The American Library Association once compared the situation to someone owning the ingredients for making a cake: "Flour by itself is flour, but add eggs, sugar and water and you have a cake batter—a unique presentation of flour. [Database legislation] would hinder users who want to take 'flour' (data from one database) and the other 'ingredients' (data from other sources) and make a 'cake' (a new database)." Locking up the key "ingredients" of facts and data would have disastrous consequences for the basic processes of science, education, journalism, and culture.

The idea that facts might be "branded" as proprietary franchises seems absurd, of course. But this trend is already under way in the area of weather forecasting. Private companies that prepare weather forecasts for private clients such as insurance companies and local broadcasters consider their data proprietary. They increasingly object to the availability of public-domain weather forecasting data, as prepared and released by the government's National Weather Service.

The reason that the National Weather Service was created, of course, was to assure that weather forecasting data would be available to everyone as a public good. Small farmers, boaters, tourists, and local civil defense agencies need reliable weather data as much as big agribusiness concerns and commodities futures speculators. Furthermore, there are certain efficiencies and social equities in having a reliable government source of weather data. But private vendors of weather data would like to rein in government weather forecasts and make the data more proprietary and branded. They see zip code–specific forecasts and other special analyses as encroaching on "their" markets.

Welcome to the new frontiers of intellectual property, where "cloudy with a chance of showers" may well become "Cloudy with a Chance of Showers©."

CHAPTER 8

Stifling Public Dialogue through Copyright

The Court has perhaps advanced the ability of the historian, or at least the public official who has recently left office, to capture the full economic value of information in his or her possession. But the Court does so only by risking the robust debate of public issues that is the 'essence of self government.'

— Justice William Brennan,
Harper & Row v. Nation Enterprises (1985)

Historically, copyright law has presumed that if a work can be encased in property rights, it is more likely to be sold in the marketplace and be given wide dissemination. This is an important function of copyright law, and it often functions in precisely this way. The problem arises when the *limited* monopoly of copyright protection is declared to be an *absolute* property right. In fact, copyright law has always been a "bargain" that balances the private monopoly given to authors with the public's creative and free speech needs.

Nowadays, that bargain is a one-sided deal. Copyright holders enjoy enormous control over how the public may access and use a work. Many vital functions in a democratic society—news coverage, political dialogue, cultural commentary—are being stifled. This chapter explores some of the more noteworthy examples of this trend.

Gerald Ford Uses Copyright Law to Stifle the News

In 1977, a year after losing his race for the presidency, Gerald Ford signed a contract with Harper & Row to write his memoirs. In light of the tumultuous years that Ford's book, *A Time to Heal*, chronicled—the Watergate scandals, the Nixon resignation, his anti–inflation crusade—it was of considerable public interest.

For example, the book disclosed that before Nixon's resignation, Chief of Staff Alexander Haig had broached the idea of the next president granting a blanket pardon to Richard Nixon. Ford also revealed that Nixon had nearly selected Ronald Reagan as his 1972 running mate; that Nixon had proposed the selection of Nelson Rockefeller as vice president; and that Ford had had a prickly relationship with Henry Kissinger.

Shortly before the book's publication, *Time* magazine agreed to pay Harper & Row $25,000 in order to publish a 7,500-word excerpt. *Time* paid half the money immediately and agreed to pay the other half upon publication.

But the final payment was never made. Before *Time* could get the excerpt to press, an undisclosed source leaked the book manuscript to Victor Navasky, editor of *The Nation* magazine, a liberal political weekly. Realizing the news value of the material, Navasky quickly published a 2,250-word article that culled highlights from Ford's book. *The Nation* article used paraphrases, facts, and verbatim quotations. Only 300 words were directly drawn from the 200,000-word memoir. When it became clear that *The Nation* had scooped *Time*, *Time* refused to make its second payment of $12,500 to Harper & Row, which then sued *The Nation* for damages.

Even though the actual damages in this case were small, the larger implications of the case were (and are) quite significant. Did *The Nation's* use of the Ford memoir infringe upon Ford's copyright? Does the use of 300 verbatim words drawn from a 200,000-word memoir constitute fair use?

Essentially, Gerald Ford was attempting to assert a copyright interest in material that has direct value to the democratic process and stemmed from his official duties as president. Ford was asking the court to protect his private right to profit from his public service against the public's right to know that information through news reporting.

The case reached the U.S. Supreme Court in November 1984, and in May 1985 the court ruled by a 6-to-3 margin that *The Nation's* use of 300 words from Ford's memoirs did not constitute fair use and therefore violated Ford's copyright. Writing for the majority, Justice O'Connor held that "*The Nation's* liberal use of verbatim excerpts posed substantial potential for damage to the marketability of first serialization rights in the copyrighted work." It was a fairly stark ruling: the market value of a book trumps the public's fair use right to news.

In dissent, Justice Brennan pointed out: "The progress of arts and sciences and the robust public debate essential to an enlightened citizenry are ill-served by [the court's] constricted reading of the fair use doctrine. . . . Harper & Row had every right to seek to monopolize revenue from that potential market through contractual arrangements, but it has no right to set up copyright as a shield from competition in that market because copyright does not protect information. *The Nation* had every right to seek to be the first to publish that information."

Harper & Row v. Nation Enterprises stands as a distressing landmark in the jurisprudence of fair use. By elevating property rights in information over the public's right to know, the court sent a troubling message—the market value of information about our public servants is a higher priority than a democratic people's free access to and use of such information.

Extra, Extra—Newspapers Snuff Out Free Expression!

Americans are accustomed to seeing major national newspapers champion their allegiance to the First Amendment. They claim to be defenders of the public's right to know and surrogates for the little guy. Imagine the surprise of Free Republic, an online forum for conservatives, when the *Washington Post* and the *Los Angeles Times* announced they were suing the organization for infringing on their copyrights.

Free Republic is a self-styled cybercommunity of conservatives who trade news and views at its Web site, www.freerepublic.com. Run by founder Jim Robinson from Fresno, California, Free Republic is not affiliated with any political party or news source, but is an "independent grassroots discussion group" funded by its 60,000 registered members. Through Robinson's Web site, Free Republic members would routinely post news articles from various online sources and then launch debate on the quality (or bias) of the journalism. Thomas Jefferson would have been proud.

The *Washington Post* and *Los Angeles Times*, however, were not happy. They alleged that the postings represented unauthorized copying and thus infringements on their copyrights. The newspapers felt that the article postings, despite being on a noncommercial Web site, potentially interfered with the market for their articles. So in 1997, the two newspapers sued Free Republic for copyright infringement.

At issue in the case was an online practice known as "framing," in which one site can link to a second site and display the contents of the second site within a "frame" on the first site. This linking is tremendously efficient and useful because it seamlessly brings together in one place disparate information sources. But linking can also cause some readers to be confused about which Web site originated the content. It can also wreak havoc with advertising metrics that determine which site "gets credit" for a Web visit and can therefore charge higher advertising rates.

Free Republic argued that its use of the newspaper articles was covered under the fair use exceptions under copyright law and protected by the First Amendment. Without access to the verbatim articles, the Web site argued, visitors to the site could not express their views about political news or press bias. Could any other values be more central than these First Amendment concerns?

Yes—copyright law. On March 30, 2000, a federal district judge rejected Free Republic's claims and found for the two newspapers. The parties agreed to an amended final judgment in June 2002. The three defendants associated with Free Republic were "permanently enjoined from copying, uploading, downloading, posting, distributing, displaying, using . . . [etc.]" the works of the *Los Angeles Times* and *Washington Post*, and paid fines of $5,000 to each newspaper.

The clash between the newspapers' property rights and the free speech interest of citizens, writes the Yale University law professor Yochai Benkler, could be called "the Free Republic problem." Should the goal of "making markets in information goods" trump the speech interests of citizens? Privileging marketable speech invariably favors large-scale, commercial vendors of speech. But giving priority to citizen speech will favor smaller, more diverse kinds of speakers, both professionals and amateurs.

Benkler concludes that the Free Republic suit "crystallizes a pervasive tension between property in the information economy and the freedom to exchange ideas in the information society." If copyright is allowed to expand to new extremes, as many newspapers seek, it will jeopardize fundamental values that lie at the core of our democratic freedoms.

International Olympics Committee Legally Locks Up the News

Athletes weren't the only ones setting records at the 27th Olympic Games in Sydney, Australia, in 2000. Copyright maximalists also broke new ground in their ceaseless quest to propertize and control more aspects of culture through contracts and copyright law.

"Concerned that the power of the Internet could eventually undermine the economic foundation of the modern Olympic movement, the Olympic committee is going to great lengths to control how and where the images and accounts of the Sydney extravaganza reach the public," the *New York Times* reported.

Athletes were forbidden from talking to their hometown newspapers or chatting online with local reporters. Video streaming of events was banned. The International Olympic Committee (IOC) sued 1,800 "cyber-squatters" whose Internet domain names supposedly used words owned by the committee. More than 20 "web monitors" prowled the World Wide Web searching for violations of IOC copyrights and trademarks.

Essentially, the IOC asserted a new centralized control over the outflow of information from the Olympic Games. Christie Ambrosi of the U.S. women's softball team was not allowed to write an Olympic diary for her hometown newspaper, the *Kansas City Star*. Siri Mullinix of the women's soccer team was prohibited from having online chats with the *Greensboro News & Record*.

An IOC spokesman, Franklin Servan-Schreiber, insisted that free speech was not an issue. "I don't think the IOC can be seen in any way limiting speech about the Olympics," he said, citing the fact that some 20,000 journalists were on-site, covering the games. But he added that information controls were needed to make sure that "the association between the athlete, the sport, the values and the symbol that represents all this is clear."

In other words, copyright was a necessary instrument of "brand management." Too bad that such controls require squelching the free dialogue that lies at the heart of an open society.

"The readers miss that connection with their local athlete," complained Mike Fannin, the sports editor of the *Kansas City Star*. "Christie Ambrosi's a softball player in the Kansas City suburbs. When she walks into a bar, people know who she is. The Olympics—it's all about representing your hometown, your city, your country." It is interesting that at least one newspaper, the *Newark Star-Ledger*, published a diary of a U.S. Olympic athlete—Joetta Clark Diggs, an 800-meter runner—without objections or penalty.

The IOC even tried to assert copyright control over the athletic scores posted on the IOC Web site, which regarded the Associated Press, Reuters, and three other news agencies as publishing competitors. The IOC had lined up Swatch and IBM as sponsors of the Olympics Web site, and so wanted any other Web postings of competition results delayed by an hour and credit given to the sponsors.

Servan-Schreiber complained that the news agencies "want to take the real-time results and resend them, with no value added, to other Web sites—and give us no compensation." In other words, the IOC wanted to be paid for staging the competitions while controlling how they would be communicated to the world: a rather novel definition of "news."

I Have a Dream . . . That Someday
All of Public Life Will Be Copyrighted

Everyone agrees that it makes sense for the creator of a work to be able to earn money from a new work. That is what copyright law is all about. But what happens when a work becomes so culturally important or so publicly disseminated that it arguably "belongs" to everyone?

Martin Luther King Jr.'s famous "I have a dream" speech, delivered on August 28, 1963, is a work that arguably belongs to everyone. It is a fascinating paradox that one of the greatest speeches in American history is in fact a strictly controlled piece of private property. It is owned by King's estate, consisting of Coretta Scott King and her four children. The estate actively licenses the right to reproduce Dr. King's works, and has sued news organizations and scholars for using excerpts of his speeches without permission or payment. One of the most meaningful moments in American public life, a bracing call to human dignity and progress by one of America's great leaders, is available only to those who can curry favor with the King family or pay them enough money.

But aren't public events considered part of the public domain? Isn't a speech text and its public performance unprotected by copyright law, particularly when it was a national event covered by dozens of news organizations and personally witnessed by a throng of 400,000?

That question lay at the heart of a 1997 lawsuit in which King's estate sued CBS for using video footage of the speech without authorization. CBS had signed a contract with the Arts & Entertainment Network to produce a television series, *Twentieth Century with Mike Wallace*, one episode of which was devoted to the speech.

Although Martin Luther King Jr.'s "I have a dream" speech may be one of the most famous orations of modern times and the centerpiece of a federal holiday, it remains the private property of the King estate.

Under copyright law, even important works by public figures delivered to national audiences are considered private property. This principle was affirmed by the Supreme Court's 1985 ruling in *Harper & Row Publishers v. Nation Enterprises* (see page 167). Notwithstanding his interest in launching a movement, Dr. King registered his speech with the U.S. Copyright Office in September 1963 (at the time, copyright protection was not automatic, but required formal registration).

The validity of the copyright was tested in 1963 when a company called Mister Maestro, in partnership with Fox Movietone News, sold audio recordings of the "I have a dream" speech without Dr. King's permission. The defendants argued that the speech had been delivered to one of the largest audiences imaginable, and that copies of it had been distributed to the press in advance. But a federal court ruled that even these acts are not enough to make a work part of the public domain. "It is clear," wrote the court, "that this was a limited, as opposed to a general, publication. There is nothing to suggest that copies of the speech were ever offered to the public; the fact is clear that the 'advance text' was given to the press only." Without a finding of "general publication," copyright protection for the speech remained valid.

This ruling proved to be important thirty-four years later when CBS and the Arts & Entertainment Network began selling a videotape documentary with lengthy excerpts of the speech. The King estate sued in federal district court. But a July 1998 ruling held that CBS could use the video footage because the speech was a news event and therefore in the public domain.

An appeals court reversed that ruling in November 1999, declaring—amazingly—that Dr. King's delivery of the speech did not constitute a "general publication." If the speech had been distributed to the general public "in such a manner as allows the public to exercise dominion and control over the work," or if it had been exhibited or displayed in such a manner as to permit unrestricted copying by the general public, then it would have been divested of its copyright protection. But this did not occur, the court held. The distribution of advance copies of King's remarks to the press; the delivery of the speech to a vast television audience; and even a reprinting of the speech in the Southern Christian Leadership Conference's newsletter, constituted "only a limited publication," the court ruled.

The appeals court sent the case back to the district court for a review of some material facts. But before that could occur, the case was settled in July 2000 without any resolution of the competing legal claims. The practical upshot is that most public uses of the "I have a dream" speech must be licensed from King's estate. While some uses might be considered legal, fair use adjudication is notoriously unpredictable and litigation expenses are daunting.

Dexter Scott King, Dr. King's son, believes that people should not be allowed to exploit Dr. King's memory without paying something to the estate. As he told the *New York Times*, "It has to do with the principle that if you make a dollar, I should make a dime." For her part, Coretta Scott King said she only wants to promote Dr. King's message. "It's difficult and it's challenging when people desire in their own way to exploit the message and the mission of Dr. King for their own personal gain," she told the *Times*. "Yet when we seek to perpetuate the legacy in the way the Holy Ghost has told us to perpetuate it, and we just so happened to be blessed financially by it, it saddens me that people are confused. If it were your daddy, what would you do?"

The King estate clearly is not confused about its interests. It wants to leverage the speech for some serious money. In 2001, it licensed the rights to the speech to Alcatel, a communications firm, for a television and print ad campaign. The ad features the Reverend King delivering his soaring sermon to a vast empty space; through the miracle of digital editing, the Mall is utterly empty. A narrator intones: "Before you can inspire, before you can touch, you must first connect. And the company that connects more of the world is Alcatel, a leader in communication networks."

The family also licensed Dr. King's speech to Cingular, the wireless telephone carrier. A company spokesman explained it wanted to use Dr. King's image because the wireless marketplace is "a ghetto of competing rate plans." Ouch.

It is tempting to dismiss the King family's fierce reliance on copyright law as a simple matter of bad taste. In truth, an expansive reading of copyright law has enabled the privatization of a public event that arguably belongs to all Americans. It is not a value-free proposition, after all, for the law to classify our greatest cultural experiences as property so they can be sold in the marketplace. Now that Martin Luther King Jr.'s birthday is a national holiday, it is especially odious that uses of the speech must be cleared by the King family.

Copyright maximalists might cringe at the dubious taste of it all, but then, principled behavior sometimes means having to live with awkward outcomes. To help us understand what a world of wall-to-wall copyright control might look like, an irreverent journalist, Philip Van Munching, came up with his own version of the "I have a dream" speech:

I have a dream that, even in death, especially in death, historical figures like myself can line the pockets of not only the crassest of marketers, but also of our families, who have replaced our purity of motive with pure profit motive.

I have a dream that my four children will one day live in a nation where they will not be judged by the color of their skin, but by how readily they sell out their father's legacy to cash-rich providers of quality high-speed Internet access.

I have a dream where images of the greatest men of our century, men like Albert Einstein and Gandhi, will incite our children to stand up, and with real excitement in their voices, proclaim, "Hey, that's the Apple Computer pitch guy!"

Uppity Alice Randall and
the Cultural Icon Protection Act

To African Americans, the antebellum South conjured up by *Gone with the Wind* is not a society of romantic balls, charming gentlemen, and beautiful ladies. It is a savage society based on slaveholding and a complex social web of inequality, cruelty, and indignity. Yet the nostalgic illusions peddled by *Gone with the Wind*, or *GWTW*, remain powerful today, especially among white Americans. Since its publication as a novel by Margaret Mitchell in 1936, and the film version by David O. Selznick in 1939, *GWTW* has been the preeminent popular depiction of the Old South.

Alice Randall, an accomplished screenwriter and songwriter, was disturbed that a cultural icon like *GWTW* has indoctrinated generations with grossly inaccurate and racist understandings of the Civil War era. She found this especially troubling because as a young African American girl, she herself found the story enthralling. Only later, rereading the book as an adult, did she realize how morally offensive and historically inaccurate it is.

"Where are the mulattos on Tara?" asked Randall. The world conjured up by *GWTW*, she said, is a "South without miscegenation, without whippings, without families sold apart, without free blacks striving for their education, without . . . Frederick Douglass." The blacks in the novel and film are "buffoonish [and] lazy . . . routinely compared to 'apes,' 'gorillas,' and 'naked savages.' "

Henry Louis Gates Jr., chair of the Department of Afro-American Studies at Harvard University, remembers watching audiences weep during the film version of *GWTW*. "If you are a black person, as I am, the death of the 'Old South' meant the liberation of one's ancestors! It is an occasion for celebration." Gates says the book form of *GWTW* "is widely regarded in the black community as one of the most racist depictions of slavery . . . in American literature."

Randall decided that if she wanted to persuade contemporary readers that the Old South was not the happy, sentimental place depicted by *GWTW*, she would have to take on *GWTW* itself. The story needed to be retold—this time, from a slave's perspective. Randall set about devising a new version of the *GWTW* story, liberally drawing upon the plotline, characters, scenes, and snippets of key dialogue from the book. Her book was not written as a sequel. It was a radical reimagining of the story that frankly sought to subvert its popularity and original meanings.

Randall started by titling her book *The Wind Done Gone*, which bluntly ridicules the sentimentality of *Gone with the Wind*. The protagonist of Randall's book is an entirely new character, Cynara, who is Scarlett O'Hara's illegitimate, mulatto half sister—the daughter of Scarlett's father, the plantation owner, and his slave Mammy.

Randall reimagined and renamed other characters. Scarlett became known simply as Other. Rhett Butler became R., who is portrayed as graying and effete, and who eventually marries a slave whom he meets in a brothel who, in a reversal of the *GWTW* story line, later leaves *him*. Ashley Wilkes, referred to as Dreamy Gentleman, is gay. The prostitute Belle is reimagined as a lesbian. A cameo character, Aunt Pittypat, becomes Aunt Pattypit. Many of the white characters in *GWTW* are revealed as having black ancestors or carrying on affairs with black characters.

The literary strategy used by Randall is parody—an attempt to turn "everything upside down and inside out" in an effort to ridicule. By remaking key aspects of the white and black characters, she wanted to reveal the characters and moral universe of *GWTW* as pernicious myths while entertaining readers in the process. Parody is an important genre for African Americans and other socially subordinate groups because it allows them to remake the prescribed meanings of mainstream culture to describe the reality *they* experience.

Just as the book was about to be published by Houghton Mifflin in April 2001, Randall was shocked to learn that her book might be found illegal. The estate of Margaret Mitchell, author of *GWTW*, asserted that *The Wind Done Gone* represented a copyright infringement.

Mitchell had died in 1962, at which point the copyright in her book had been passed along to her nephews, Eugene Mitchell and Joseph Mitchell. The rights were held in trust by a committee controlled by two retired Atlanta attorneys who had been law partners of Mitchell's brother.

At the time that *GWTW* was published, in 1936, the book was entitled to have up to fifty-six years of copyright protection, which meant that it should have entered the public domain in 1993. But because Congress had extended the term of copyright protection eleven times since 1960, the copyright on *GWTW* remained in force. It is not due to enter the public domain until 2032—seventy years after Mitchell's death and ninety-six years after its publication. (Of course, Congress in the interim may choose to extend the copyright term yet again.)

Margaret Mitchell's estate, which continues to make money from licensing rights to *GWTW*, naturally was not pleased with Randall's book. Not only did it ridicule the beloved myths embodied by *GWTW*, it threatened to undermine the revenues earned by book sales and licensing rights. Accordingly, the Mitchell trusts sought a preliminary injunction in federal district court to prevent publication of *The Wind Done Gone*. They claimed that it constituted an unlawful plagiarism of *GWTW.*

The court found that Randall had borrowed a total of fifteen characters from *GWTW* and had drawn upon many specific scenes and snippets of dialogue. The plaintiffs also produced testimony from literary experts that *The Wind Done Gone* was "a subliterary parasitical work," and that it had breached "the line between parody and plagiarism." Another concluded that "racial stereotypes" have "long since been exploded."

On April 20, 2001, the district court agreed with Mitchell's estate (represented by its trustee, Suntrust Bank), and granted a preliminary injunction ordering Houghton Mifflin to halt "further production, display, distribution, advertising, sale or offer for sale of the book *The Wind Done Gone.*"

The ruling provoked front-page headlines and a firestorm of criticism from leading writers—Pat Conroy, Toni Morrison, Harper Lee, Shelby Foote. Wendy Strothman, an executive with Houghton Mifflin, said in a statement, "Today's ruling, if allowed to stand, will have a chilling effect on all those who seek to use free expression and parody to explode myths and provoke new thinking. The Mitchell trusts are threatening to redefine American parody as we know it."

In a statement to the court, the novelist Toni Morrison had said: "Who controls how history is imagined? Who gets to say what slavery was like for the slaves?" In his ruling, Judge Charles A. Pannell Jr. responded, "The question before the court is not who gets to write history, but rather whether Ms. Randall can permeate most of her new critical work with copyrighted characters, plot and scenes from *Gone with the Wind.*"

Judge Pannell labeled Randall's novel as "unabated piracy," and found that it would deprive the Mitchell trusts of revenue from *GWTW* sequels. It would also deprive the trusts of the right to control *GWTW* characters. For example, the trusts have decreed that Scarlett O'Hara cannot die—a stipulation that Alice Randall's novel violated.

Houghton Mifflin quickly appealed the district court ruling. A month later, in May 2001, the Eleventh Circuit Court of Appeals struck down the preliminary injunction and cleared the way for publication of Randall's book. The court found the injunction to be "an unlawful prior restraint in violation of the First Amendment."

Randall was fortunate that the Supreme Court, in the 1994 case of *Campbell v. Acuff-Rose Music, Inc.*, had issued a landmark ruling about how much of an original work a parodist could legally use. The rap group 2 Live Crew had used Roy Orbison's song "Oh, Pretty Woman" and turned it into a raunchy rap version. The Supreme Court ruled that a liberal appropriation of Orbison's song "for comic effect or ridicule" was a permissible form of fair use (see pages 21–22).

Now, confronting *The Wind Done Gone*, the circuit court expanded this broad fair use definition to literary works as well: "For the purposes of our fair-use analysis, we will treat a work as a parody if its aim is to comment upon or criticize a prior work by appropriating elements of the original in creating a new artistic, as opposed to scholarly or journalistic work. . . . The fact that Randall chose to convey her criticisms of *GWTW* through a work of fiction, which she contends is a more powerful vehicle for her message than a scholarly article, does not, in and of itself, deprive *The Wind Done Gone* of fair-use protection." *The Wind Done Gone* reflects transformative value, wrote Judge Stanley F. Birch Jr., "because it can 'provide social benefit, by shedding light on an earlier work, and in the process, creating a new one.'"

While the Mitchell trusts initially announced their intention to appeal further, a year later they reached an undisclosed settlement with Houghton Mifflin. Both sides reaffirmed their legal positions. Randall's book would continue to bear the label "unauthorized parody," and at the request of the Mitchell trusts, a donation was made to Morehouse College. A year after *The Wind Done Gone* was published, Houghton Mifflin had sold 150,000 hardcover copies and 60,000 paperbacks.

CHAPTER 9

The DMCA's Attacks
on Free Speech

Very frankly, I am opposed to people being programmed.

> —Fred Rogers (Mister Rogers), as cited in
> *Sony v. Universal City Studios*, 464 U.S. 417
> (1984)

From 1556 to 1694, the Stationers' Company of London held a monopoly on the publication of written works in England. Only members of the guild were authorized by the Crown to own printing presses and publish works. Any copying of published works was prohibited. The abuses that resulted were entirely predictable: competition was stifled, the company reaped monopoly profits, members of the guild received preferential treatment, outsiders were excluded, and the flow of creativity and information to the public was strictly controlled.

This regime was overthrown in 1709 when the English parliament enacted the first copyright law, the Statute of Anne, whose principles became the basis for modern copyright law and a cultural renaissance.

History does not always move in straight lines toward something known as "progress." With the enactment of the Digital Millennium Copyright Act (DMCA) in 1998, Congress took a major step backward. Although the law was intended to help copyright industries protect their works against digital copying and infringement, its effect has been to override some of the key principles of copyright law as they apply to digital content.

The DMCA makes it a crime to circumvent any technical measure that controls access to a copyrighted digital work. In addition, it makes it a crime not only to make or distribute technologies that can bypass copy-protection measures, but even to *share* information about them. The law thus creates a whole new class of "forbidden knowledge"—about software encryption, digital watermarking, and other copy-protection measures—that is potentially illegal to discuss.

Passed by Congress with little public debate and little awareness of its likely consequences, the DMCA has become one of the most controversial laws of the Internet era. It radically empowers the film, record, publishing, and information industries to control their content in unprecedented ways, and revokes many of the access and usage rights that the public, academics, librarians, computer programmers, and various non-profit constituencies have enjoyed. Under the DMCA, large media companies can now use technologies to eliminate all sorts of customary fair use practices, such as making a personal backup copy of a CD.

In a backhanded way, the DMCA also trumps the term limit that has always been part of the copyright law. It used to be that a work would enter the public domain after a specific period of time; now copy-protected digital content can in effect be locked up forever. To be sure, the DMCA applies only to copyrighted works, not those in the public domain. But when copy-protection technologies are used to lock up all works, copyrighted and public domain alike, one cannot access the public-domain work without circumvention tools, which the DMCA makes illegal.

The DMCA also gives companies the ability to bypass the first-sale doctrine, which is the legal rule that allows libraries to lend copies of books to the public and video stores to rent videos to customers. Now with DMCA-authorized technology locks, copyright holders may control all "downstream" uses of their product even after its purchase. They have new powers to prevent competitive aftermarkets from emerging (e.g., used bookstores) and to control how people may use a work after purchase (e.g., no sharing with family or friends; no outright purchases of a book, just "rentals"). By limiting the public's ability to own, share, and reuse works, the DMCA subverts the core purpose of copyright law—to promote the widest dissemination of knowledge, innovation, and competition.

To the casual observer, it seems perfectly acceptable for a company to be able to control their digital works with copy-protection systems or any other system. After all, companies should be able to control the content they create. For someone else to use it without authorization is the same as someone breaking into their house or stealing their car. Such are the metaphors routinely invoked.

These comparisons are misleading, however, because they assume that copyright is an absolute property right. This is simply not the case, and never has been. Copyright is a social bargain between the public and the creator, in which the public grants creators a limited monopoly right in their work in return for stipulated forms of public access and use of those works. The DMCA overrides the public's end of the bargain—our right to various fair uses in digital works, our freedom to use purchased works as we please, and our ability to access works that enter the public domain (which is now effectively eliminated for digital works). The public has a broader set of interests than propertizing all content; creators cannot create new works without access to prior works and the citizens of a democratic society need to be able to share and reinvent content. American culture is more than a pay-per-use marketplace.

This chapter looks at some of the disturbing consequences of the DMCA and why it urgently needs to be rolled back.

New Genres of Forbidden Science and Speech

Once the DMCA went into effect, it became potentially illegal for academic researchers and software programmers to openly discuss the nature of copy-protection systems. Many of these experts spend a lot of time exploring the flaws of encryption systems as part of their ongoing attempts to build better, stronger ones. But a discussion that is too explicit or public may well violate the DMCA's anticircumvention provisions, which make it illegal to disclose how to thwart a copy-protection system.

The Princeton University computer scientist Dr. Edward Felten got a swift lesson in the DMCA's power when he accepted a public challenge from a music industry group known as the Secure Digital Music Initiative (SDMI). The group invited computer experts to defeat some "digital watermarking" technologies that it believed to be effective in preventing copying of digital music. Felten joined researchers at Princeton, Rice University, and Xerox Corporation to see if they could defeat the watermarking system and copy music. In short order, they did.

But when Felten tried to present the findings at a professional conference sponsored by the U.S. Navy, the SDMI threatened legal action under the DMCA if the work was published or publicized. The threat provoked an explosion of criticism in the computer science community, and Felten and his fellow scientists began to explore a legal response. With the help of the Electronic Frontier Foundation, they ended up suing the SDMI, arguing that the DMCA violated their First Amendment rights. Perhaps worried about a public backlash and the strength of its legal case, the SDMI responded by claiming its letter was a "mistake," and withdrew its threat (while reserving the right to sue in the future).

Felten went ahead and presented some of his research findings at an August 2001 USENIX conference of computer security experts. But he and other researchers remained troubled that the music industry might sue again or require them to seek permission to publish their future research. Ultimately, a federal judge held that there was no current dispute that could be tried. While the constitutionality of the DMCA was not addressed, scientists—until further notice—seem to have the freedom to pursue their research and speak publicly about it.

The root problem of the DMCA is that it casts too broad a net and squelches legitimate scientific inquiry. "That the DMCA can be used to deny researchers their constitutional freedom to exchange ideas—in print and in speech—shows what is wrong with overly broad legislation," said Eugene Spafford, a co-chair of the Association for Computing Machinery. "In this case, the threat inhibits our ability to explore, to understand, and to advance science and technology."

Felten came up with a parable about *bricks* to mock the music industry's use of the DMCA. When the brick (read deencryption technology) was invented, said Felten, people worried that bricks might be used to hit other people over the heads. So Congress enacted the Detached Masonry Control Act to ban not only bricks, but brick-making tools and even discussions of bricks.

This seemed to make everyone feel safer, and in fact, no one was being hit over the head with bricks. But meanwhile, neighboring kingdoms were using bricks to build new structures and roads, which improved their standard of living. In the "Land of RIAA," however, scientific innovation languished. The kingdom's fortifications were built out of simple wood, making everyone vulnerable to attack.

In Felten's parable, the DMCA is repealed. In real life, of course, the DMCA's overly broad provisions remain in force. They continue to intimidate other researchers from talking publicly about security vulnerabilities.

As described in the Electronic Frontier Foundation's periodic reports on the DMCA's effects, a Dutch cryptographer and security systems analyst, Niels Ferguson, discovered a flaw in an Intel video encryption system, High Bandwidth Digital Content Protection. But because he feared possible prosecution under the DMCA, Ferguson would not publish his work. He also removed all references to the security flaws from his Web site.

On another occasion an educational software company, Blackboard Inc., invoked the DMCA to stop two students from presenting their research findings on the security problems of one of the company's products. Other digital security researchers—Fred Cohen, Dug Song, and others who prefer to remain anonymous—have suppressed their research results lest they be prosecuted under the DMCA. The law has criminalized the very kinds of inquiry that are needed to help identify security weaknesses and allow them to be openly discussed and fixed.

The power of the DMCA to disrupt science was again demonstrated in the summer of 2001 when the Russian programmer Dmitry Sklyarov came to Las Vegas to speak at a conference. Federal authorities arrested him on charges that he was working on a software program that could be used to open Adobe Systems' electronic books. Sklyarov's program let users convert files from Adobe's eBook format into the "portable document format" (or "pdf" format), also made by Adobe. This angered the company because the conversion would allow eBook consumers to remove control restrictions embedded in eBook files, enabling eBooks to be read on another company's software or resold without Adobe's approval.

The government did not accuse Sklyarov of violating anyone's copyrights or contributing to an infringement. His "crime" was to work on a tool that, despite many legitimate uses, might be used by third parties to copy an eBook without the copyright holder's permission. What Adobe called a "burglar's tool" was, from the public's perspective, simply a tool by which the purchasers of eBooks could exercise their traditional fair use and first-sale rights. The imprisoned Sklyarov must be puzzled, wrote Professor Lawrence Lessig, "about how a free society can jail someone for writing code that was legal where written, just because he comes to the United States and gives a report on encryption weaknesses."

Sklyarov was freed after five months in jail, but the government continued a criminal case against Sklyarov's employer, ElcomSoft. At trial, no evidence was found that ElcomSoft's software had been used to make illicit copies, and a jury acquitted the company. But the chilling effects of the case linger on. Many foreign scientists now avoid travel to the United States lest they run afoul of the DMCA, and others in computer science want to hold their conferences offshore both as a matter of protest and as a way to ensure full and open dialogue.

"It's critical in the high-tech world that people be able to talk about this stuff, study it, take it apart, adapt it to their use," said Edward Felten, who has gone on to become something of a missionary on the subject of technology controls and scientific freedom. His Web site, www.freedom -to-tinker.com, is dedicated to discussion about computer security and technology regulation. The Electronic Frontier Foundation also documents and publicizes the pernicious influence of the DMCA through its Web site, www.chillingeffects.org.

You May Not Teach Your Robot Dog New Tricks

Thanks to the Digital Millennium Copyright Act, you may not be allowed to teach a robot dog new tricks—literally. In 1999, the Sony Corporation came out with a fanciful new electronic product, the "Aibo Entertainment Robot." Sony explains that "Aibo" is an acronym for "artificial intelligence robot" and also happens to mean "compassion" in Japanese. The electronic novelty is essentially an electronic, programmable pet.

With versions that now sell for as much as $1,600, the Aibo is touted as providing "the greatest degree of autonomous behavior and functionality yet to be achieved by Sony robotic engineers." The latest versions of Aibo (now in its third generation) feature tactile touch sensors and an "Illume-Face" that is capable of a variety of facial expressions. Aibo also has the ability to recognize the owner's face and voice, and the ability to understand more than one hundred words and phrases.

When a consumer buys an Aibo as a pet, she should not be deceived into thinking she actually owns it. In critical ways, Sony keeps the dog on a short leash by way of the DMCA. This "gotcha" became clear when an enterprising Aibo enthusiast and hacker attempted to reprogram the source code of one of Sony's robotic Aibo dogs so as to "teach" it new tricks. The renegade consumer, who only allows himself to be identified as AiboPet, maintains a Web site, www.aibohack.com, at which Aibo owners can download free homemade programs to make their pets dance.

As recounted by the journalist Brendan I. Koerner, "By expertly tweaking Aibo's code, hobbyists have enabled the robo-beast to boogie to Madonna's 'Vogue,' double as a breadbox-sized surveillance camera, or growl 'Bite my shiny metal robot ass!' All these behaviors are infinitely cooler than the bland canine-like moves that unenhanced Aibos perform."

AiboPet was not trying to market his tricks or compete with Sony. He was merely posting new tricks to his Web site for the benefit of an active online community of Aibo lovers. But Sony did not find this love of their product to be endearing, and in fact believed that his homemade programs violated the anticircumvention provisions of the DMCA. Sony wrote to AiboPet: "We do not support the development of software that is created by manipulating existing Sony Aibo-ware code, copying it and/or distributing it via the Internet. This is a clear case of copyright infringement, something that most Aibo owners can appreciate and respectfully understand."

AiboPet was forced to shut down most of his site as a result of Sony's pressure. At the time, the only other way for Aibo owners to enhance the performance of their robo-pets was to buy a $450 "performance kit" from Sony. AiboPet said that Sony actually incorporated some of the software innovations he had developed (such as a program to snap digital photos) into later models of Aibo. "I really don't care about them stealing ideas and more from me," said AiboPet, "as long as they let me keep doing my stuff."

In the meantime, however, Sony got some religion. As Linux and the open source software movement demonstrated the power and imagination of uncontrolled software, Sony developed a new set of software tools that *resemble* open source software. In May 2002, Sony released an open way of programming their robots (without making it open source software). Sony gives users access to the interface protocols for programming Aibo, so they can make their own software extensions, but they cannot access or modify the actual source code used inside Aibo.

AiboPet has mended his breach with Sony, and now has "semi-official, unofficial approval" from the company, he said. And why not? It is hard to imagine a better salesperson for Aibo than a smart, motivated hobbyist. Sony apparently learned that strict control of the sort authorized by the DMCA is a great way to undermine a loyal user community and a nascent market. Give users sufficient freedom and a good product and they are likely to make the product their own—and spend huge sums.

These Words May Not Be Read Aloud

Adobe Systems inadvertently revealed the alarming reach of the DMCA when it drafted the license for an e-book version of *Alice's Adventures in Wonderland*. The book, which is now in the public domain and no longer protected by copyright, was offered on Adobe's new Acrobat eBook Reader. Not many people take the trouble to read the fine print of eBook licenses. But those who did so in 2001, including the Stanford law professor Lawrence Lessig, made a startling discovery. Consumers who buy the eBook are not allowed to read the text of the book aloud!

In his column in the now-defunct *Industry Standard*, Lessig found that Adobe had added a number of licensing restrictions to eBook versions of works that had entered the public domain. Among the bizarre stipulations found in the license for *Alice's Adventures in Wonderland*:

- "No text selections can be copied from this book to the clipboard."
- "No printing is permitted on this book."
- "This book cannot be lent or given to someone else."
- "This book cannot be read aloud."

Lessig scratched his head in perplexity: "A plain reading of the 'permissions' makes it sound as if the firm is trying to control, in addition to everything else, whether parents may read a children's story to their own children."

When people pointed out the absurdity of this licensing provision, Adobe backtracked and tried to clarify. "Read aloud" does not mean "read aloud," but rather "Read Aloud," which, said Adobe, refers to the voice-reading capacity within the eBook Reader software that enables it to "speak" the book aloud.

"So by this 'permission' not to 'read aloud,'" explained Lessig, "what Adobe meant was that its reader did not have the capacity to 'read aloud' the electronic text. 'Permission' means 'capacity.'" Lessig continued:

Remember, this is *Alice's Adventures in Wonderland*, and the adventures don't stop there. It turns out that Adobe has a special meaning for just about every word on its "permissions." When Adobe says "lend" it doesn't mean lend; it is referring to a function that enables users to forgo the rights to a book temporarily, while someone else has them. "Give" does not mean give; when Adobe says "give," it is referring to a function that enables users to permanently forgo the rights to a particular book, when they "give" it to someone else. And when Adobe says "print" (as in "No printing is permitted on this book"), it doesn't mean printing on the book; it apparently means printing of the book.

Apparently embarrassed, Adobe quickly came out with a new set of permissions for *Alice's Adventures*. But the new ones still insisted the eBook could not be lent or given—though it could be "read aloud." And a new stipulation allowed users "to copy 10 text selections every 10 days" and "to print 10 pages every 10 days."

Despite its modest changes, the basic problem remained: Adobe was creating more stringent restrictions on the use of the eBook than exist on any physical book that you might find in a library.

Adobe's eBook license brings to mind the famous colloquy between Alice and Humpty Dumpty: "'When I use a word,' Humpty Dumpty said, in rather a scornful tone, 'it means just what I choose it to mean—neither more nor less.'"

"'The question is,' said Alice, 'whether you *can* make words mean so many different things.'"

"'The question is,' said Humpty Dumpty, 'which is to be master—that's all.'"

The Ingenious Use of Copyright Law to Squelch Competition

Under the DMCA, copyright holders can legally eliminate the public's traditional rights to share, reuse, and resell digital works. But the effect of this giveaway is much greater. This extension of copyright protection amounts to a license for anticompetitive conduct by the makers of virtually any consumer product using electronic microchips. Here's why: since the "digital content" processed by the microchips can be protected under the DMCA, any competitor who tries to use that electronic data to make a compatible generic product is probably violating the law. The result: less consumer choice, less technological innovation, and higher prices.

Consider the lucrative aftermarket for computer printer cartridges. The real money for printer manufacturers comes from selling the toner cartridges; that is one reason manufacturers greatly discount the price of their printers. The user base for a given printer represents a lucrative market franchise. So imagine if one could use copyright law to lock up this user base by making the printer cartridge proprietary and preventing generic competition.

That is essentially what Lexmark, the second largest laser printer vendor in the United States, is trying to do. In the electronic microchip used in its printer cartridges, Lexmark inserted a control technology with "authentication routines" that were used to verify the compatibility of Lexmark cartridges and Lexmark printers. These digital codes were inserted precisely to prevent would-be competitors from producing generic printer cartridges that might undercut Lexmark sales.

One company, Static Control Components, reverse-engineered the Lexmark "Smartek" chips and copied fifty-six bytes of code so that competitors could produce generic refill cartridges. This prompted Lexmark to invoke Section 1201 of the DMCA and claim that Static Control was circumventing Lexmark's control technology—a copyright violation.

Many consumers share the views of attorney Robert L. Ellis of Columbus, Ohio, who told the Politech online forum: "For years we could buy cheap aftermarket toner cartridges for our printers and copiers. Now in my office, for example, we have a crappy little digital copier that automatically shuts down when it decides its toner cartridge is empty—whether it's empty or not. We can't refill it. We can't even buy an aftermarket toner. Hell, we can't even shake it and get a few more copies out of it. Our toner cartridge has an encrypted chip in it, so we no longer actually run out of toner, we run out of chip. The machine will work only if we put in a new, 'genuine' replacement toner that likewise has an encrypted chip. And guess what—the 'genuine' replacement costs about twice as much as similar toner cartridges for unchipped products."

After Lexmark obtained an injunction against Static Control enjoining sales of the reverse-engineered chips, Static Control appealed the ruling and filed an antitrust countersuit as well. The case illustrates how far copyright law has drifted from its original aims, and how it can be abused for anticompetitive purposes.

Now that the DMCA grants such sweeping authority over digital information, it is not difficult to imagine manufacturers finding contrived reasons to insert electronic chips into their consumer products. In the guise of quality or safety, companies can insert "digital content" into their product, invoke the DMCA, and then sue any competitor that tries to bypass the electronic encryption of the proprietary digital information.

Such cases are in fact proliferating. In 2003 a company selling garage door openers, the Chamberlain Group, sued the maker of a universal garage door remote control, Skylink, for violating the anticircumvention provisions of the DMCA. Skylink had created a cheaper, generic remote control that was interoperable with the one sold by the Chamberlain Group.

As explained by the Electronic Frontier Foundation, "Even though the Skylink clicker does not use the 'rolling code' sent by the Chamberlain transmitter, Chamberlain claims that it 'bypasses' its 'authentication routine' to use the computer program that controls the garage door's motor. On this view, a consumer who replaced his lost or damaged Chamberlain clicker with one of Skylink's cheaper universal clickers would not be allowed to 'access' his own garage. The same argument would apply equally to ban universal remote controls for televisions."

In November 2003, a federal court ruled that the Skylink interoperable remote controls did not violate the DMCA, an opinion that the Second Court of Appeals later upheld. This was a welcome development, to be sure, but we have not likely seen the end of such abuses of the DMCA.

Those Notorious Weapons of Piracy—the Shift Key and the Magic Marker!

The music and film industries often insist that their copy-protection systems are remarkably strong and cannot be decrypted. Then some enterprising techie discovers that the techno-lock amounts to a silk ribbon . . . but to disclose that fact publicly would be illegal under the DMCA! Two recent episodes demonstrate how telling the truth can be a crime.

John "Alex" Halderman, a graduate student in computer science at Princeton, was skeptical about the claims by SunnComm Technologies that its new MediaMax CD3 Copy Prevention System made it difficult to rip music CDs from computer hard disks. BMG Music had adopted MediaMax as a new "copy management" system for its music CDs. Based on testing, SunnComm claimed that "none of the ripper programs used in the testing process was able to produce a useable unauthorized copy of the protected CD." The company said its product provides "a verifiable and commendable level of security."

To test this claim, Halderman bought a copy of a recently released Anthony Hamilton album, *Comin' From Where I'm From*, and tried to rip some music. He not only came to a radically different conclusion, he found that defeating the system was easy. "I assert that [SunnComm's] claims are patently deceptive," Halderman wrote in his paper. "In practice, many users who try to copy the disc will succeed without even noticing that it's protected, and all others can bypass the protections *with as little as a single keystroke*" [original emphasis]. The decryption procedure could be communicated to a novice in a single sentence: "Press the Shift key every time you insert the CD, and that's it."

After Halderman posted a formal report about his analysis on his Web site, SunnComm's stock dropped by over $10 million, or about one-third of its total value. The company immediately announced that it would sue Halderman for violating the DMCA.

A wave of ridicule from the computer science community immediately descended upon SunnComm. One wag suggested that keyboard makers should be sued for creating such a nefarious anticircumvention device, the shift key. A mock press release announced, "Jack Valenti [then head of the Motion Picture Association of America] slammed keyboard companies for what he called 'the next thing to armed robbery,' adding that 'They even put two of these keys on each model, and make them two or three times as large so you can't miss it. That's not incitement to piracy?'"

The CEO of SunnComm, Peter Jacobs, told *Wired News* that the shift key was not a defeat mechanism, but a "design element" of the system, and that the company's real beef was Halderman's disclosure of the copy-management file names and instructions on how to remove them. "I don't think researchers have a right to publish a 'how-to' on how to perform illegal activities under the guise of research," Jacobs said.

That was a Thursday. On Friday, the company changed its tune and announced it would not be suing Halderman. The public outcry on blogs and online forums may have been influential in this decision. The company may have also been wary of inviting a court to rule that the DMCA eliminates a traditional form of fair use for the purpose of criticism. CEO Jacobs told the press, "I don't want to represent a company that would do anything to cause any kind of chilling effect on research."

This was not the first time that a music industry copy-protection system proved to be as permeable as a soggy paper towel. In May 2002, Sony introduced a new "Key2Audio" technology that purported to make it impossible to burn music CDs onto blank recordable CDs or onto computer hard drives. When the news organization Reuters attempted to burn a copy of Celine Dion's latest release, *A New Day Has Come*, the copy protection worked as claimed. But after blackening the edge of the shiny side of the CD with a black felt-tip pen, the reporter had no problem copying the CD to his computer's hard drive.

The apparent idea behind the copy-protection system was to introduce a "security track" with bogus data on the outside rim of the CD. Since computers typically read data files first, a computer would refuse to "read" the security track and never get to the music tracks. But blacking out the security track defeated the copy protection. Inevitably, Internet wits began speculating that DMCA defenders would soon be calling for a ban on Magic Markers as anticircumvention devices and jail time for those who shared this information.

The dangers of a law that criminalizes the disclosure of computer security flaws took on a more serious tone in August 2003 when accusations were raised that a manufacturer of computerized voting machines had knowingly sold machines with security problems. The company, Diebold Election Systems of Ohio, had sold its voting machines to California, Maryland, Georgia, and other states, but potential vulnerabilities in the security for the machines were allegedly ignored.

In the summer of 2001, someone leaked or stole more than 13,000 internal company e-mails and documents that seemed to verify the worst suspicions about the security flaws of electronic voting machines. The documents had been leaked to activist Bev Harris and *Wired News*. Some documents said that identified security flaws had not been aggressively corrected. Memos said that software "patches" were sometimes installed on voting machines that had already been certified for use. In one memo, a Diebold employee suggested installing a bug fix rather than going through the long process of recertifying the integrity of voting machines.

In the wake of these revelations, activists who have raised questions about the reliability of electronic voting machines called for a full investigation. Inevitably, the documents soon appeared on a number of Web sites.

I'm sorry Dave. That information is protected under the Digital Millennium Copyright Act.

HAL 9000

Diebold technology: It's a secret. Get over it.

DIEBOLD
We won't rest.

When students at Swarthmore College raised questions about the security of Diebold electronic voting machines, the company invoked the DMCA to stifle public debate. The episode prompted the students to found a new "international student movement for free cuture" (www.freeculture.org).

Diebold swung into action, sending cease-and-desist letters to more than a dozen people who had posted the documents or links to them. Their crime: infringing the copyrights to employee e-mails. Diebold sent cease-and-desist letters to colleges and universities in their capacities as Internet service providers, or ISPs, demanding that they remove copyrighted materials from their systems. Here, too, the DMCA granted broad, unilateral rights to copyright holders. It did not really matter whether the students had a right to post the materials on their Web pages; through the DMCA, copyright holders could unilaterally demand the withdrawal of "their" materials from Web sites without the trouble of due process.

When news of Diebold's legal action became known, students at Swarthmore, near Philadelphia, began a campaign of civil disobedience against the company, and students at a number of other colleges followed suit. The Electronic Frontier Foundation and the Stanford Law School

Internet and Society Cyberlaw Clinic entered the fray with legal assistance for the colleges and students. Said EFF attorney Wendy Seltzer: "Diebold must not be permitted to use unfounded copyright claims to stifle public debate on the accuracy of electronic voting machines."

In December 2003, Diebold backed off and rescinded its lawsuit. But that did not mean that the DMCA could not be invoked again, or by another company, to thwart a legitimate public discussion. To address this eventuality, EFF is seeking a court ruling that the posting of Diebold documents did not, in fact, violate copyright laws because the publication clearly constituted fair use.

As these many DMCA stories suggest, the overexpansion of copyright laws can wreak havoc on all sorts of important values in American life. Maintaining a delicate balance is key to the success of copyright law. The DMCA is justly reviled because it represents such a blunt, aggressive departure from the basic principles of copyright.

PART FOUR

Absurd New Frontiers of Control

The Digital Millennium Copyright Act has certainly inaugurated a broad new class of outlandish copyright claims. But it is only one front in a multipronged onslaught of intellectual property excesses. Part Four looks at some of the daffy new property rights being claimed in knowledge, creativity, and culture.

We first look at how the DMCA ethic is metastasizing into a fuller, even more alarming ideal: the quest for perfect control. As we will see in chapter 11, the real purpose of the DMCA and so many other intellectual property and technological initiatives is to empower content industries to utterly control the sale and aftermarket uses of their works. Fair use, in the new absolutist regime, becomes more of a nominal legal right than a meaningful guarantee to quote, reuse, share, or transform. Indeed, a number of industry figures have explicitly denied that fair use is a public right. They regard it as an indulgence, tolerated only so long as the means to charge money for works is lacking. Once copyright holders find a technology to exploit their works, goes this line of thinking, then fair use rights can be overridden at will.

By this logic, singing in the shower is fair use only until a means is discovered for metering the activity. The same for personal copying of CDs for use on one's car stereo, recording TV shows for later viewing, or singing songs at camp without a performance license.

Inevitably, the pursuit of perfect control overreaches and incites public resistance. Should broadcast networks actually be able to force TV viewers to watch the ads and prevent personal copying, as one industry executive urged? Should the law allow property claims for letters of the alphabet;

trademarks for smells; patents in common business methods and life-forms; and copyrights for sequences of yoga postures? The attorney Charles F. Gosnell years ago recalled that "one member of a self-appointed committee of copyright lawyers has boasted that they have developed restrictions on every means of transmission of thought except smell, taste and extra-sensory perception." Yet as we will see, even smell and taste are being redefined as protectable forms of property via the law governing trade dress.

There finally comes a point at which the absurd frontiers of intellectual property law merge so completely with parody that it is nearly impossible to tell the difference. Chapter 12 takes a romp through this growing field.

Happily, the news from the world of copyright and trademark law is not all discouraging. The conclusion of this book looks at a number of imaginative new initiatives that articulate a new, more constructive vision. Bypassing some of the property categories of intellectual property discourse, this movement is attempting to reinvent and reclaim the cultural commons. The movement takes many forms—artistic protests, grassroots mobilizations, public policy advocacy, litigation, alternative licenses for content, and new online commons. While this movement is still emerging and finding its voice, its preliminary successes, aided by the burgeoning Internet culture, suggest that intellectual property law is likely to move in some positive, public-spirited directions in the years ahead.

CHAPTER 10

The Quest
for Perfect Control

The more prohibitions you have, the less virtuous people will be.
The more weapons you have, the less secure people will be.
The more subsidies you have, the less self-reliant people will be.

—Lao-tzu, *Tao Te Ching*

I n the drive to assert perfect control over how content may circulate
in our culture, the logic of copyright and trademark maximalists
sometimes reaches some scary extremes. A leading senator has
declared that the computers of three-time copyright infringers should be
destroyed. A publishing industry official has called some librarians "Ruby
Ridge or Waco types" for wishing to share information. To fight piracy, a
congressman introduced legislation to authorize copyright holders to
hack into the computers of people they regard as copyright infringers.

These are signs of desperation and intransigence. They also suggest a
disturbing belief that the public does not have any serious copyright
interests of its own. Determined to secure absolute control over their
works, copyright maximalists tend to ignore the artistic and civic importance of quotation, sharing, creative collaboration, and transformative
uses of prior works. The unacknowledged doctrine of "perfect control"
that animates so many leaders of the content industries is not a benign
advance, but rather a deeply troubling threat to an open, democratic
culture.

TV Executive: You Are *Required* to Watch the Ads

The idea that people have the right to copy and share video content has stuck in the craw of the film industry ever since the landmark 1984 Supreme Court ruling *Sony v. Universal City Studios*, often known as the Betamax case. (Sony's VCR product was the "Betamax.") That ruling held that it is legal for consumers to "time-shift"—record a television program for later viewing—so long as it is for personal, noncommercial purposes. A new technology cannot be summarily banned, held the court, so long as it is capable of "substantial, non-infringing uses."

With the rise of the "personal video recorder," or PVR, Hollywood is revving up its propaganda machine against consumer choice again. This time it is worried that computerized recording systems such as TiVO and ReplayTV will be used to skip ads and destroy the historic business model for commercial television.

In the eyes of Jamie Kellner, who in 2002 was the chairman and CEO of Turner Broadcasting, a Time Warner Company, TV viewers have an affirmative legal obligation to watch ads. TiVO and ReplayTV are unfairly interfering with this time-honored "contract" between network television and viewers, said Kellner: "[Ad skips] are theft. Your contract with the network when you get the show is you're going to watch the spots. Otherwise you couldn't get the show on an ad-supported basis. Any time you skip a commercial or touch the button you're actually stealing the programming."

Mr. Kellner's startling claim that avoiding commercials is theft has some dire implications for America's bladders. Are bathroom breaks legal? Kellner magnanimously concedes, "I guess there's a certain amount of tolerance for going to the bathroom." But he adds, "if you formalize it and you create a device that skips certain second increments [ReplayTV 4000 skips forward in 30-second increments], you've got that for only one reason, unless you go to the bathroom for 30 seconds. They've done that just to make it easy for someone to skip a commercial." In Kellner's universe, TV viewers are nothing more than passive automatons who are obligated to watch the ads.

It is revealing that Kellner's authoritarian vision is not even supported by empirical marketing research. As reported by *Advertising Age*, a marketing research report by Next Research found that PVRs do not affect the viewing of advertising much at all:

> The study . . . showed that viewers' likelihood of watching commercials when viewing programs with PVRs vs. live TV is nearly the same. Only 1 percent said they always watch the ads when using a PVR or watching live TV, while 60 percent said they occasionally watch them with PVRs and 62 percent with live TV.

Not surprisingly, Kellner's remarks provoked a firestorm of ridicule and outrage. One visitor to Slashdot, a leading Web site for computer techies, suggested that TV viewers may have to be straitjacketed and forced to watch TV as part of their reeducation, much as the character Alex in Anthony Burgess's *Clockwork Orange* was forced to watch disagreeable video content as part of his moral "reeducation." As Alex put it:

> What I was taken to, brothers, was like no cine I'd been before. I was bound in a strait jacket and my gulliver was strapped to a head-rest with like wires running away from it. Then they clamped like lidlocks on my eyes so I could not shut them no matter how hard I tried. It seemed a bit crazy to me, but I let them get on with what they wanted to get on with. If I was to be a free, young malchick in a fortnight's time, I would put up with much in the meantime, my brothers.

Forced viewing of advertisements is not just a dystopian fantasy. It exists today. Some studios have placed commercials at the beginning of their DVDs with digital code that disables the fast-forward button (and trying to circumvent the code would likely violate the DMCA). A major newspaper prohibits "deep linking"—hyperlinks to specific articles on its Web page—because that would enable visitors to bypass advertising on the home page. "Product placement" on TV shows and films has now morphed into a genre known as "embedded advertising," in which the programming and the advertisement are so intertwined that viewers cannot avoid the (undisclosed) marketing.

Since it is now becoming morally suspect—and who knows, potentially illegal—to avoid ads, one can only wonder what new copyright crimes could materialize in the future. On the LawMeme Web site, Ernest Miller extrapolated from Jamie Kellner's reasoning to imagine his own David Letterman–type list of illegal acts:

10. *Watching PBS without making a donation.* You know who you are, you cheap . . .

9. *Changing radio stations in the car when a commercial comes on.* Future radios will prevent listeners from changing channels when a commercial comes on. The RIAA [Recording Industry Association of America] has not yet taken a position on whether it is permissible to switch channels when the listener doesn't like the song.

8. *Channel surfing during commercials, especially with Picture-in-Picture capability.* Similar to radio, skipping through channels, particularly when combined with picture-in-picture (which permits viewers to know precisely when an ad block ends), will be prohibited.

7. *Getting into a movie after the previews, but just in time for the main feature.* Theaters will be required to close their doors once the advertising and previews have begun. The MPAA has not yet taken a position on the time-in-seat requirements for advertising in the pre-preview slide show or whether audiences should be compelled to watch the credits at the end of the movie.

6. *PBS.* How can commercially sponsored broadcast networks compete with a government-sponsored network?

5. *Inviting friends over to watch pay-per-view.* When you call to authorize viewing, you will be required to indicate the number of people present to watch. Compliance will be monitored and viewers must identify themselves.

4. *Blocking pop-up ads on the Internet.* Yeah, Mozilla and Opera [browser] viewers, this means you!

3. *Not buying things from the advertisers on television shows.* Part of your contract is that not only do you watch the advertisements, but that you subsequently buy from the advertisers. If you don't buy from the advertisers, the whole system breaks down.

2. *Watching MTV if you are older than 35 or Matlock reruns if you are younger than 45.* Advertisers buy ads to reach a particular demographic. If you aren't part of that demographic, you are, effectively, a thief.

1. *Libraries and librarians.* This is why we have the Racketeer Influenced and Corrupt Organizations (RICO) Act.

Kellner's remarks about ad-skipping were not careless rhetoric; the television industry has a serious commitment to preventing viewers from being able to use digital video recorders to skip television ads. To fight this objective, the Electronic Frontier Foundation in 2003 sought a declaratory judgment against twenty-eight entertainment companies, asking a federal court to rule that "time-shifting and "space-shifting" (sending digital content to another electronic device) are lawful fair uses under copyright law. Before the case could be tried, however, ReplayTV went bankrupt and the entertainment companies agreed not to sue the EFF's clients for using the ReplayTV devices, prompting the court to dismiss the case.

Senator Hatch: Destroy the Computers of Infringers

At a Senate hearing on illegal downloading of copyrighted music in June 2003, the chairman of the Senate Judiciary Committee, Senator Orrin Hatch, asked one of the technology experts appearing before the panel if some way could be found to damage the computers of file traders. As reported by the Associated Press, Randy Saaf of Media Defender, a Los Angeles company that devises technical means to frustrate file sharing, responded, "No one is interested in destroying anyone's computer."

"I'm interested," said Hatch, who argued that it "may be the only way you can teach somebody about copyrights." Hatch is himself a songwriter who earned a reported $18,000 in royalties in 2002.

"If we can find some way to do this [prevent copyright infringement] without destroying their machines, we'd be interested in hearing about that," Hatch said. "If that's the only way, then I'm all for destroying their machines. If you have a few hundred thousand of those, I think people would realize the significance of their actions. There is no excuse for anyone violating copyright laws." Senator Hatch said that he would favor technology that would warn copyright infringers twice and "then destroy their computer."

Legal experts have pointed out that hacking into a personal computer and causing harm violates federal anti-hacking laws. Therefore, if copyright holders are going to be allowed to act as cyber-vigilantes, a legal exemption would have to be enacted.

Even the Recording Industry Association of America did not seem to embrace Senator Hatch's surprise proposal. An RIAA spokesman said that Hatch was "apparently making a metaphorical point that if peer-to-peer networks don't take reasonable steps to prevent massive copyright infringement on the systems they create, Congress may be forced to consider stronger measures."

A few months later, in October 2003, Senator Hatch returned to this topic at a speech before the National Press Club and confessed that his idea of destroying computers for copyright infringement "struck a nerve." His goal, he said, was "to spark a policy discussion about serious consequences for serious actions. . . . I am one of those old school law-and-order types who is skeptical of the term victimless crime. With apologies to Gertrude Stein, a crime is a crime is a crime."

That seems to be precisely what is being contested, however—*what should be considered a crime?* (And should Senator Hatch be allowed to rip off Gertrude Stein's famous phrase with impunity?) A January 2004 Harris Interactive Survey found that 75 percent of adult Americans agree that "downloading and then selling the music is piracy and should be prohibited, [but that] downloading for personal use is an innocent act and should not be prohibited." Some 70 percent of respondents agreed with the statement, "If the price of CDs was a lot lower, there would be a lot less downloading of music off the Internet."

Until recently, anyone who questioned the entertainment industries' ethic of "total control" was cast as a beyond-the-pale radical. When a panelist at a 2001 conference defended information-sharing via the Internet, the chief attorney for intellectual property rights at a major film studio exclaimed, "I haven't heard such wonderful speeches since I left City College of New York, where we had a corner over there called 'Little Kremlin.'" Yet by 2004, the business-oriented Committee for Economic Development had issued a report warning that the entertainment industry's get-tough approach to copyright enforcement was actually bad for business and the economy. The report warned that many of the legal and technological protections sought by industry threaten to upset the delicate balance of rights between content industries and the public. While the report found that digital rights management systems were acceptable, they should not place excessive burdens or restrictions on consumers. "In the music business, 'cheap and great' is likely to be at least as attractive to consumers as 'free and crummy,'" the report said.

Despite such attempts to forge a new middle ground, the champions of "perfect control" are not likely to retreat soon. They are likely to be frustrated because digital technologies practically invite the reuse and sharing of works, and consumers, for their part, have long been frustrated by high CD prices and industry resistance to online music distribution. One thing is certain: destroying computers is not likely to be an effective copyright enforcement mechanism.

The Great Cultural Lockdown

If piracy, broadly construed, is going to be stamped out in the digital environment, then it necessarily follows that copyright holders must have near-perfect control of content flows. This, in turn, requires that virtually all consumer electronics and computers be built with government-mandated copy-protection mechanisms. This is the only possible way that no one will be able to use a copyrighted work in an unauthorized way, say the film and music industries.

To fulfill this industry vision of a closed, controlled system, Senator Fritz Hollings in 2002 introduced the Consumer Broadband and Digital Television Promotion Act. "The reality is that a lack of security has enabled significant copyright piracy which drains America's content industries to the tune of billions of dollars every year," he said in introducing the bill.

Senator Hollings's proposal was immediately derided as an attack on technological innovation and on the public's ability to play their purchased CDs and DVDs on whatever device they want. "In the old days, when you bought an album" wrote Alex Salkever, the online technology editor of *Business Week*, "you could play it on your turntable or take it to a friend's party and play it there. You could tape it on cassette. Once you bought a piece of music, it was pretty much yours. Under the Hollings proposal, these activities could become criminal or, at the very least, punishable by a fine."

Although the bill made a token recognition of fair use rights, its real purpose, it was clear, was to allow content owners to expand their control over how their products may be used after their sale. The power to determine whether a given CD could be rented or sold, played on some playback devices but not others, or played on machines in some regions of the world but not others, would reside with the film and music companies—not consumers.

Since the bill's definition of a "digital media device" requiring regulation was so broad, computer scientist Ed Felten developed a daily listing of electronic devices that would be required to contain copy-protection technology. His first listing: "Big Mouth Bill Bass," the animatronic fish mounted on a wall plaque. "Fight piracy—regulate singing fish novelties," urged Felten. Number two on the "Fritz Hit List" was the "Amana Messenger refrigerator," because it would qualify for regulation as a "digital media device." "Fight piracy—regulate kitchen appliances!" urged Felten.

And so on. After several dozen listings, Felten retired the project, having made his point. The idea that fighting piracy requires copy-protection regulation of musical chip-and-dip bowls, digital church bells, digital sewing machines, and digital hearing aids, suggests the impracticalities of achieving a perfectly controlled system.

While the Hollings bill was not reintroduced, its history is instructive because it represents the prevailing industry vision for the future. Mandatory copy-protection technologies were stymied by technical complications and politics, but the overriding goal remains—to assert as much post-purchase control of works as possible.

The film and music industry's two preferred "tethering" strategies include copy-protection technologies and "region coding" of content. Copy protection prevents traditional fair uses (quotation, personal copying, noncommercial uses), while region coding assures that a DVD or CD bought in one geographic region of the world will play only on playback devices sold in the same region.

DVDs are currently copy-protected through a system called CSS, for Content Scrambling System. This industry-imposed system of copy protection effectively overrides the public's fair use rights in digital content such as movies and music. Not only is a work made inaccessible by the CSS program, but under the DMCA it is illegal to circumvent the code to use the content as one wishes. Thus, when fifteen-year-old Norwegian programmer Jon Johansen developed a program, DeCSS, that could play purchased DVDs on a Linux-based computer operating system, and not Windows—an act that would normally be considered fair use—he was promptly charged with violating the DMCA. Under the law, film companies, using the CSS coding, dictate what a consumer may do with his purchased content.

A judge later acquitted Johansen, but not before his case became a cause célèbre in the computing world. The film industry appealed the case and lost a second time. Meanwhile, the film industry turned their attention to Eric Corley, the editor of a Web site called *2600* that had published the DeCSS program as part of its news coverage of the debate about copy protection. As the *Corley* case worked its way up to a U.S. appeals court, it too caused outrage within the computer community and highlighted the absurdities of the DMCA.

The court of appeals ultimately ruled that decryption codes can be legally suppressed under the DMCA as a way to fight piracy. While conceding that copy protection may make it more difficult to exercise fair use rights (because the content is encrypted), the court said that Congress has the power to make antipiracy measures a higher priority.

The court not only banned DeCSS, it prohibited Web hyperlinks that pointed to Web sites that hosted the program. This sparked an outpouring of "electronic civil disobedience" as hundreds of Web sites posted DeCSS. Others defiantly posted the banned DeCSS code in other media—T-shirts, bar codes, haiku, a movie script—to communicate how the program could be re-created and to dramatize the First Amendment implications.

Region coding is another way that the music and film industries seek to control aftermarket uses of their works. With this tethering scheme, the world is divided into six marketing regions, and DVDs are coded to play back only on those players with matching region codes. Region coding not only allows DVD makers to charge different prices for different regions, it prevents a "gray market" of "parallel importing" of the sort that now exists for pharmaceutical drugs. Region coding also prevents a person who buys a DVD while on vacation in India (region 5) from playing it back when she returns to the United States (region 1). While there are ways that hardware and software can be made to bypass region coding, the legality of these measures under the DMCA is questionable.

The point of all these measures—the DMCA, CSS, region coding, and all the associated surveillance, enforcement, and public relations—is to achieve a great cultural lockdown of content. Naturally, this brave new world of strictly controlled content has some serious implications for an open, democratic society.

When all works are either coded as authorized or presumptively "pirated," a closed, centralized system of control is created. Permission to read, share, reuse, collaborate, and create—all become conditional freedoms.

Cartoonist Mike Keefe predicts the inescapable next step in the recording industry's enforcement dragnet.

Surveillance of reading, viewing, and computer usage becomes imperative lest "piracy" (often the practices formerly known as fair use) become too prevalent. When ferreting out pirates becomes an overriding priority, the very idea of anonymous reading, listening, and viewing becomes problematic because these activities escape antipiracy surveillance.

Inevitably, a vast policing apparatus is needed to patrol the key checkpoints of distribution lest contraband information is passed along. Hardware systems that enable unauthorized copying must be neutralized; software innovations that threaten to "spill the beans" about encryption flaws or deencryption strategies must be suppressed; aggressive litigation dragnets of the sort already launched by the RIAA are imperative to catch suspected infringers and deter would-be scofflaws.

The logical end point of all these measures is captured by a parodist in a mock news article, "RIAA Wants Background Checks on CD-RW Buyers." Hilary Rosen, then the head of the RIAA, warns, "A CD-RW can be a dangerous weapon when it falls into the wrong hands. You wouldn't sell a gun to a convicted felon and you shouldn't sell a CD-RW drive to a Gnutella user. A three-day waiting period gives us time to verify that no copyrighted material is on the purchaser's hard drive and to make sure they have a membership in the Columbia House CD club."

Funny, but close to the bone. Is a nation that has long cherished its First Amendment freedoms and thrived on the open ethic of the Internet prepared to accept the great cultural lockdown?

The Morality Lectures of Industry Virtuecrats

Since technology controls and draconian laws are not sufficient to achieve perfect control of content, aggressive forms of "public education" are inescapable. We already see this in the Motion Picture Association of America's antipiracy propaganda trailers in movie theaters, the steady drumbeat of antipiracy PR from the film and music industries, and even curricula for elementary school children touting the virtues of copyright. The top executives of some of America's most cutthroat industries have a new calling these days—giving high-minded lectures to the American people about personal character and ethics.

If you are skeptical that the Fox Network, the television network responsible for *Married . . . With Children, Who Wants to Marry a Millionaire?* and *Joe Millionaire*, is indifferent to the nation's moral fiber, think again. Peter Chernin, the president of the News Corporation, the owner of the Fox Network, was so concerned about the prevalence of pornography, spam, and piracy on the Internet that he denounced it as a "moral free zone."

Chernin told the Progress & Freedom Foundation in August 2002: "The stall tactics and smoke screens of those who have purposely ignored digital shoplifting can no longer be tolerated and can no longer mask the ulterior motives that have driven them all along. The truth is that anyone unwilling to condemn outright theft by digital means is either amoral or wholly self-serving."

The moral correctives that Chernin favored? Legislation to authorize copyright holders to disrupt peer-to-peer networks and hack into people's computers, and legislation to require copy-protection systems in all computer hardware and software devices. After a huge public outcry, both bills, introduced on behalf of the movie and recording industries, were quietly retired.

To listen to the content industries, the democratization of creativity made possible by computers and the Internet threatens to repeal the

Renaissance and roll back the Enlightenment. Here is Richard Parsons, the chairman of Time Warner, who (as president of the company) warned in 2000: "This is a very profound moment historically. This isn't just a bunch of kids stealing music. It's about an assault on everything that constitutes the cultural expression of our society. If we fail to protect and preserve our intellectual property system, the culture will atrophy. And corporations won't be the only ones hurt. Artists will have no incentives to create. Worst-case scenario: The country will end up in a sort of cultural Dark Ages."

Jack Valenti, the former longtime head of the Motion Picture Association of America (MPAA), is famous for cloaking his frequent diatribes against "piracy" in lofty, didactic terms. Perhaps his most classic declaration about the immorality of "piracy" (which in his definition seems to conflate mass counterfeiting with personal fair uses) came in testimony at a 1983 congressional hearing. The film industry was seeking to prevent consumers from using VCRs to videotape television shows. Valenti considered the "time-shifting" of shows to be copyright infringement. Eager to convey the true horror of the VCR to a congressional committee, he told legislators a howler that continues to circulate today: "The VCR is [to the movie industry] as the Boston strangler is to women home alone."

Of course, the Supreme Court ruled in the landmark Sony Betamax case in 1984 that the VCR is a legal device so long as it is capable of "substantial non-infringing uses." The VCR (and its successor, the DVD player) ended up becoming a lucrative boon for Hollywood, generating a vast new global aftermarket for films. Videocassette sales have actually exceeded revenues from theatrical exhibitions of movies since the mid-1980s. By 2003, sales of videocassettes and DVDs brought in $22.5 billion, or more than twice as much money as box-office receipts ($9.2 billion).

Like the VCR, the arrival of new digital technologies has provoked similar "the sky is falling" denunciations. In 2003, Valenti gave a number of speeches in which he linked the moral decline of America's best and brightest to music file sharing. Recounting an appearance before two hundred students during the Napster craze, Valenti asked "the finest of the breed at one of the most prestigious universities in the land" how many of them had used Napster in recent months. All two hundred students raised their hands. Clearly some stern moral education was in order:

I fixed my gaze on a young man who I was told was going to graduate near the top of his class. "You are," I said, "about to graduate
from one of the best schools in the world. You are now an educated,
civilized human being, those best fitted to meet life's changes and
challenges with versatility and grace. Now, tell me, how do you
square that with the fact you're stealing?"

He was crestfallen at first. Then his face brightened and he said,
"Well, maybe it is a kind of stealing, but everyone else is doing it
and besides music costs too much." I smiled as I thought to myself,
"for this version of a moral value, parents are paying a small fortune
in tuition."

The great moral crusader from Hollywood saw grave consequences
for the nation's ethical future: "If choices chosen by young people early in
their learning environment are infected with a moral decay, how then can
they ever develop the judgment to take the right fork in the road?"

Book publishers are another industry that has often squared off against
one of their largest, most loyal customers—public libraries. Publishers like
to sell their books, and libraries like to buy them. But libraries are dedicated to *sharing* their purchased books. It is part of an old-fashioned idea
that easy, free citizen access to printed materials is a great way to encourage literacy, education, and democratic culture (not to mention seed the
market for book-buying). To some publishing executives, however, the
idea that some people may get information "free" (after the library buys
it) seems almost anti-American.

One of the most contentious issues dividing publishers and libraries is
the terms that will govern the lending of electronic books and journals,
and the definition of fair use in digital information. Should interlibrary
loans be allowed? Should libraries be able to own digital content, or just
rent it? How many copies of an e-book should be available to a library
that purchases one? As Pat Schroeder, the president of the Association of
American Publishers, told the *Washington Post* in 2001, "We have a very
serious issue with librarians."

As librarians have pushed back on publishers, advocating for the fair
use rights of library patrons and the public, publishers have ratcheted up
the rhetoric: "They've got their radical factions, like the Ruby Ridge or

Waco types" who want to share all content for free, said Judith Platt, a spokeswoman for the Association of American Publishers, in 2001.

The morality lectures are not likely to end soon, and for a simple reason—a public that has developed its own social practices and norms, and that remains committed to the idea of fair use and free expression, will always need "moral re-education." There will always be a surplus of industry virtuecrats to exhort them to stay on the right path.

CHAPTER 11

Intellectual Property Goes Over the Top

They want to own the Mc. They want to own the M. They want to own it all.

—Mary Blair, owner of McMunchies, a sandwich shop
whose name was challenged by McDonald's

The mania to assign property rights to every imaginable intangible is a sickness that is, alas, beyond the scope of this book. Yet it is important that we stop and contemplate some of the jaw-dropping excesses of copyright and trademark law in order to appreciate what the philosophical crack-up of a venerable legal tradition looks like. How are citizens supposed to take intellectual property law seriously when the idea of "authorship" is being extended to letters of the alphabet and sequences of yoga postures? Why should we respect copyright law when it is successfully used to protect the concept of *silence* as a musical performance? Such trends are not confined to copyright and trademark law. They are also roiling patent law, which has officially recognized enforceable property rights in peanut butter and jelly sandwiches, swinging sideways on swings, and "one-click" online shopping. It's a mad, mad, mad, mad world.

As Difficult as A®, B®, C®

In light of the ferocious propertization of everything, it was perhaps inevitable that private claims would eventually be made for letters of the alphabet. Like the scramble to trademark commonly used words and to register them as Internet domain names, the quest to own letters is a brash tactic to assert a symbolic monopoly. The owner may not actually be able to sue people for *any* use of the letter, but a trademark in even specific, limited uses of a letter sends an unmistakable signal: *My brand is elemental and preeminent in the global culture!*

That is certainly the message that the McDonald's Corporation seems to be sending as it prowls the planet for restaurants and carryouts that have the temerity to use the Scottish prefix "Mc." In 1977, McDonald's began using "Mc" to invent such words as McService, McPrice, McFries, McMuffin, among dozens of other marketing novelties. With more than ten thousand restaurants, tens of millions of customers, and an advertising budget of more than a billion dollars a year, McDonald's has virtually universal brand recognition. As its marketing popularized "Mc" coinages, the company essentially invented a whole new class of seemingly generic words. *Seemingly.* The "Mc" words are not really generic words, but rather proprietary terms that can be used only with permission.

As Naomi Klein reports in her book *No Logo*, McDonald's has "sued the McAllan's sausage stand in Denmark; the Scottish-theme sandwich shop McMunchies in Buckinghamshire; went after Elizabeth McCaughey's McCoffee shop in the San Francisco Bay Area; and waged a twenty-six-year battle against a man named Ronald McDonald whose McDonald's Family Restaurant in a tiny town in Illinois had been around since 1956." McDonald's may have been within its legal rights to sue McMunchies, but its public reputation took such a drubbing that it later relented and let it keep the name.

When a major hotel chain, Quality Inns, tried to start a new chain of motels called "McSleep," McDonald's successfully sued in federal court, claiming a trademark violation. Quality Inns chose the term because, like McDonald's, it wanted to offer lodging that would be "consistent, convenient, quality product at a low price."

Years before, it seems, McDonald's had invented the term "McStop" to describe a cluster of fast-food and convenience stores on a highway plaza. As a result, McDonald's said it already had dibs on "Mc" in a traveler-related line of business. A rule known as the "Aunt Jemima doctrine" strengthened McDonald's case; a 1917 ruling by Judge Learned Hand decreed that a maker of pancake batter using the "Aunt Jemima" mark—a common racist stereotype of the time—could stop a syrup maker from using the same mark.

But can the Scottish prefix be "taken private" just because it has acquired a new set of secondary meanings associated with McDonald's? For the Quality Inns litigation, a linguist was commissioned to review hundreds of journalistic uses of the prefix, such as "McMedicine," "McFashion," and "McPaper"; he identified twenty-seven different definitions of the prefix, suggesting widespread popular adoption of the term. In the end, however, a federal judge rejected the notion that McDonald's "has lost its right to enforce its marks because 'Mc' has become a prefix with a single meaning that has become part of the English language and beyond McDonald's control." If a motel chain could be named McSleep, the judge ruled, too many consumers would be misled into believing that it was associated with McDonald's.

Another letter that has inspired a litigious rivalry is the letter "O." In 1995, the German publisher Ronald Brockmeyer bought a trademark in the letter "O" from a bankrupt erotic art magazine with that name. With the tagline, "The Art, the Fashion, the Fantasy," Brockmeyer revamped O into a magazine that featured scantily clad women in fetish outfits and sexual fantasy scenarios.

Flash forward to April 2000. Oprah Winfrey, the businesswoman and talk show host, launched her own magazine devoted to women and life-style, O, The Oprah Magazine, which quickly became a huge success. Oprah's O is not likely to be confused with the German soft-porn magazine: her magazine sells for about half the price, comes out monthly rather than irregularly, and deals with losing weight, looking fit, and attaining spiritual peace.

Yet because Brockmeyer's O was also distributed in the United States, one could argue, as Brockmeyer did, that his magazine O had first claim on the letter. "I know that lawsuits are a burden on your life but I had no choice," he told ABC News. "O is my trademark. I built it up and protected it for years. The defendants knew about my rights but went ahead anyway, and they refused to stop when I asked them to." Brockmeyer's suit against Winfrey's publishers, the Hearst Corporation and Harpo Print LLC, sought to prevent them from using the term "O Magazine" and the letter design for "O."

In July 2002, a federal judge ruled in favor of Oprah, saying that the magazines were so different that there was little chance that anyone would confuse the two. The judge also held that the irregular publication schedule of Brockmeyer's O and his delay in bringing a suit against Oprah's O made his case less compelling.

One of the most famous squabbles over the ownership of a letter (and in this case, a numeral as well) was provoked by the appropriationist band Negativland, which in 1990 produced a spoof of a song by the rock group U2. The thirteen-minute vinyl single known as *U2/Negativland* used about thirty seconds of the U2 song "I Still Haven't Found What I'm Looking For," and mixed it with Negativland's vocals and some obscenity-laced outtakes from *Casey Kasem's Top 40* radio show. Kasem was taping an introduction of the then unknown band U2 and kept flubbing his lines; he was also castigating his staff about a listener's song dedication to her dog Snuggles, who had just died. The cover of the record featured a drawing of a U-2 military spy plane, the letter "U," the numeral "2," and the word "Negativland."

What followed was a three-year legal odyssey in which representatives of the band U2, its record label, and Casey Kasem sued the band and sought to have the record destroyed. The most persuasive aspect of their complaint was the charge that the record cover would mislead consumers into thinking the record was made by the band U2. But clearly U2, Island Records, PolyGram International, and Casey Kasem were also displeased by the spoof, and refused to negotiate a deal. The five members of Negativland were equally adamant about protesting "the criminalization of artistic appropriation, a significant creative technique which continues to be unrecognized, ignored or consciously suppressed by our current copyright laws."

In the end, Negativland persuaded everyone except Kasem to allow the Negativland single to be released under certain conditions, such as repackaging it to prevent consumer deception. The band's success may have been helped by a major Supreme Court ruling in the interim, *Campbell v. Acuff-Rose*, which held that musical parody is protected under the fair use doctrine (see pages 21–22). But because of Kasem's veto, the Negativland single has never been officially rereleased and remains an underground classic. The band, meanwhile, has become a hero in certain circles both for its "sonic collage" music and its fair use advocacy.

The band memorialized its epic legal fight by publishing a book collecting all the correspondence, faxes, memos, news clippings, and other materials. *Fair Use: The Story of the Letter U and the Numeral 2* offers a rare unfiltered glimpse into the mind-numbing complexities and agonies of a copyright infringement dispute. The crux of the battle, the band always maintained, was the "ownership" of "U" and "2." The term, after all, was coined by the U.S. government for its spy plane before U2, the band, appropriated it. In a wry tribute to this fact, Negativland invited Francis Gary Powers Jr., the son of the U-2 pilot shot down over the Soviet Union, to write the foreword to *Fair Use.* "In 1991, a very different letter U and numeral 2 was shot down," Powers wrote.

Perhaps acronyms should represent a different class of symbols than letters of the alphabet, but only barely. Once again, a whiff of arbitrariness hangs over the adjudication of what will and will not cause confusion. While the public is not likely to confuse a German porn magazine with Oprah Winfrey's *O,* another court believes that the public *will* confuse an organization devoted to saving wildlife with an organization devoted to lowbrow, theatrical wrestling. Both groups—the World Wildlife Fund and the World Wrestling Federation—laid claim to the letters "WWF."

The World Wildlife Fund has used the initials "WWF" to identify itself since it began its environmental and conservation work in 1961. Its public image is associated with its cute panda logo and its international activism. The British-based WWF was alarmed, therefore, when the U.S.-based World Wrestling Federation began to expand its raucous, scripted brawls to new overseas venues. It did not help that American prosecutors had begun criminal proceedings against the federation and a magazine accused the wrestling circuit of sanctioning drugs, sexual harassment, and other crimes.

The wrestlers had signed an agreement with the panda-lovers in 1994 to stop using the initials "WWF." But the wrestlers ignored the contract and even used the letters on their Web site. So the "real" WWF went to court, and a London high court in August 2001 found that the wrestlers had to stop using WWF, lest the panda-lovers become confused with the mayhem-lovers and their "very insalubrious image." The world just ain't big enough for two radically different types of enterprises to share the same initials "WWF."

An account of dueling acronyms cannot fail to include the battle over "WWJD," which stands for "What Would Jesus Do?" The phrase had its origins in the 1890s, coined by the Congregationalist minister Charles Sheldon as a part of a series of rousing sermons. He exhorted the faithful to ask themselves, "What would Jesus do?" before every decision they faced. The sermons were later collected into a book and published under the title *In His Steps*. Because of a copyright mix-up (the magazine in which the sermons were originally published was not copyrighted), the inspirational book became a public-domain title. This was a key reason why it has been published by eighty different publishing houses, translated into twenty languages, and has sold more than ten million copies over the past century.

As Janie Tinklenberg, a church youth group leader, contemplated how she could inspire teenagers to lead more Christian lives, she came up with the idea of bracelets with the acronym WWJD. As she told *Salon* magazine, "I figured a bracelet was perfect: They could wear it all the time and it was even kind of cool."

Little did she know that her idea would spawn a massive, multimillion-dollar fad within Christian publishing and merchandising circles. More than sixteen million bracelets bearing "WWJD" have been produced. Dozens of books and a wide array of T-shirts, pencils, and other merchandise trade on the popularity of "WWJD."

This situation raised some interesting ethical questions for the Christian merchandising industry: Would Jesus have tried to claim a property right in "WWJD" or would he have been pleased to see the term spread freely through the air, without restriction? Would Jesus have tried to cash in, the better to help his ministry, or would he have wanted the message to be circulated outside of the marketplace? The Christian merchandising sector had certainly made its own judgment on these issues.

For Tinklenberg, however, it was the tasteless knockoffs—a "Christian" version of the Polo Ralph Lauren horse and $400 necklaces—that prompted her in 1998 to apply for a trademark on WWJD in jewelry. She planned to use any revenues to support the church youth group. Tinklenberg eventually won the trademark, but others own trademarks for the use of "WWJD" in videos, books, concert tours, and dozens of other products.

As more people become aware of their intellectual property rights and the stampede to own letters and acronyms gains greater momentum, one can only wonder if the idea of a common culture, collectively enjoyed, is a quaint anachronism. Coming attractions? George W. Bush sues W Hotels, Quincy Jones (aka "Q") sues the maker of Q-Tips, and C-Span tries to kneecap Hi-C and C++.

A Legal Monopoly over Silence

Does silence belong to all of us, or can someone own it and charge money for it? It sounds like a silly question. But not, apparently, to the British licensing agency that collects royalties for the performances of composers' works.

A controversy over the sounds of silence began in 2002 when the avant-garde composer Michael Batt performed "One Minute's Silence," which was exactly that. In the program notes for the performance, Batt decided to pay tribute to the experimentalist composer John Cage, who in 1952 had pioneered a similar performance piece called 4'33" which was precisely four minutes and thirty-three seconds of silence. Batt also put "One Minute's Silence" on his album *Classical Graffiti*, performed by the Planets.

At the debut of Cage's version of silence in Woodstock, New York, the pianist David Tudor sat down at a piano, opened the keyboard lid, used a stopwatch to clock four minutes and thirty-three seconds, then closed the lid. The point, as Cage wrote in his book *Silence*, was: "There is no such thing as an empty space or an empty time. There is always something to see, something to hear. In fact, try as we may to make a silence, we cannot . . . sounds occur whether intended or not." Cage's performance, then, was of all the sounds we do not intend.

In the program notes for Batt's performance, he listed the composers of "One Minute's Silence" as "Batt/Cage." He gave a credit to Cage "just for a laugh," he later told the *Independent* of London. This attribution was sufficient, in the eyes of the Mechanical-Copyright Protection Society, the British agency that collects royalties for music performances, to demand payment. MCPS sent Batt its standard license form, seeking a royalty on behalf of Cage's estate.

Batt was nonplussed: "My silence is original silence, not a quotation from his silence. Mine is a much better silent piece. I have been able to say in one minute what Cage could only say in four minutes and thirty-three seconds." Batt's mother asked her son, "Which part of the silence are they claiming you nicked?"

Gene Caprioglio, speaking for Cage's American publisher, Edition Peters, told a reporter, "The [*Independent*] article tries to make us sound ridiculous for taking this position, but Batt [was the one who] listed Cage as the composer. . . . If Mr. Batt wants to produce a minute of silence under his own name, we would obviously have no right to the royalties." The

Sun newspaper (London) reported that Nicholas Riddle, a director of Edition Peters, intended to sue Batt for royalties if necessary: "John [Cage] always said the duration of his piece may be changed, so The Planets' piece doesn't escape by virtue of its shorter length." It was pointed out, however, that Batt's recording of silence was not identical to Cage's. Batt's recording was completely silent while Cage's recording contains coughing by the audience and the rustling of candy wrappers.

In a more legalistic vein, Batt told a reporter, "I didn't credit 'John Cage' on my silence. I just credited 'Batt/Cage'—the Cage being *Clint Cage*, no relation to John, but a pseudonym for myself (properly registered with the collection societies). I explained all this to the record company at the time. Somebody else presumed it was Little Johnny Cage and added the detail voluntarily and wrongly, after it left me!"

Who knows what transpired in private talks between Edition Peters and Batt, but in September 2002, Batt agreed to pay "an undisclosed six-figure sum" (in British pounds) to the John Cage Trust "in recognition of my personal respect for John Cage." Edition Peters reiterated its conviction that "the concept of a silent piece, particularly as it was credited by Mr. Batt as being co-written by 'Cage,' is a valuable artistic concept in which there is a copyright."

Owning the Smell of Freshly Cut Grass

The next frontier in the commodification of life is sensory experience. Realms of subjective perception that have hitherto been too elusive to be enclosed by property rights—sounds, tastes, and flavors—are starting to win legal recognition as property. Two legal decisions in particular have opened the door to this new frontier, one involving the trademark for a distinctive smell used in yarn, the other for a shade of green-gold used on press pads by a dry cleaner. Given the expansionist history of intellectual property law, one can only wonder if some food company is going to capture the smell of chicken noodle soup and a media corporation will come to own a special shade of green.

Here is the story so far. A number of sounds have enjoyed trademark protection for some time. NBC owns a trademark in its distinctive three-note chimes (the notes G–E–C, an aural allusion to NBC's ownership by General Electric Corporation). MGM, the studio, has a trademark on the roar of the MGM lion that announces the beginnings of its films. The

Harlem Globetrotters basketball team owns the song "Sweet Georgia Brown" as a trademark. And AT&T owns a trademark in the musical flourish that can be heard after dialing an AT&T telephone call.

To be sure, there have been some setbacks in the trademarking of sounds. Harley-Davidson, the motorcycle maker, tried for six years to win a trademark for its distinctive "hog call"—the low, guttural engine noise ("potato-potato-potato") that its "47 degree V-twin single crankpin motor" produces. But Japanese motorcycle makers strenuously fought the trademark application, and eventually Harley-Davidson relented and withdrew its application.

This came as some relief to many legal practitioners, who worried that the makers of vacuum cleaners and kitchen blenders might try to trademark their allegedly distinctive sounds. Historically, few sounds have been trademarked. In 1998, the U.S. Patent and Trademark Office reported that only twenty-five American trademarks were sounds. The idea of owning distinctive sounds was culturally alien to American society in earlier periods, and not seen as strategically valuable for competing in the marketplace.

But we live in different times now. With greater competition for people's attention and a more cluttered cognitive environment than ever before, owning property rights in sounds or colors seems to be more compelling to some companies. One landmark ruling that is encouraging companies to contemplate "sensory trademarks" was a 1985 circuit court ruling that the color pink could be a trademark when used in housing insulation (the case was brought by Owens Corning). In 1995, the potential for trademarking color got another boost with a Supreme Court ruling, *Qualitex Co. v. Jacobson Products*. In this case, a dry cleaner produced press pads that were a distinctive shade of green-gold, which it claimed had acquired a "secondary meaning" that identified and distinguished his company from others.

The case has been controversial in some quarters because it declares that a trademark could consist of a color "pure and simple," without regard for other components of a trademark (shape, texture, and so forth). But by recognizing that a color, pure and simple, could be a distinguishing mark eligible for trademark protection, the Supreme Court seemed to suggest that other nontraditional marks, such as smells and flavors, may also be possible. One hurdle would have to be surmounted at the outset: any sensory mark must have acquired a secondary meaning as a distinc-

tive symbol widely identified with the company or product. But in prin
ciple, the law would not stand in the way.

A "scent" case, *In re Clarke*, gave new impetus to the trademarking of
smells and, by implication, other sensory indicia. In 1990, a trademark
examiner refused to grant a trademark to Celia Clarke for "a high impact,
fresh, floral fragrance reminiscent of plumeria blossoms" in embroidery
yarn and sewing thread that she sold. When Clarke appealed to the Trademark Trial and Appeal Board, however, it granted her a trademark in the
smell. The board noted that the precedent would apply only if the smell
were not an "inherent attribute" of the product; perfumes, colognes, and
scented household products would continue to be ineligible for trademark registration (a rule that allows knockoff fragrances to compete with
the more famous ones).

The rationale for these new sensory marks is that they reduce confusion in the marketplace by helping people identify products more readily.
But given the slippery slope of expanding protection that is endemic to
intellectual property law, this new frontier of trademark law is troubling.
Just as other aspects of the public domain have been made privatized, in
the current legal climate one can imagine common sensory stimuli—
smells, colors, flavors—becoming proprietary as well.

Already British and European companies are forging ahead with "creative product-scent relationships," such as a cinnamon scent used on phar-
maceuticals and a floral scent "reminiscent of roses" used on auto tires.
The European Court of Justice in February 1999 recognized the "smell
of freshly cut grass" as a trademark used in conjunction with tennis balls.
In the United States the maker of toner cartridges for laser printers is trying to obtain trademark registration for a lemon scent. The maker of an
oil-based metal-cutting fluid has a "scent mark" for the smell of bubble
gum. Pharmaceutical companies may wish to acquire "flavor marks" for
their pill capsules.

Perhaps the ultimate propertization of sensory experience may be a
"service mark" on the living body of Elayne Angel, owner of the Rings
of Desire body-piercing studio. On November 5, 2002, the U.S. government granted the first ever service mark to a body tattoo—a full set of
angel wings tattooed on the back of Angel. Service mark 2,645,270 gives
Elayne Angel legal protection relating to her body-piercing business, and
is duly registered with an ® symbol between two of the angel "feathers"
on her right buttock.

This may be the logical culmination of "branding"—the literal branding of human flesh with a proprietary symbol. Since many people choose to have various trademarked designs tattooed on their bodies—the Nike swoosh, automobile logos, cartoon characters—one can only wonder what would happen if a disgruntled trademark owner went to court. If an infringement were found, could the owner win a court order for a tattoo removal? Could a court award damages if someone copied another artist's tattoo design? In both cases, the answer, in theory, is yes, according to a fascinating article by New York attorney Marisa Kakoulas in *Body Modification* ezine.

Just when it seemed as though the logic of commodification could not proceed any further, and that some things would remain a part of the commons of human experience, intellectual property law always manages to thrash its way to a new beachhead. One can only wonder what will happen when, in the tradition of Ralph Lauren appropriating the word "polo" from the equestrian sport, the owners of scent marks begin to accuse others of "diluting" and "tarnishing" their trademarked smells.

No Photos, Please, of the Inside of a Starbucks

Three women decide to spend the weekend together in Charleston, South Carolina. In the course of their visit, they stop for coffee at a Starbucks. To commemorate their time together, one of them pulls out a disposable camera. They then pass it around, taking pictures of each other in a round-robin sequence.

At this, the manager of the Starbucks approaches the women angrily, screaming, "Don't you know it's illegal to take photographs in a Starbucks?" and demands that they hand over the camera. The whole interior "environment" is protected by trademark law, the manager explains, and so cannot be used without Starbucks' express permission, even for a personal snapshot.

Another town, a different Starbucks, the same scenario. A Web log correspondent recounted what happened to him:

> As we approached the counter to order our stuff, a man stood up from a table of about eight people, and was going to take a picture of all his friends around the table. The guy behind the counter called out, "Sir, I'm sorry, but there's no taking pictures here."

"What?"

"It's company policy, you can't take pictures in here."

The customer looked bewildered, incredulous, and annoyed and didn't take the picture. I asked the guy behind the counter why there's no pictures allowed. He said, "The company doesn't want pictures to end up in magazines, so all pictures have to go through corporate communications."

How dumb is this? Here's a customer clearly having a good time in the store, and wants to take a picture of his friends. He's got a typical point-and-shoot camera for taking snapshots. Because Starbucks is worried about the less-than-microscopic chance that this picture will end up in a magazine and somehow make Starbucks look bad (how, exactly?), they've squashed these peoples' good time, and made themselves look like the corporate weasels they are in front of at least twenty customers. Nice going.

Why do big corporations have to act like such soulless control freaks, even when it is in their own worst interest?

When word of such "no photos" incidents at Starbucks reached Professor Lawrence Lessig in May 2003, he told the readers of his popular Web log and invited reactions. It turned out that a lot of people had had similar encounters at Starbucks around the world—in San Francisco and Bangkok, Manhattan and Durham. While dozens of people had not had their Kodak moments thwarted, a good number *had*. Sherlock Holmes was not needed to deduce that there might be a common reason for these seemingly isolated incidents . . . perhaps a corporate policy.

A rollicking discussion quickly materialized on various Internet venues and in a few daily newspapers. Ridicule was the keynote. Was Starbucks behaving like some backward tribesman who feared that a photograph could steal his spirit? One person quipped, "When cameras are outlawed, only outlaws will have cameras." Some respondents pointed out that the owners of private property can do whatever they want with their property, including banning photographs. Others, including former Starbucks employees, insisted the whole issue was moot because there was no such policy.

Still others with experience in retailing said that it is a common practice to prohibit photography in stores. It prevents would-be thieves from finding security breaches, assures the comfort of store patrons, prevents competitors from spying on prices or retail display, and yes, prevents the imitation of trademarked designs. This last issue could easily be a concern for Starbucks, a company that sells an image as much as coffee and has clearly invested a great deal in the look and feel of its groovy interiors.

What seemed to rankle people about the "no photos" incidents was their inhospitable tone. Starbucks, after all, has styled itself as a welcoming "third place," a convivial neighborhood hangout for friends and strangers. A ban on casual photography among friends suggested that the bonhomie of a Starbucks might actually be a myth, a marketing illusion. Online chatters wondered: Could Starbucks really be more concerned about protecting the intellectual property of the interior design than respecting the social milieu that makes its stores appealing?

Scott Leverenz decided to take the bull by the horns. He invited Starbucks customers around the world to post photographs of themselves *inside* a Starbucks of their choice. Could any corporate policy possibly suppress such a puckishly defiant act of customer sovereignty? The Web site (www.starbucksphotos.com) quickly collected dozens of photos of people slurping coffee and posing with friends inside Starbucks' proprietary interiors. It also featured a spoof Starbucks logo—a camera-shy person holding a hand over his face.

So did Starbucks, in fact, have a policy against customers taking photographs in their shops? After the flurry of Web controversy, the Starbucks public affairs senior specialist Sanja Gould told one inquisitor: "Starbucks does not have a photo policy for the general public. Our policy is not to allow media to photograph within our stores without prior approval from our media relations marketing team."

So if individuals can take snapshots in a Starbucks, why all of these reports of staff interventions? Gould said: "While I'm sure every instance is different, I can't comment about that because I haven't been able to talk to the managers involved. I can tell you what our policy is, and our policy is for the media only."

While some in the blogosphere admired Starbucks' PR skills, others had their doubts about the official explanation. Could the prevalence of so many identical incidents be chalked up to the random acts of coffee-jangled store managers?

Perhaps sensing the futility of resistance in the face of an Internet uprising, Starbucks may have opted to abruptly "revise" its no-photo policy, if indeed it had one. If there was such a policy, it was certainly applied inconsistently. My queries to the Starbucks press office in 2004 seeking clarification went unanswered.

Professor Lessig himself confessed, "I couldn't quite tell whether the extremism of these stories was an exception or a policy. And I guess I was relieved to read, and to find, at least some stores where the manager of a place that loves to imagine itself a public place was actually giving members of the public a freedom to feel like they are in public. I understand of course—as everyone should—that this 'feeling' is just virtual. It can be withdrawn at any time."

Send in the Yoga Police!

The mantle of copyright has spread from writings and maps in the 1700s to piano rolls and sculpture in the 1900s. But now the ownership of intangibles has reached a ludicrous new threshold—a sequence of yoga postures. Like so many entrepreneurs who sought to privatize and commercialize something that belongs to everyone, as in a commons, Bikram Choudhury decided he wanted to personally own and control yoga traditions that are thousands of years old. In Choudhury's hands, a discipline that seeks to nurture humility and compassion is being transformed into a moneymaking franchise worthy of Starbucks or McDonald's.

While yoga has produced many masters over the ages, Choudhury is a self-styled yoga entrepreneur. "Headstrong but beloved by many students," writes the *New York Times*, "Mr. Choudhury is well known for his collection of Rolls Royces and Bentleys (about three dozen of them) and his lavish lifestyle in Beverly Hills, where he trains 500 to 600 teachers a year, charging each a fee of $5,000. An advanced seminar, at $2,400, is scheduled at a Ritz-Carlton hotel on Maui in August."

Choudhury, a native of India, won a number of yoga competitions in the 1960s before moving to the United States to teach yoga. He developed his own style of yoga practice, as set forth in his 1978 book, *Bikram's Beginning Yoga Class*, whose devotees later came to include Brooke Shields, Ricardo Montalban, and Raquel Welch. Bikram certified his yoga instructors, who then went off to start their own yoga studios.

None of this is especially noteworthy. Yoga is a practice with many different traditions and styles developed over the centuries. Some have larger followings than others—there is Ashtanga, Anusara, and Kundalini yoga, for example—but none of them is regarded as the legal property of anyone. While the founders of other lines of yoga practice have claimed copyrights in their books and videos and trademarks in their names and logos, none claimed to own the yoga tradition itself.

The regimen developed by Choudhury is a version of Hatha yoga that he dubbed "Bikram Yoga." (Choudhury is widely known by his first name alone.) Bikram does not feature meditation, headstands, or just any of yoga's eighty-four poses. It is a tightly scripted ninety-minute sequence of twenty-six specific poses and two breathing exercises performed in front of mirrors and in 105-degree rooms. The mirrors are supposed to help people straighten their poses, and the heat is supposed to loosen muscles and foster well-being.

By 1996, there were about ten schools in the nation that taught Choudhury's style of yoga. By 2003, that number had soared to more than seven hundred worldwide. If an Eastern yogi would be gratified simply at the spread of a venerated discipline, the Americanized Choudhury saw the possibility of getting rich. He apparently figured: Why not use copyright law to declare his twenty-six yoga postures a form of property; invoke trademark law to protect its name, Bikram Yoga; and begin to franchise yoga studios in classic Starbucks fashion?

In 2002, Choudhury's Web site (www.bikramyoga.com) asserted copyright ownership of Bikram Yoga:

> In addition to exact copying of the [yoga] sequence, the copyright prohibits others from creating derivative works of the sequence. Virtually all modifications or additions to exact copying of the sequence will constitute copyright infringement, including: the unauthorized use of even a small number of consecutive postures; the addition of different postures or breathing exercises to the sequence or portions of the sequence; the teaching or offering of the sequence with or without the Dialogue [the official script for Bikram Yoga]; or by the addition of extra elements to the sequence, like music.

Any infringers, the Web site warned, would be liable for damages of up to $150,000 per infringement. In 2002, Choudhury also began a system for licensing Bikram teachers and franchising his style of yoga practice, charging between $200 and $500 per month per studio, as well as one-time fees for new Bikram studios.

Choudhury did not state that he invented the yoga poses, but he does claim that Bikram Yoga represents an original "selection, arrangement and ordering of physical movements" eligible for protection under copyright law. Choudhury also copyrighted a document describing Bikram Yoga's teacher training and the verbatim dialogue to be used in beginners' classes. Finally, he also sought trademarks in "Bikram Yoga," "Bikram Hot Yoga," "Bikram's Yoga College of India," and "Bikram's Beginning Class."

Choudhury told *Yoga Journal*: "It's become the Bikram system, but there's no such thing as Bikram Yoga; yoga is yoga, yoga is Hatha yoga. It's not anybody's property; it's like God, it's love, it's nature. But anybody picks up a few postures in a sequence and makes it a book, it's a copyright, so somebody copies my book, I sue them."

Attorneys compare the situation to music or dance: individual notes or individual steps are in the public domain, but the specific sequence of notes that constitute a song or a dance can by copyrighted. But other attorneys question whether the asserted copyrights over Bikram Yoga could actually affect "derivative works" that depart from the twenty-six-pose sequence.

To enforce his alleged rights, Choudhury in 2003 sent out cease-and-desist notices to about twenty-five yoga studios that he claimed were violating his copyrights and trademarks by teaching and practicing Bikram Yoga. After he reached a settlement with one yoga studio, Choudhury claimed a "significant legal victory."

The yoga community was aghast. Many teachers who had Bikram certification were scared it would be revoked or become worthless if Choudhury's copyright claims were upheld. Others consider the propertization and sale of the great Shiva consciousness handed down through generations to be a sacrilege.

Chuch Miller, an Ashtanga yoga teacher in Santa Monica, California, told *Yoga Journal*, "As a teacher, I feel I don't own this; I'm just passing it on. But as a business owner, there's a certain sense of wanting to protect the entity and not let people siphon it off."

If only to resolve the legal challenge to their practice, some members of the yoga community organized themselves as a nonprofit group, Open Source Yoga Unity. In a July 2003 complaint filed in federal court, the group sought a declaratory judgment prohibiting Choudhury from enjoining anyone from teaching or practicing the "Bikram Sequence." The group argued that the Sequence "is functional and constitutes physical facts and/or ideas, not expression protectable by copyright. The individual asanas [poses] in the Sequence have been in the public domain for hundreds of years." By mid-2004, Bikram had moved on to his third set of attorneys and the case was still mired in procedural wrangling.

Some members of the yoga world believe that Bikram's purported copyright would have profoundly negative effects on the evolution of yoga practice. They argue that it would consolidate a diverse community of practice into a single, highly commercialized monopoly, centralized control, and a standard version of Hatha yoga.

For his part, Choudhury believes that copyright control is the only way he can assure quality control for Bikram Yoga: "I brought Hatha yoga to the Western world. Now Hatha yoga is being crucified in America; people are messing with our Indian tradition and culture. So I think this franchising and copyrighting will help another ten kinds of yoga to build up their business and help more people."

There remain many doubters that a spiritual discipline with physical aspects can or should be propertized. But in a nation where genes, smells, and colors can be owned, Bikram Choudhury understandably wondered: Why not yoga too?

Patenting Side-to-Side Swinging

It is enough to survey the excesses of copyright and trademark law without taking on the mountain of ridiculous patents. But readers should at least be aware that this important field of intellectual property law has corresponding defects. While patent law has a different framework for protecting inventions, the drive to overpropertize knowledge is strikingly similar. The U.S. government grants monopoly rights to all sorts of "inventions" of dubious originality. As a result, the public is forced to pay higher prices for something that ought to be freely available to all, and genuine innovation is impeded.

A representative example of how far patent law has drifted from its constitutional purpose—to promote the useful arts and sciences—is the 1999 patent that the J.M. Smucker Co. of Orrville, Ohio, claimed for a "sealed crustless sandwich," which it dubbed "Uncrustables." U.S. Patent No. 6,004,596 painstakingly describes why this sandwich is so unique. Its "first bread layer [has] a first perimeter surface coplanar to a contact surface," and its crimped edge has a "plurality of spaced-apart depressions for increasing" the bond between the two crustless bread slices. A dispute over the ownership of the sandwich arose in January 2001 when Smucker's complained that Albie's Foods of Gaylord, Michigan, was selling a crustless peanut butter and jelly sandwich.

A similar dispute arose that year when Mrs. Smith's Bakeries of Georgia sued the Gardner Pie Co. in 2001 for stealing its method of producing a pseudo-latticework pie crust top. The attorney for Mrs. Smith's explained that the patent involves a way of creating a latticework crust top from a single sheet of dough "so it looks like the pie crust was formed by interweaving dough."

Another great leap forward in human progress is guaranteed by U.S. Patent No. 6,368,227, which is "a method of swinging on a swing." Steven Olson of St. Paul, Minnesota, came up with the brilliant idea: "a user positioned on a standard swing suspended by two chains from a substantially horizontal tree branch induces side to side motion by pulling alternately on one chain and then the other." The inventor notes in his patent application that the movement required by side-to-side swinging "resembles in some measure the movements one would use to swing from vines in a dense jungle. The swinging method of the present invention may be referred to by the present inventor and his sister as 'Tarzan swinging.' The user may even choose to produce a Tarzan-type yell while swinging in the manner described. Actual jungle forestry is not required."

It remains unclear whether trademark approval is needed from the estate of Edgar Rice Burroughs to call this method of swinging "Tarzan swinging."

There have always been a lot of wacky patents granted; some Web sites exclusively devoted to them (such as the British Web site "Patently Absurd!") make for amusing reading. While some goofy patents may end up finding a market—who knows?—the alarming fact is not that wacky patents are sometimes granted but that the government is casually granting legal monopolies on some rather common "inventions" and practices.

Some of the most worrisome examples are in Internet- and software-related fields, where patents on mathematical algorithms and basic Internet practices could be compared to monopolies on wooden pencils and standard-sized stationery. One of the most prominent basic patents granted for an online business method is the "one click online shopping" patent that Amazon.com obtained for its Web site. By holding U.S. Patent No. 5,960,411, "Method and System for Placing a Purchase Order via a Communications Network," Amazon founder Jeff Bezos sought to force competitors to make their online ordering system more complicated—and thus less attrative to Web shoppers. When Amazon.com sought to stop Barnesandnoble.com from infringing the patent, a federal court issued a preliminary injunction against Barnesandnoble.com during the Christmas season of 1999. But the judge held that even a trivial work-around in software code would not infringe the patent, and so Barnesandnoble.com did precisely that.

Another patent that drew criticism is one described as "A Method and System for Interactive Contributions Solicitation and Donation." Its owner, Witold A. Ziarno, says his patent covers all forms of electronic fund-raising by charity Web sites. After the U.S. Red Cross launched a new Web site, www.DisasterRelief.org, to raise funds, Mr. Ziarno sued the charity in May 1999 for allegedly violating his patent; the claim was ultimately rejected by an appeals court.

Patent law has traditionally required that any new invention be novel and nonobvious in order to qualify for patent protection. But as patents began protecting not just physical inventions but intangible ideas and business methods, their scope has expanded radically. Even if the claimed scope for a given patent is dubious, it can nonetheless be used to intimidate supposed infringers.

Ron Wilson, one of the executive editors of *Electrical Engineering Times*, a high-tech trade journal, wrote in an editorial that "U.S. intellectual property law is rapidly reducing itself to absurdity." Tim O'Reilly, a publisher and advocate of open source software, called the Amazon patent "one more example of an 'intellectual property' milieu gone mad." He characterized the system as "a land grab, an attempt to hoodwink a patent system that has not gotten up to speed on the state of the art in computer science."

Because of slacker standards for granting patents, the business world does not necessarily regard them as indicative of genuine innovation anymore. The practical value of patents, in many instances, is as a legal threat and bargaining chip in dealings with competitors. As Greg Aharonian, the editor of the Internet Patent News Service, explained, large companies "just want to have as many as possible because they trade them like base-ball cards. When you have a thousand patents and your company has 1,500, you don't care what they are, you just swap them."

A whole other realm of controversial patents involves the patenting of common agricultural crops and life-forms. The U.S. Patent and Trademark Office has granted a patent in novel lines of basmati rice and grains (No. 5,663,484), which many critics in underdeveloped countries regard as "biopiracy"—an attempt to "take private" food crops that have been accessible to everyone for millennia. Harvard University owns the patent on a genetically modified laboratory mouse with a cancer-prone gene, often called the "onco-mouse." The Harvard patent covers not just the mouse itself but also later generations of mice if they contain the unique gene.

As more biotechnology companies seek to own key segments of genetic information, the patenting of "disease genes" is becoming more prevalent. In order to prevent medical schools and biotech firms from profiting off their rare "disease tissue," some patients have even taken to "patenting themselves" so that they can retain some measure of control over their tissue, and perhaps make some money. Ironically, the overprop-ertization of genes and biological materials only makes it more likely that future research will be stymied because the rights-clearance problems become astronomically more difficult. This, indeed, is a serious impedi-ment in the search for malaria treatments. How can scientific research pro-ceed when proprietary biologics and research tools are scattered among dozens of rights-holders?

The absurd reach of contemporary patents prompted one parodist, Adam Scott, to fantasize about "a new phase of the battle to patent living organisms"—an attempt by the parents of the Harvard student who "invented" the onco-mouse to patent their son: "'Clearly our Harvard Son meets the test of being a composition of matter that is novel, useful and not obvious,' said the mother. While refusing to divulge all the details of the process used to create their son, the scientist's parents maintain that it is unique. 'Only one specific pattern of spouse selection, intercourse and parenting could have resulted in the creation of a son so unique and talented as to develop the Harvard Mouse.'"

The parody continues, "The parents allege that they are entitled not only to ownership of the process used to create their son, but also the son

himself and all his offspring that display an aptitude for genetic manipula-
tion. . . . The parents are not seeking a patent for boy-children as they
exist in nature, but for one particular type of boy-child that would not
exist without their own considerable investment. If they prove ownership
of their son, the parents will remove him from Harvard and use him for
yard work, another area where he has demonstrated usefulness."

CHAPTER 12

Just Kidding or Dead Serious?

Many a truth is spoken in jest.

—English proverb

C opyright and trademark law has been stretched and pulled in so many extreme directions over the past few decades that it is sometimes difficult to take it seriously. That is one reason it has become an increasingly popular source of material for comedians. This arcane body of law contains a veritable mother lode of yuks.

The content industries solemnly urge that children take "copyright education" courses so they can learn about the virtues and utility of intellectual property law. But when a game show hostess can win a $403,000 award for a robotic "appropriation" of her publicity rights; when letters of the alphabet can be trademarked by private companies; and when a fashion house can steal the word "polo" from the equestrian sport—all in the name of "authorship" and "originality"—it is awfully hard to keep a straight face. Veneration and respect have to be earned, after all.

Since jesters and comedians have long been the truth-tellers of last resort, it is worth hearing what some inspired pranksters make of copyright and trademark law. It is my firm conviction that a well-executed gag can be as illuminating as a dozen law review articles. In the words of countless stand-up comedians, "I'm not making this stuff up!"

Who Owns the "Frowny" Emoticon :-(?

What happens when a company obtains a trademark on one of the most frequently used symbols of online life, the "frowny" emoticon? For millions of Internet users, the symbol rendered as ":-("—a sequence of the colon, dash, and parenthesis mark—is an arch way to convey sadness in e-mail messages.

But is this widespread practice still legal? In 2001, Despair, Inc., a Dallas-based maker of spoof inspirational merchandise for the corporate world, played a colossal practical joke that exposed the absurdities of current trademark policies.

In the spirit of the cartoon *Dilbert*, which makes shrewd fun of life in corporate cubicles, Despair makes spoof-inspirational posters, mugs, and other merchandise with "megalomaniacal maxims" and "idiotic insights." A sample: a "Delusions" poster that reads, "There is no joy greater than soaring high on the wings of your dreams, except maybe the joy of watching a dreamer who has nowhere to land but in the ocean of reality," and an "Elitism" poster that reads, "It's lonely at the top, but it's comforting to look down upon everyone at the bottom."

Given its puckish inclinations, it is not surprising that Despair sought to have its corporate logo, the "frowny" emoticon, declared a legal trademark. It applied in 1998, and two years later, the U.S. Patent and Trademark Office actually awarded Despair a trademark in the emoticon (registration #2347676). On January 2, 2001, Dr. E. L. Kersten, the founder and COO of the company, announced plans to sue "anyone who uses the so-called 'frowny' emoticon, in their written email correspondence. Ever."

Playing the gag for as much as it was worth, the Despair press release announced that the company had "filed suit yesterday in a U.S. District Court in Dallas, alleging trademark infringement against over seven million individual Internet users. The company has requested separate injunctions granted against each. It is believed to be the largest single trademark dispute in history." The company even claimed it had used the FBI's controversial "Carnivore" Internet wiretapping system to identify the seven million individuals who had illegally used the :-(symbol in e-mail.

In a clear swipe at Amazon.com for its dubious patent for "1-Click" shopping, the Despair press release quoted an intellectual property specialist who said the Amazon patent was directly analogous to Despair's trademark: "HTML cookies have been commonly used by programmers since Netscape introduced them years ago, yet Amazon has received a patent for one. Emoticons have been in circulation even longer, yet Despair has trademarked one."

E. L. Kersten deadpanned that Jeff Bezos, the founder of Amazon, was indeed an inspiration: "Once again, Jeff has proven to be a true innovator. He's really inspired a new movement in the dotcom universe—frivolous, destructive intellectual property lawsuits. I couldn't be happier to be part of the revolution."

Kersten ended his frighteningly realistic warning by eerily echoing a Jack Valenti antipiracy jeremiad: "Let our message to trademark violators be clear. Whether you are a fourth-grade nothing using your momma's AOL account, or you are Time Magazine's 'Man of the Year,' we are going to hunt you down, and when we do, we're really going to give you something to :-(® about."

Freedom of Expression™

Can freedom of expression be privatized through intellectual property law? University of Iowa professor Kembrew McLeod demonstrated that it is possible in the most literal sense. He applied for a trademark in the phrase, "Freedom of Expression," and the U.S. Patent and Trademark Office granted him a private monopoly on the term. Trademark No. 2,127,381 entitled McLeod, an intellectual property professor and author of *Owning Culture*, to stop some (but not all) unauthorized uses of the phrase for ten years.

In 1997, as McLeod watched corporate trademark owners bully help-less individuals into surrendering certain words and phrases, he wondered if the very phrase "Freedom of Expression" could be taken private. He decided to try by paying a $245 nonrefundable fee to the U.S. Patent and Trademark Office to register the trademark. "I had this uneasy feeling that someone in government would see that my application was nothing more than a satirical joke, a comment on what I have labeled 'the private ownership of culture,'" McLeod confessed.

And in fact, his application was initially deemed "not acceptable"—but not for any philosophical or legal reasons. He had merely failed to fill out the application properly. On January 6, 1998, McLeod's trademark was duly registered under Class 16 of the international schedule of goods and ser-vices. While he was not authorized to monopolize "Freedom of Expres-sion" in all circumstances, the trademark did cover its use in printed matter.

To test the scope of his trademark protection, McLeod—then a student at the University of Massachusetts and a part-time music critic—knew that he had to have a bona fide product. So he started a quarterly zine— a self-published fan magazine—called *Freedom of Expression*, which sold about a hundred copies an issue. He then recruited an old high school friend, Brendan Love, to pose as the publisher of a punk rock magazine also entitled *Freedom of Expression*. To complete his elaborate spoof, McLeod hired an attorney (without letting her in on the joke) to send a cease-and-desist letter to the "infringing" competitor. The letter read in part:

> We represent Kembrew McLeod of Sunderland, Massachusetts, the owner of the federally registered trademark, FREEDOM OF EXPRESSION. . . . Your company has been using the mark Freedom of Expression. . . . Such use creates a likelihood of confusion in the market and also creates a substantial risk of harm to the reputation and goodwill of our client. This letter, therefore, constitutes formal notice of your infringement of our client's trademark rights and a demand that you refrain from all further use of Freedom of Expression.

McLeod then took the story to the local newspaper, the *Daily Hampshire Gazette*, of Northampton, Massachusetts. The reporter, taking the story at face value, quoted Brendan Love's mock reaction to the letter: "To go on with a different name would fly straight in the face of what I've been trying to do all along. It's a battle between who came along first and who is the opportunist." In response, McLeod deadpanned, "I didn't go to the trouble, the expense and time of trademarking Freedom of Expression just to have someone else come along and think they can use it whenever they want."

So much for gags. In 2003, a real case presented itself. AT&T had the temerity to use McLeod's trademark as the slogan in print ads promoting long-distance telephone service to college students. McLeod's attorney, Gregory Williams of Iowa City, sent AT&T a cease-and-desist letter on January 22, 2003, demanding that it stop its use of McLeod's registered mark.

"I want A&T to think twice the next time they try to use 'Freedom of Expression' without my permission," said McLeod, who conceded the irony of owning a phrase that means the opposite of private ownership. "But 99.999 percent of the time it is corporations that shut down individuals' freedom of expression—so it's satisfying that trademark law allows me to do the same to AT&T."

In the end, AT&T demonstrated McLeod's point about brand-name bullies. It ignored his letter. As a matter of law, McLeod's trademark was not likely to cover AT&T's particular use of "Freedom of Expression," and even if the case were more promising, McLeod could not have afforded to pay a stable of attorneys to pursue the case. So the rights to "Freedom of Expression" remain more or less available to everyone. McLeod would not be displeased.

The Automatic Injunction Generator

As we have seen, large corporations with legal departments routinely send out threatening cease-and-desist letters even if the alleged infractions have not been substantiated. Indeed, the legal basis for threats may not exist, but that often does not matter when recipients cannot afford a lawyer.

An Austria-based group, UberMorgen (www.ubermorgen.com), decided that the ability to send cease-and-desist letters ought to be democratized. Why shouldn't *every* user of the Internet be able to send a threatening warning to individuals or Web sites they dislike? Why shouldn't there be a "public shutdown service"?

In a subversive act of culture-jamming, UberMorgen developed an ingenious Web-based software program, "The Injunction Generator," which allows anyone to "auto-generate an 'injunction,' a standard court order, claiming the target-website to operate on an illegal basis." The site also sends the injunction to the owner of the appropriate registrar of the domain name service, and to journalists if so requested.

Of course, the legal force of such "injunctions" is nonexistent. But that is precisely the point: many "real" cease-and-desist letters have an equivalent legal standing, but nonetheless succeed in intimidating domain-name owners into submission.

UberMorgen called its Web site the "Internet Partnership for No Internet Content," or IP-NIC, an acronym apparently meant to bring to mind the "Internet Protocol—Network Information Center." The opening visual of the site is an official seal that looks like an actual law enforcement seal. Using the UCDR, the Universal Content and/or Domain Removal form, a complainant can insert the name of the "defendant-target Web site," the court venue and country, the kind of court order sought (temporary or preliminary), the alleged crimes and misconduct—consumer fraud, corruption, hate crime, terrorist activity, illegal MP3s, trademarks and copyrights, biochemical warfare, among others. Other toggles on the Web form allow visitors to the site to register customized complaints against the defendant, send the complaint to other e-mail addresses, and even obtain printed copies of the court order.

The IP-NIC Web site is a curious case of art imitating life. In 2000, UberMorgen put up a Web site, www.vote-auction.net, that invited American citizens to put their votes up for auction. The site provoked a firestorm of outrage and legal actions by individuals and state attorneys general. In one case, an American court sent an e-mail injunction to UberMorgen's Swiss Internet service provider, which immediately took the site down even though Switzerland is not within the U.S. courts' jurisdiction and e-mail documents are generally not considered legally valid.

The IP-NIC site went on to win an award at a Helsinki, Finland, software arts festival in 2003. By blurring the lines between real and fake cease-and-desist letters, UberMorgen imitates the methods of the scam artists it seeks to condemn. Yet it also performs a useful function in prodding people to contemplate the moral legitimacy of laws that sanction cease-and-desist abuses.

Dialing for Dollars: Licensing the "Music" of Phone Tones

The musician Nigel Helyer and the composer Jon Drummond once made a public art project, *An Unrequited Space*, in a flooded underground bunker beneath a park in Sydney, Australia. They installed a large bell in the cavernous space, and then tolled it at midnight every night while mixing in live sound effects and prerecorded stories. The project, which sought to explore the underground as a psychological and physical space, was aired live on Australian Broadcasting Corporation for three weeks in 1992.

The project was so popular that a television program called *Police Rescue* built an episode around the bell. When Helyer objected that the artists' copyright in the project was being ignored, the producer was unmoved.

As Helyer told the journalist Rick Karr of National Public Radio: "Because I was an individual artist and they were a large video and film production house, they told me to go for a long walk off a short pier, basically."

The artists settled out of court, but not before the seeds were planted for a brilliant new experimental art project. The idea was to take the philosophical premises of copyright law so seriously that its absurdities would become blazingly evident. Their brainchild was a Web site called Magnus-Opus (www.magnus-opus.com), which uses a mathematical algorithm to generate 18,446,744,070,000,000,000 different musical melodies based on the tones made by touch-tone telephones. "We are," said Drummond and Helyer (who dubbed himself "Dr. Sonique" for this project), "the world's most prolific composers."

The two artists then issued a stern warning to the world: "All of the melodies contained within the Magnus-Opus series are protected by copyright. You may inadvertently be in breach of international copyright law by using a telecommunications device (telephone, mobile telephone, modem and other Internet devices) to transmit and perform one of the Magnus-Opus melody series." (This warning may be inspired humor, but lawyers would likely argue that it is technically incorrect: to violate copyright law, a complainant must either have proof of actual copying or a showing of "access" to the work and "substantial similarity.")

The Web site invites people to test whether their phone number corresponds to one of the compositions in the Magnus-Opus database. Naturally, *every* mathematically possible telephone number in the world generates a series of tones that Drummond and Dr. Sonique claim as their intellectual property. As they calculate it, anytime someone dials a phone number, Drummond and Dr. Sonique's property rights are being violated.

The artists even go so far as to provide an official online license agreement to obtain permissions—five U.S. cents for a one-time use, an annual license for $100, and $10,000 for a permanent license. People who decline to buy the license can click the option, "I do not wish to purchase a copyright license from Magnus-Opus and want to know the best way to discontinue the use of my telecommunications device." A convenient FAQ offers advice on how to recycle your unlicensed, copyright-infringing telephone equipment.

Drummond and Helyer took their joke a step further by asking the Australian Performing Rights Association to begin to collect royalties on their copyrighted "compositions." While conceding that "the majority of our pieces are currently being played and broadcast via telecommunications media rather than in more conventional music venues . . . we trust that APRA will be able to find an appropriate method for assessing and collecting the royalties due to us."

A first response from an APRA official declined to accept the registration of Magnus-Opus works because they were not in material form. APRA also objected that the pieces are not original compositions because they are algorithmically generated. In response, Drummond and Helyer offered to provide APRA with a CD-ROM of the music, and pointed out that a number of works in the Western musical tradition—Guido's automated chant composition, Mozart's Musikalisches Wurfelspiel, and Xenakis's stochastic composition—are the result of algorithmic composition.

Furthermore, the artists argued, the phone-tone compositions are original because they are "based upon a specific selection of eight frequencies used in sixteen unique diads which do not conform with equal tempered tunings. When combined with a flexible and arrhythmic structure these form a unique and constrained set of compositions which do not infringe upon the copyright of pre-existing works." Drummond and Helyer insisted that Magnus-Opus's copyright claim "is for a limited (although large) set of compositions and not (as has been incorrectly reported) a universal or exhaustive copyright claim on composition per se."

The legal debate between the artists and APRA attorneys continued for yet another letter, turning the mannered formalism of copyright discourse into high farce. Only Groucho Marx, in his exchanges with Warner Bros.' attorneys over the use of the word "Casablanca" in a film title, achieved greater hilarity at the expense of literal-minded attorneys.

Helyer said he does not consider Magnus-Opus an attack on copyright law, but rather on how it is used to diminish the public domain. He believes in the goal of copyright law, for example, namely that artists should get paid for their work. But that goal is being subverted, he argues: "The kind of argument we're pushing is more a critique of how large, often transnational corporations are able to, by sheer dint of economic power and size, kind of corrupt that original meaning [of copyright law] so they can control the economic lives of literally millions of people."

At least one American took the Magnus-Opus licenses seriously enough that he asked to buy the rights to his phone number. He thought that by owning a copyright in his number he might be able to stop telemarketers from calling him.

Tanzania Loses Name to Tanning Salon Company, and Other Spoofs

Groucho Marx once asked guests on his television show, *You Bet Your Life*, whether they were going to believe him or their own two eyes. So today: Are you going to believe the copyright experts or your own two eyes? Increasingly, Americans believe what they see and experience. That is surely one reason why *The Simpsons*, the *Onion*, the *New Yorker*, and other general-audience enterprises are finding so many belly laughs in intellectual property law. They realize that these issues are spreading fast in popular consciousness. People's daily lives are directly affected yet the content industries' narratives increasingly do not make sense. For humorists, who constantly prowl the borders between the official line and everyday experience, the laughs are there for the taking.

In September 2003, the *Onion*, a weekly tabloid that mocks the conventions of the mainstream press, served up a rich satire on trademarks out of control. Under the headline, "Tanzania Loses Name to Tanning-Salon Company," the story read: "The country formerly known as the United Republic of Tanzania has lost the use of its name to Tampa-based Tanzania Tanning Salons, the Florida Supreme Court ruled Monday. 'Any use of my country's name constitutes infringement on the plaintiff's trademark,' said Benjamin Mkapa, president of the currently unnamed republic. 'We've lost our national identity. This is a very sad day for the people once known as Tanzanians.'"

The story goes on to say how the salon came up with its name by combining the "words 'tan' and 'zany' to suggest a lighthearted, fun approach to indoor-tanning retail." The existence of an African country by that name was later discovered through an Internet search. After a two-week court battle, the State of Florida granted rights to the word "Tanzania" to the Tanzania Salons founder and CEO Jerry Yeltzer: "It was easy to establish that my client's company had a greater vested interest in the Tanzania brand name," said Yeltzer's lawyer Ben Knowles. "Tanzania, the salon chain, is a rapidly growing business, adding nearly 50 locations each year. Tanzania, the African nation, is languishing under a debt of $7 billion."

As a magazine that validates and explains many cultural trends, the *New Yorker*, with its cover of September 29, 2003, created a rare and memorable landmark in the public understanding of copyright law. Days earlier, the Recording Industry Association of America had launched its infamous legal crackdown on hundreds of alleged music file sharers. The much-publicized lawsuits were meant to frighten file sharers and so deter illicit music downloading. But many of the lawsuits seemed like simple bullying. One lawsuit named an honor roll student from elementary school; another targeted a grandmother who had never downloaded music.

In an inspired spoof by the illustrator Istvan Banyai, the cover of the *New Yorker* featured a vulnerable young girl standing against a brick wall, with a police spotlight shining in her eyes. Her school backpack, teddy bear, and CDs are strewn on the ground in disarray, and she is shielding her frightened face from the glare of the light in her eyes. The illustration, *Nabbed*, is a devastating riposte to the RIAA litigation strategy.

One of the more subversive pop spoofs about copyright law came from a 1996 episode of the *Simpsons* cartoon series. This is both surprising and appropriate because Matt Groening, the creator of *The Simpsons*, has been on both sides of the copyright fence—as a satiric appropriator of others' work and as a zealous protector of his own characters.

Groening's most famous role as a copyright maximalist came in 1995 when Noel Tolentino, the publisher of the zine *Bunnyhop*, drew a hilarious parody of Groening's Binky the Rabbit punching out the Trix rabbit. The drawing was done without permission, attribution, or signs that it was a parody. Groening threatened legal action and forced Tolentino to destroy the copies—and apologized years later.

Tolentino told an interviewer: "We ended up decapitating Binky's head from the covers and mailing 300 of them in a bag to the lawyers. I wrote a cold, minimal apology—and anyone with a keen eye could recognize a little sarcasm there. The whole experience was incredibly disheartening." The irreverent now-defunct *Suck* Web site later derided Groening for "a prima facie example of artistic hypocrisy" because his career with *The Simpsons* and other ventures "can almost be said to be built upon the masterful use of cultural appropriation."

One wonders if the experience had any influence on an inspired episode of *The Simpsons* that aired only a year later, on March 17, 1996, and dealt with these very issues. Written by John Swartzwelder, "The Day the Violence Died" is a thinly veiled satire about Walt Disney's appropriation of cartoon characters from other artists.

One day Bart Simpson meets a homeless man, Chester J. Lampwick, who says that he invented the Itchy character in Bart's favorite cartoon, *Itchy and Scratchy*, which features a hyperviolent cat and mouse. Lampwick says that he did the cartoon short "Steamboat Itchy" but that Roger Myers (read Walt Disney) stole the Itchy character from him. (Disney's 1928 cartoon "Steamboat Willie" was the first incarnation of Mickey Mouse, which itself drew upon cartoon characters of the time, especially "Oswald the Rabbit.") Chester complains, "He stole the character from me in 1928. When I complained, his thugs kicked me out of his office, and dropped an anvil on me. Luckily, I was carrying an umbrella at the time."

In the course of the episode, the *Simpsons* writers inject a good number of zingers about Myers/Disney: "He's a good man; every Christmas he goes down to the pound and rescues one cat and one mouse and gives them to a hungry family." And a note from Chester to Myers/Disney reads, "To Roger Myers, Keep drawing, your moxie more than makes up for your lack of talent."

When the theft of the Itchy character goes to trial, the son of the Disney manqué finally admits, "Okay, maybe my dad did steal Itchy, but so what? Animation is built on plagiarism! If it weren't for someone plagiarizing *The Honeymooners*, we wouldn't have *The Flintstones*. If someone hadn't ripped off *Sgt. Bilko*, they'd be no *Top Cat*. Huckleberry Hound, Chief Wiggum, Yogi Bear? Hah! Andy Griffith, Edward G. Robinson, Art Carney. Er, don't forget Yogi Berra. Your honor, you take away our right to steal ideas, where are they gonna come from? Her? [points at Marge Simpson]."

Bart's success in winning justice for the penniless cartoonist causes its own problem, however. After paying out its penalty, the Myers studio no longer has any money to produce *Itchy and Scratchy* episodes. Bart and his sister Lisa are desolate. In a postmodern twist, they are saved by earlier cartoon variants of themselves, Lester and Eliza, who had appeared in a cartoon on *The Tracy Ullman Show*. Lester and Eliza discover that old man

Myers once drew a stick figure, the "Manic Mailman," who was ripped off by the U.S. Postal Service when it created "Mr. Zip." The discovery of this "infringement" by the government gives Myers Jr. a huge cash settlement, with which he resumes production of *Itchy and Scratchy*.

So long as the pretensions of copyright and trademark law fail to square with the lived experiences of people, humorists will continue to have a rich vein to mine. Which is to say, for a long time to come.

Conclusion:
Reclaiming the Cultural
Commons

Only one thing is impossible for God: to find any sense in any copyright law on the planet.

—Mark Twain's Notebook, 1902–1903

As we have seen, the expansion of intellectual property law over the past generation has produced some rather disturbing results. They include a tighter lockdown on musical and visual creativity . . . the privatization of folk culture . . . broad trademark claims on words . . . attempts to own facts . . . litigation to squelch parodies . . . broad protections for a celebrity persona . . . retroactive copyright extensions for dead authors . . . assorted enclosures of the public domain . . . copyright litigation that stifles the news and free speech . . . technological locks to override fair use rights . . . and claims to own letters, silence, smells, and yoga postures.

If this be the past, what of the future?

Despite the troubling trajectory that intellectual property law has taken over the past generation, a new movement to assert the public interest is starting to take shape and gain momentum. Key constituencies such as consumers, artists, librarians, computer professionals, academics, and scientists have become active players in the debates, and partners in advocacy. The general public, too, has become far more attentive. Ever since the Napster controversy dramatized the everyday implications of copyright law, ordinary people are more aware that technological and legal battles can directly affect them. Now that tens of millions of people use the Internet, networking software, CD burners, iPods, WiFi, and dozens of other innovations, few will knowingly accept a great cultural lockdown without a fight.

Knowingly is a key word. Too many key decisions about the emerging digital culture are still shrouded in obscurity, making it difficult for the American people to assert their interests. But this too is rapidly changing. While the mainstream news media have been unprepared to report on many copyright issues, the *Eldred* copyright term extension case was a wake-up call. So is the ongoing saga of music distribution and copy protection.

Meanwhile, the Internet is spawning its own burgeoning community of expert news sources, pamphleteers, Web archivists, and agitators. Many Web logs are closely watched bellwethers for breaking news and commentary, efficiently channeling timely content to the mainstream press. Professor Lawrence Lessig's Web log demonstrated this power with the "no photo" incidents at Starbucks; blogs run by Ed Felten, Siva Vaidhyanathan, Dave Winer, Clay Shirky, Mike Godwin, Susan Crawford, Ernest Miller, Wendy Seltzer, and dozens of others set the pace for traditional media.

Copyright abuses can no longer be swept under the rug, thanks to a number of enterprising Web sites that gather information and publicize stories. The Electronic Frontier Foundation's ChillingEffects.org collects cease-and-desist letters from copyright holders; Public Knowledge has regular updates on Washington policymaking; Donna Wentworth's "Copyfight: The Politics of IP" explains the "nexus of legal rulings, Capitol Hill policymaking, technical standards development and technological innovation"; Harvard Law School's Berkman Center and Yale Law School's LawMeme host a wide variety of initiatives and legal discussions; and so on. The online resources are exploding.

Innovative protests and grassroots organizing are proliferating as well. The DMCA has provoked hundreds of protest Web sites and acts of "electronic civil disobedience." When the World Intellectual Property Organization (WIPO) sponsored an essay contest on the virtues of maximum copyright protection, a competing essay contest called WIPOUT quickly arose to solicit and publicize essays from a public-interest perspective. The "Illegal Art" exhibit of 2003 helped showcase the issues in a stylish way, catalyzing mainstream discussions about first principles in copyright law. The "Grey Tuesday" civil disobedience protest in February 2004—the defiant mass downloading of Danger Mouse's *Grey Album*—dramatized how copyright law is impeding artistic creativity and how consumers want to hear alternative kinds of music. The entrepreneur Jed Horovitz's scathing DVD *Willful Infringement* describes how various companies have intimidated individuals into suppressing their music and art. From such unexpected outbursts "from below," a new literature and public consciousness are growing.

One of the most promising recent developments may be the activism of artists. Historically, the artists most concerned about copyright issues were on the fringe: self-styled provocateurs like the band Negativland, and conceptualist-artists associated with the online community The Thing. Now the circle is expanding. Musicians are finding their voice. The Future of Music Coalition has become a focal point for hundreds of independent musicians eager to advance their creative and economic interests. This is a remarkable change. For years the recording industry has presumed to speak for artists. Now a growing corps of performers, many with marquee reputations, is insisting upon speaking for themselves. Some are battling the unconscionability of standard industry contracts; others are trying to bypass the traditional music distribution system by developing their own online ventures. Meanwhile, new linkages are being forged between artists and public policy advocacy. Public Knowledge, for example, has begun to collaborate with various creative sectors to help mobilize their members and fight for artists' self-determination.

Public education is a key challenge in nurturing a broader social movement. While the blogs and Web sites are of incalculable value, expert intermediaries who can advocate the public interest in traditional policy arenas—Congress, the courts, state legislatures—are more important than ever. Organizations like Public Knowledge, the Electronic Frontier Foundation, the Consumer Project on Technology, the Center for Democracy and Technology, the American Library Association, and other advocacy players are not only helping to interpret technological and policy issues for the press and general public, they are also helping to introduce new terms of debate. The very politics of copyright law are starting to change now that so many fresh voices are creating a new policy literature, new public platforms for grassroots opinion, new technical expertise, and better press outreach. Copyright issues are starting to be addressed through open public debate, not privately brokered industry deals.

One of the engines of the new politics of copyright law has been a new generation of legal scholars, academic centers, and policy-oriented legal clinics that are collectively forging a new public-spirited vision.

While there is no single, coordinated agenda, legal scholars are collaborating closely on a wide range of research, litigation, and policy advocacy projects. Among the many topics that legal scholarship is addressing are the economic dynamics of commons versus markets, alternative business models for music distribution, the "geography" of the public domain, and the tensions between the Internet and copyright and trademark law.

Stanford Law Professor Lawrence Lessig may be the most visible and prolific of the loose network of scholars, but the circle includes many innovative thinkers: Professors Pamela Samuelson (UC Berkeley), Yochai Benkler (Yale), James Boyle (Duke), William Fisher (Harvard), Eben Moglen (Columbia), Jessica Litman (Wayne State), Siva Vaidhyanathan (NYU), Peter Jaszi (American University), Jonathan Zittrain (Harvard Law School's Berkman Center), and Julie Cohen (Georgetown University). These scholars represent a new breed. They combine high-tech sophistication with economic analysis, innovative legal theory, and policy activism.

One of the most exciting outgrowths of this scholarly ferment was the establishment of the Creative Commons in 2001. Inspired by the success of the free software and open source software movements, Professor Lessig and other founders of the Creative Commons are seeking to promote similar sorts of creative collaboration among authors, musicians, filmmakers, and other artists. Their chosen tool is special legal licenses. As the group's Web site explains, "People who want to copy and reuse creative works have no reliable way to identify works available for such uses. We hope to provide some tools that solve both problems: a set of free public licenses sturdy enough to withstand a court's scrutiny, simple enough for non-lawyers to use, and yet sophisticated enough to be identified by various Web applications."

For example, one Creative Commons license, "Attribution," permits people to copy, distribute, display, and perform a work and derivative works based upon it, but only if credit is given to the author. A "Noncommercial" license permits others to copy, distribute, display, and perform a work and derivative works based upon it, but only for noncommercial purposes. By making license terms known in advance through standard contracts and simple logos, the Creative Commons hopes that its licenses will promote the kinds of content-sharing that simply are not feasible under current copyright law.

Beyond those scholars who prowl the ramparts of high technology and copyright theory, a growing corps of copyright law professors is stepping up to criticize the new extremes of the law and to file briefs in major copyright cases. These professors recognize that copyright law has historically embodied a balance between the rights of owners and the public, and that the public's rights are being drastically curtailed. Such widespread activism on the part of many law professors is a fairly new development, one that helps the courts realize that Hollywood and the record labels may not be the most reliable interpreters of copyright law and its goals. Indeed, one sign of shifting attitudes toward copyright law can be seen in a March 2004 report issued by the business-oriented Committee for Economic Development. The report warned that "equating intellectual property with physical property" might be hampering innovation, and that government mandates to lock up content are a bad idea.

Toward a New Language of the Commons

At bottom, the challenge is not just to shore up the boundaries of fair use, the public domain, and other public rights, important as those rights are. What is truly needed is a new discourse that can escape the restrictive intellectual categories of copyright and trademark law. To be sure, fair use and other valuable concepts within the copyright paradigm must be fortified and expanded. But these legal doctrines are, and will always be, stepchildren in the house of copyright law. They are subordinate to the basic principles of a property discourse. They are likely to be weak vehicles for advancing a bold agenda to protect a free and open culture.

The traditional language of private property, contracts, and market transactions is a necessary but insufficient discourse for our times. The problem is, it does not adequately take account of the inherently social, collaborative nature of creativity, especially as amplified by the Internet's many innovations—Web sites, free software such as GNU/Linux, social networking software, instant messaging, peer-to-peer file sharing, massive multiplayer games, and more. It is increasingly obvious that value-added creativity does not emerge solely through individual authors, as copyright law presumes, but increasingly through online social collaborations. It is becoming clear that originality does not reside solely in the individual, but in the networked community. So why cannot the law recognize this new reality?

We can try to shoehorn the new social practices of the digital era into a brittle, complicated, nearly incoherent body of law that originated in the eighteenth century. Or we can embark on the project of developing a new language that better recognizes the realities of a networked culture. Or we can do both, and hope that a new rapprochement will eventually result.

The point is not to reject some cherished principles of copyright law (such as payment for artists), but to reconceptualize how traditional principles may be better fulfilled in the very different economic, technological, and social environment of the digital age. American society requires that people have the freedom to create without seeking permission. It requires that people have the ability to share information and collaborate with others. It requires a sufficient *absence* of property rights, and protected common cultural spaces, so that artists can express themselves, citizens can speak to each other, and Internet users can participate in open networks, all without fear of legal reprisal.

The prevailing discourse of intellectual property law is not prepared to entertain this conversation. Indeed, it has already shown that it has other priorities. Contemporary applications of copyright and trademark law are fixated on strict legal and technological control of content, the surveillance of consumers, pay-per-use access to information and creative works, the evisceration of fair use, the erosion of the first-sale doctrine and the public domain, and intimidating displays of legal enforcement and deterrence. The clear priority of corporate copyright owners is to use strict and overwhelming controls—legal, technological, and economic—to prevent any unauthorized acts of reading, viewing, listening, and sharing. One can only wonder what happened to the open, self-confident vision of copyright law that once prevailed in American life.

On the other hand, critics must shoulder a greater burden to develop an alternative vision that would foster a culture of openness, access, and freedom. Developing a new vision will require that we begin a new conversation, one that puts forward a different critique of key problems and suggests a new set of solutions. It will require new terms of analysis and new narratives that reframe the prevailing categories of copyright law.

For example, rather than conceive the public domain as a "dark star" in the constellation of intellectual property—a cultural wasteland that hardly deserves much inquiry or analysis—we need to develop a new language that explains why the public domain is so indispensable to creativity, culture, democracy, and commerce. Rather than assume that value-creating transactions occur only when money changes hands in the marketplace, we need a new set of stories that reveals how online communities of trust and social reciprocity create enormous value—often more efficiently than conventional markets. Rather than assume that all value results from "individual originality," we need an economics and public policy language that understands the value of "public knowledge" and affirmatively seeks to protect and replenish it.

I believe that "the commons" offers an attractive new approach to these challenges. The commons articulates a set of values that is being systematically eliminated from contemporary copyright law (the ability to share, reuse, and transform) while naming important creative practices that traditional copyright law cannot really comprehend (networked collaboration without any mediation by markets).

While the commons is clearly akin to the public domain and fair use, it is a fresh term that avoids some of the prejudicial legal meanings and associations of those terms. The commons is useful because it helps describe and defend robust cultural spaces and social practices without precedent in copyright law. Trying to apply "fair use" and the "public domain" to the contemporary creative environment is akin to trying to dress a twenty-first-century citizen in the fashions of the eighteenth century. The clothing may be serviceable and even adaptable, but the cut is wrong. "Fair use" can only be understood in the context of copyright law, and copyright law has its own strong philosophical prejudices about how property rights, markets, and creativity work.

A number of legal scholars such as Lawrence Lessig, Yochai Benkler, and James Boyle have embraced the commons paradigm precisely because it offers a better account of the dynamics of creativity and online communities than the conventional language of property, contracts, and markets. An example is Professor Benkler's stellar 2002 essay "Coase's Penguin," which explains why some types of "peer production" (open source software, collaborative Web sites, social networks like Friendster) are more efficient and innovative than market-based production. Because copyright law focuses on the individual as the source of all value-creation, it has trouble understanding why social collaborations, or commons, can be valuable in economic, social, and creative ways. Yet as we have seen in the preceding chapters, some of the most significant forms of creativity—from hip-hop and folk art to modern art and online peer production—derive from a cultural commons.

The commons is an important concept because it can help us develop a new vision of law and politics. It offers a new vocabulary for talking about roles, behaviors, and relationships that cannot be adequately captured by market theory and copyright law. It gets us beyond market-speak in which everyone must be either a producer or a consumer, each with prescribed economic roles, and instead describes a cultural ecology in which people may play a variety of roles—citizen, creator, collaborator, community member.

By getting beyond property-speak, in which everything must be strictly owned by an individual or a corporation, the commons identifies the shared cultural spaces that are increasingly important. Who owns the Internet? Who owns online knowledge? Who owns words, letters, and smells? Who owns the fictional characters of mass culture? Rather than granting fair use exceptions to the default norm of property ownership (on a parsimonious, case-by-case basis!), the commons reverses the terms of debate. It asserts that many cultural and creative intangibles presumptively belong to all of us, and that a strong case must be made before exclusive rights to privatize them are granted. In this way the commons provides a more muscular, effective articulation of the public domain.

The point of speaking about the commons is to re-situate creative works in a larger context. Creative works are not simply artifacts of the market. They are not simply or always "property." They also exist as important aspects of our personal, social, and shared cultural lives, and they deserve legal recognition as such. In market discourse, everyone is presumed to be an interchangeable participant in the market seeking to rationally maximize his economic well-being. In a commons, by contrast, the different social roles played by different individuals and institutions can be fully recognized for what they are.

Thus, instead of conceiving public libraries as mere consumers of books from whom publishers should extract maximum economic rents, the commons paradigm frames libraries as vital social and democratic institutions. In its implementation, copyright law casts many modern painters as common thieves stealing others' visual property, when in fact they are artists who necessarily must draw upon others' images to create meaningful art. Current applications of copyright law conceive ordinary citizens as consumers of intellectual property, not as sentient human beings who have their own creative urges and needs to use the artifacts of their culture, including perhaps trademarked Disney characters, to comment upon their life and times.

The point of a language of the commons is to change the frame of reference from property-speak to a more humanistic frame of reference. The commons enables us to escape the ideological straitjacket and meta-physical presumptions of intellectual property law. This is not to say that the commons is hostile to property or the market. It is to say that there should be distinct limits to property rights and market activity, and that the integrity of the commons must be affirmatively protected.

The dozens of stories recounted in this book are essentially variations on that basic theme. If there is a moral, it is that we must strike a new and better balance between intellectual property rights and irreducible cultural and civic needs. In many cases, the only realistic human response to the many extreme expansions of copyright and trademark law is laughter. How else shall a mature person regard the claims to own the "zilla" in Godzilla and the "Mc" in McDonald's, an evocation of Vanna White and the word "Olympics"? If the law is going to recover the public respect that its champions say it deserves, its most zealous champions will need to surrender their imperial ambitions and learn to respect the cultural commons as an equal.

Notes

Introduction

4   *Einstein's inspiration by railroad timekeeping*   Peter Galison, "The Clocks That Shaped Einstein's Leap in Time," *New York Times*, June 24, 2003, p. D1.

7   *Ray Bradbury's objection to Fahrenheit 9/11*   Paul Chavez, "Moore Film Title Angers Ray Bradbury" Associated Press, June 19, 2004.

PART ONE
ART AND CULTURE: USE ONLY AS DIRECTED
1: The Crusade to Lock Up Music

ASCAP Stops the Girl Scouts
from Singing around the Campfire

13–17   *Newspaper accounts*   Elisabeth Bumiller, "Battle Hymns Around Campfires," *New York Times*, December 17, 1996; Lisa Bannon, "The Birds May Sing, But Can't Unless They Pay Up," *Wall Street Journal*, August 21, 1996, p. A1; Ken Ringle, "ASCAP Changes Its Tune; Never Intended to Collect Fees for Scouts' Campfire Songs, Group Says," *Washington Post*, August 24, 1996, p. B1.

13–17   *San Francisco Chronicle*   Thaai Walker and Kevin Fagan, "Girl Scouts Change Their Tunes; Licensing Order Restricts Use of Favorite Songs," August 23, 1996, p. A1; Thaai Walker and Tara Shioya, "From C to Shining C, Scouts Sing Free Again," August 27, 1996, p. A1; editorial, *San Francisco Chronicle*, August 27, 1996, p. A20.

16   *DeLong quotation*   James V. DeLong, "ASCAP vs. Girl Scouts," *National Law Journal*, March 10, 1997.

16   *ASCAP clarification of its position*   Press release, August 26, 1996.

The Blurry Line between Originality and Copying

17   *Musical imitation by classical composers*   William Austin, "Bartok's Concerto for Orchestra," 18 *Music Review* 21 (1957), p. 37, as cited in Geri J. Yonover, "The 'Dissing' of Da Vinci: The Imaginary Case of Leonardo v. Duchamp: Moral Rights, Parody and Fair Use," 29 *Valparaiso University Law Review* 935 (Spring 1995), p. 972.

18   *Vaidhyanathan research*   Siva Vaidhyanathan, *Copyrights and Copywrongs: The Rise of Intellectual Property and How It Threatens Creativity* (New York: New York University Press, 2001), chapter 4.

18–19 *Vaidhyanathan quotation*   p. 124.

19   *Dylan's alleged plagiarism*   Jonathan Eig and Sebastian Moffett, "Did Bob Dylan Lift Lines from Dr. Saga?" *Wall Street Journal*, July 8, 2003; Jon Pareles, "Plagiarism in Dylan, Or a Cultural Collage?" *New York Times*, July 12, 2003, p. B7; Steven Winn, "The Lines, They Were A-Changin', But Not Enough to Save Dylan from Plagiarism Accusations," *San Francisco Chronicle*, July 17, 2003, p. E1.

20   *We Shall Overcome Fund*   Pete Seeger, *Where Have All the Flowers Gone: A Singer's Stories, Songs, Seeds, Robberies* (Bethlehem, Pa: Sing Out Corporation, 1993), pp. 32–35; and David Dunaway, *How Can I Keep From Singing?* (New York: Da Capo Press, 1990), pp. 222–23. I am grateful to Carolyn Toll Oppenheim of the Council on International and Public Affairs for alerting me to the We Shall Overcome Fund and Pete Seeger's longtime commitment to honoring the communities that originate folk music. At press time Oppenheim and Seeger were organizing a November 2004 conference, "Music, the Public Domain and the Cultural Commons," at the Connie Hogarth Center for Social Justice, Manhattanville College, Purchase, New York, which called on key musicians and industry participants to explore voluntary innovations like the We Shall Overcome Fund to honor sources of music, with both recognition and royalties.

21   Stephen Fishman, *The Public Domain: How to Find and Use Copyright-Free Writings, Music, Art and More* (Berkeley, Calif.: Nolo Press, 2001), p. 4/37–39.

21–22 *Legal commentary on Campbell v. Acuff-Rose Music, Inc.*   Roxana Badin, "An Appropriate(d) Place in Transformative Value: Appropriation Arts Exclusion from *Campbell v. Acuff-Rose Music, Inc.*," 60 *Brooklyn Law Review* 1653 (Winter 1995).

22   *2 Live Crew and "Oh, Pretty Woman"*   *Campbell v. Acuff-Rose Music, Inc.*, 510 U.S. 569 (1994).

22   *House report on indeterminacy of fair use*   H.R. Rep. No. 1476, 9th Congress, 2d Session, reprinted in 1976 U.S. Code Cong. and Ad. News 5679.

22   *David Nimmer law review article*   David Nimmer, "'Fairest of Them All' and Other Fairy Tales of Fair Use," 66 *Law and Contemporary Problems* 1 and 2 (Winter/Spring 2003), pp. 263–88.

How Illegal Rap Sampling Revived the Music Business

24   *Demers quotations*   Joanna Demers, "Sampling as Lineage in Hip-Hop," Ph.D. dissertation, Princeton University, 2002, chapter 3, "Sampling Ethics and the Law."

24   *Commentary on sampling*   Sheila Rule, "Record Companies Are Challenging 'Sampling' in Rap," *New York Times*, April 21, 1992, p. C13; Henry Self, "Digital Sampling: A Cultural Perspective," 8 *UCLA Entertainment Law Review* 347 (Spring 2002).

25   *Neil Strauss quotation*   Neil Strauss, "Sampling Is (a) Creative Or (b) Theft?" *New York Times*, September 14, 1997, Section 2, p. 28.

26   *Attorney comment on Tuff City Records litigation*   Lawrence Stanley, as reported in Sheila Rule, "Record Companies Are Challenging 'Sampling' in Rap," *New York Times*, April 21, 1992, p. C13.

26   *James W. Newton Jr. and the Beastie Boys*   James W. Newton, Jr. v. Michael Diamond, 204 F. Supp. 2d 1244 (2002); Geoff Boucher, "A Musician Writes It, A Rapper Borrows It, a Swap or a Theft?" *Los Angeles Times*, September 21, 2002, p. F1; Teresa Wiltz, "The Flute Case That Fell Apart," *Washington Post*, August 22, 2002, p. C1.

26–27   *Vaidhyanathan quotation*   Siva Vaidhyanathan, *Copyrights and Copywrongs: The Rise of Intellectual Property and How It Threatens Creativity* (New York: New York University Press, 2001), p. 140.

27   *Vaidhyanathan quotation*   p. 143.

27   *Sixth Circuit ruling*   Bridgeport Music v. Dimension Films (6th Circ. September 7, 2004).

28   A useful Web site is the Columbia Law Library's Music Copyright Infringement Online Archive, at http://library.law.Columbia.edu/music_plagiarism/index2.html. The site points out that "judicial opinions typically turn on the court's musical analyses of the works in dispute, but these analyses are not meaningful to the reader without audio and visual representation of the musical numbers under scrutiny." To help the wider public review the specifics of musical infringement cases, the site offers text files that summarize and comment upon each case; the full text of the court's opinion; image files that show the disputed portions of musical works in standard music notation; sound files of relevant portions of the disputed numbers; and streaming audio clips taken from analog and digital recordings of public performances.

28   Joanna Demers, "Sampling as Lineage in Hip-Hop," Ph.D. dissertation, Princeton University, 2002, p. 162.

The Sequel to Sampling: Mash-ups

28–31   *Newspaper articles*   Neil Strauss, "Spreading by the Web, Pop's Bootleg Remix," *New York Times*, May 9, 2002, p. A1; Chris Norris, "Mash-Ups," *New York Times*, December 15, 2002; Pete Rojas, "Bootleg Culture," *Salon.com*, August 1, 2002, at http://www.salon.com/tech/feature/2002/08/01/bootlegs; Roberta Cruger, "The Mash-up Revolution," *Salon.com*, August 9, 2003, at http://archive.salon.com/ent/music/feature/2003/08/09/mashups_cruger; Robert Wilonsky, "Without Clearance, or, How

Eminem's Hit Single Spawned a Dozen of the Best (Illegal) Songs Ever," *Cleveland (Ohio) Scene*, October 9, 2002; Noah Schachtman, "Copyright Enters a Gray Area," *Wired News*, February 14, 2002, at http://www.wired.com/news/digiwood/0,1412,62276,00.html.

30–31   *"Grey Tuesday" protest*   Downhill Battle Web site, http://www.downhillbattle.org; Jon Pareles, "Silver, Brown, Gray: Jay-Z Every Which Way," *New York Times*, March 7, 2004, p. 27.

Copyright Colonizes the Subconscious Mind

31   *George Bernard Shaw quotation*   A. Lindey, *Plagiarism and Originality* (New York: Harper, 1952), p. 18, quoting *Standard Edition of the Works of George Bernard Shaw: Pen Portraits and Reviews* (London: Constable and Co., 1932).

32–33   *Jerome Kern's disputed ostinato and Judge Learned Hand quotation*   *Fred Fisher Inc. v. Dillingham*, 298 F.145 (S.D.N.Y. 1924).

33   *George Harrison and the Chiffons litigation*   *ABKCO Music Inc. v. Harrisongs Music Ltd*, 722 F.2d 988 (1983). See also Siva Vaidhyanathan, *Copyrights and Copywrongs*, pp. 126–31.

33–34   *The Isley Brothers and Michael Bolton*   *Three Boys Music Corp. v. Michael Bolton*, 212 F.3d 477 (2000), *cert. denied*, 531 U.S. 1126 (2001).

34   *Comment on expansion of subconscious copying doctrine*   Joel S. Hollingsworth, "Stop Me If I've Heard This Already: The Temporal Remoteness Aspect of the Subconscious Copyright Doctrine," 23 *Hastings Communications and Entertainment Law Journal* 457 (Winter 2001), p. 475.

Copyrighting "Genetic Tunes"

34–35   *Patenting and the human genome*   John Sunstein, *The Common Thread: A Story of Science, Politics, Ethics and the Human Genome* (Washington, D.C.: Joseph Henry Press, 2002).

35–36   *DNA music*   Algorithmic Arts and its Bankstep software: http://algoart.com; Noah Schachtman, "A Good Sequence, Easy to Dance To," *Wired News*, May 21, 2002, http://www.wired.com/news/print/0,1294,52666,00.html.

35   *Life Music album*   http://artists.mp3s.com/artists/18/genetic_music.html.

35   *Ramon y Cajal Hospital*   Associated Press, "Researchers Translate DNA Code into Music," January 19, 2003.

35–37   *Andre Crump and the DNA Copyright Institute*   Company Web site: http://dnacopyright.com; David Blaustein, "Clone Rangers," ABC News, August 23, 2002, available at http://abcnews.go.com/sections/scitech/DailyNews/clones010823.html; BBC News, "US Firm Offers Stars DNA Copyright," August 15, 2001, available at http://news.bbc.co.uk/1/hi/sci/tech/1492859.stm.

37   *High school teacher's "poor person's DNA copyright"*   CBS Radio Network, *The Osgood File*, "High School Students Copyright Their Own DNA," October 4, 2001, available at http://www.acfnewsource.org.

2: Creativity and Captive Images

38   *Motherwell quotation*   Jean Lipman and Richard Marshall, *Art about Art* (New York: E. P. Dutton, 1978), p. 7, cited in Geri J. Yonover, "The 'Dissing' of Da Vinci: The Imaginary Case of Leonardo v. Duchamp: Moral Rights, Parody and Fair Use," 29 *Valparaiso University Law Review* 935 (Spring 1995), footnote 407.

39–40 *Appropriationism in visual arts*   Roxana Badin, "An Appropriate(d) Place in Transformative Value: Appropriation Arts Exclusion from *Campbell v. Acuff-Rose Music, Inc.*," 60 *Brooklyn Law Review* 1653 (Winter 1995). Also, "Note: Beyond Rogers v. Koons: A Fair Use Standard for Appropriation," 93 *Columbia Law Review* 1473 (October 1993); Sven Lütticken, "The Art of Theft," *New Left Review*, January/February 2002, pp. 89–104.

Painting Mustaches on the *Mona Lisa*

41–44 *Law review articles on appropriation in the visual arts*   Geri J. Yonover, "The 'Dissing' of Da Vinci: The Imaginary Case of Leonardo v. Duchamp: Moral Rights, Parody and Fair Use," 29 *Valparaiso University Law Review* 935 (Spring 1995); John Carlin, "Culture Vultures," 13 *Columbia-VLA Journal of Law & Arts*, 103 (1988); Patricia Kreig, "Copyright, Free Speech and the Visual Arts," 93 *Yale Law Journal* 1565 (1984); Sonya del Peral, Comment, "Using Copyrighted Visual Works in Collage: A Fair Use Analysis," 54 *Albany Law Review* 141 (1989).

42   *Rogers v. Koons*, 960 F.2d 301 (2d Cir.), *cert. denied*, 113 S. Ct. 365 (1992). Also, Constance L. Hays, "A Picture, a Sculpture and a Lawsuit," *New York Times*, September 19, 1991, p. B2. This decision has received great attention in the legal literature. See, e.g., Lynne A. Greenberg, "The Art of Appropriation: Puppies, Piracy, and Post-Modernism," 11 *Cardozo Arts and Entertainment Law Review* 1 (1992).

43   *Sharon Appel quotation*   Sharon Appel, "Copyright, Digitization of Images and Art Museums: Cyberspace and Other New Frontiers," 6 *UCLA Entertainment Law Review* 149 (Spring 1999), note 120.

43   *Linda Hutcheon quotation*   Linda Hutcheon, *A Theory of Parody: The Teachings of Twentieth-Century Art Forms* (Urbana: University of Illinois Press, 2000), pp. 59, 65.

44–46 *Barry Kite's appropriationist art*   Kite's Web site for "Aberrant Art," http://www.aberrantart.com.

44–46   *Press clips*   Mike Thomas, "Collage Artist has a Gift for the Twisted," *Chicago Sun-Times*, December 12, 2000; Shannon Beatty, "Provocative Images Pair Past, Present," *Columbus (Ohio) Dispatch*, June 4, 2000; "Barry Kite Explains His Anti-establishment Art," *Independent* (London), December 13, 1997. Author interview with Barry Kite, December 18, 2003.

Illegal Art to Express Illicit Ideas

46   *Web site for "Illegal Art" exhibit*   http://www.illegal-art.org. See also *Stay Free!* magazine, No. 20, "Copyright Issue" (undated, Brooklyn, New York).

46–47   *Articles about the exhibit*   Farhad Manjoo, "Barbie, Starbucks and Freedom," *Salon.com*, July 17, 2003, at http://www.salon.com/ent/feature/2003/07/17/illegal_art. Also, Chris Gaither, "Touring Exhibit Tests the Limits of Copyright Laws that Block Artists from Using Corporate Images," *Boston Globe*, July 14, 2003; another art exhibit that bears on this subject is "Art at the Edge of the Law," which ran from June 3 to September 9, 2001, at the Aldrich Museum of Contemporary Art in Ridgefield, Connecticut (http://www.aldrichart.org).

47–48   *Borusan Art Gallery exhibit*   "Copy It, Steal It, Share It: Artists and Icons," September 20–November 8, 2003. Web site: http://www.borusansanat.com/english/galeri/kopyala_paylas/galeri2.asp.

The Untold Legal Story behind Andy Warhol's Art

49   *Patricia Caulfield and Warhol's "flowers"*   Gay Morris, "When Artists Use Photographs: Is It Fair Use, Legitimate Transformation or Rip-Off?" *ARTNews*, January 1981, p. 102.

49   *Feldman quotations*   Author interview with Ronald Feldman, September 10, 2003.

49   *Andy Warhol's artworks*   Frayda Feldman and Jorg Schellmann, *Andy Warhol Prints: A Catalogue Raisonné, 1962–1987* (4th ed., revised and expanded by Frayda Feldman and Claudia Defendi, D.A.P./Distributed Art Publishers, 2003).

50   *Bela Lugosi case*   *Lugosi v. Universal Pictures Company Inc.*, 603 P.2d 425, 160 Cal Rptr. 323 (L.A. County Ct. 1979).

The Dubious Calder Monopoly on Mobiles

56   *Fogarty and Lerner quotations*   Winnie Hu, "Store Wars: When a Mobile Is Not a Calder," *New York Times*, August 6, 1998, p. E1. An excerpt of this article can be found in *The Art Brief*, August 10, 1998, at http://www.exhibitionsonline.org/artbrief/ab83.htm.

Old Man Potter Locks Up *It's a Wonderful Life*

57   Account based on Stephen Fishman, *The Public Domain: How to Find Copyright-Free Writings, Music, Art and More* (Berkeley, Calif.: Nolo, 2001), p. 7/14.

3: Appropriating the People's Culture

58   *Justice Story quotation*   *Emerson v. Davis*, 8 F.Cas. 615, 619 (C.C.D. Mass. 1845).

59   *Wendy Gordon quotation*   Wendy Gordon, "On Owning Information: Intellectual Property and the Restitutionary Impulse," 78 *Virginia Law Review* 1992, p. 168, cited in Coombe, p. 68.

60   *Coombe quotation*   Rosemary J. Coombe, *The Cultural Life of Intellectual Properties: Authorship, Appropriation and the Law* (Durham, N.C.: Duke University Press, 1998), p. 63.

Vaudeville Comedy: Appropriation
Is the Seed of Originality

60–61   *Marx copyright holders' suit*   *Groucho Marx Productions, Inc. v. Day and Night Co., Inc.*, 523 F. Supp. 485 (S.D.N.Y. 1981), 589 F.2d 317 (1982).

61   *Fortune magazine*   Daniel Seligman, "Keeping Up," *Fortune*, November 16, 1981, p. 50.

61   *David Lange quotation*   David Lange, "Recognizing the Public Domain," 44 *Law and Contemporary Problems* 4 (1981).

61   *Groucho Marx quotation*   Groucho Marx, *Groucho and Me* (New York: AMS Press, 1959), p. 88, as cited in David Lange, "Recognizing the Public Domain," 44 *Law and Contemporary Problems* 4 (1981), pp. 161–62.

62   *Vaudeville history of "borrowing" from others*   J. DiMeglio, *Vaudeville, U.S.A.* (Madison: University of Wisconsin Press, 1973), p. 73.

Shakespeare the Imitator

63   *Twain quotation*   Twain letter to Hellen Keller, 1903, from Albert Bigelow Paine, ed., *Mark Twain's Letters* (New York: Harper & Brothers, 1917), p. 731, as cited in Siva Vaidhyanathan, *Copyrights and Copywrongs*, p. 64.

63–64   *Posner quotation*   Richard A. Posner, *Law and Literature* (2d ed., 2000), p. 399, cited in amicus brief submitted to U.S. Supreme Court in *Eldred v. Ashcroft*, by National Writers Union et al., by attorney Peter Jaszi, American University. See also Shakespeare Resource Center, "The Authorship Debate," at http://www.bardweb.net/debates.html.

64   *Justice Scalia quotation*   *Dastar Corporation v. Twentieth Century Fox Film Corporation*, 123 S.Ct. 2041 (2003).

Who Owns Quilts and Needlepoint Patterns?

64 *Shaker quotation* Lewis Hyde, *The Gift: Imagination and the Erotic Life of Property* (New York: Vintage, 1979), copyright page.

65–66 *Quilt design lawsuit* *Boisson v. Banian, Ltd.*, 280 F. Supp. 2d 10 (2003), 273 F.3d 262 (2001).

66 *On needlepoint design sharing* Lisa Napoli, "File Sharing Needles Pattern Makers," MSNBC, January 11, 2002, at http://www.msnbc.com/news/686230.asp?cp1=1.

67–68 *Fashion and creativity* David Bollier and Laurie Racine, "Control of Creativity? Fashion's Secret," *Christian Science Monitor*, September 9, 2003, at http://www.csmonitor.com/2003/0909/p09s01-coop.html. Bollier and Racine host the project, "Ready to Share: Fashion and the Ownership of Creativity," at the USC Annenberg School for Communication's Norman Lear Center.

Squabbling over the Ownership of Gettysburg Ghost Stories

68–69 Tom Troy, "Gettysburg Ghost Stories Scare Up Copyright Battle," *National Law Journal*, October 31, 2001.

Disney Privatizes the Classics and Folktales

69–72 *Disney's legal bullying* Paul Richter, "Disney's Tough Tactics," *Los Angeles Times*, July 8, 1990, p. D1; Gail Diane Cox, "Disney's Legal Army Protects a Revered Image," *National Law Journal*, July 31, 1989, p. 1; "Cartoon Figures Run Afoul of Law," *Chicago Tribune*, April 27, 1989; Bob Levin, *The Pirates and the Mouse: Disney's War Against the Counterculture* (Seattle: Fantagraphic Books, 2003).

69–72 *Books about the Disney Company* Sean Griffin, *Tinker Belles and Evil Queens: The Walt Disney Company from the Inside Out* (New York: New York University Press, 2000); Carl Hiaasen, *Team Rodent: How Disney Devours the World* (New York: Ballantine Books, 1998); Bob Levin, *The Pirates and the Mouse;* Richard Schickel, *The Disney Version: The Life, Times, Art, and Commerce of Walt Disney* (New York: Simon & Schuster, 1968); Steven Watts, *The Magic Kingdom: Walt Disney and the American Way of Life* (New York: Houghton Mifflin, 1997).

69 *Gilbert Seldes quotation* Ariel Dorfman and Armand Mattelart (translation and introduction by David Kunzle), *How to Read Donald Duck: Imperialist Ideology in the Disney Comic* (New York: International General, 1975), p. 18.

70 *Litigation over Winnie-the-Pooh* Peter Sheridan, "An Old-Age Pensioner is Taking on the Mighty Disney Corporation in a War over the World's

Cuddliest Bear," *The Express* (UK), February 20, 2004; Meg James, "Disney the Winner in a Flurry of a Lawsuit," *Los Angeles Times*, March 30, 2004.

70 *Richard Schickel quotation*   Richard Schickel, *The Disney Version*.

71 *Snow White in French AIDS awareness campaign*   "Disney Pressure Halts French AIDS Ad Campaign," *San Francisco Chronicle*, October 7, 1998.

71 *Expansion of Lanham Act test of consumer confusion about trademarks*   Jessica Litman, "Mickey Mouse Emeritus: Character Protection and the Public Domain," 11 *University of Miami Entertainment & Sports Law Review* 429 (1994), p. 434.

72 *Winnie-the-Pooh enforcement action*   Gail Diane Cox, "Disney's Legal Army Protects a Revered Image," *National Law Journal*, July 31, 1989, p. 1; Rose Sayer, "Winnie the Pooh—The Bear Facts," at http://www.tribute.ca/kids/0698/winnie_the_pooh.html.

72 *Dorfman/Mattelart quotation*   Ariel Dorfman and Armand Mattelart, *How to Read Donald Duck*, p. 18.

72 *Law review articles*   Jessica Litman, "Mickey Mouse Emeritus: Character Protection and the Public Domain," 11 *University of Miami Entertainment & Sports Law Review* 429 (1994); Michael Todd Helfand, "When Mickey Mouse Is as Strong as Superman: The Convergence of Intellectual Property Laws to Protect Fictional Literary and Pictorial Characters," 44 *Stanford Law Review* 623 (1992).

72 *Student paper*   Lauren Vanpelt, "Mickey Mouse—A Truly Public Character," Arizona State University College of Law (Spring 1999), at www.publicasu.edu/%7Edkarjala/publicdomain/Vanpelt s99.html.

Fan Fiction: You Are Not Allowed
to Imagine Batman and Robin as Gay

73 *Henry Jenkins quotation*   Henry Jenkins, *Textual Poachers: Television Fans and Participatory Culture* (New York: Routledge, 1992), p. 3.

73 *Representative fan fiction Web sites*   http://www.angstromance.net; http://www.restrictedsection.org; http://www.fanfiction.net.

73 *Tushnet quotations*   Rebecca Tushnet, "Legal Fictions: Copyright, Fan Fiction and a New Common Law," 14 *Loyola of Los Angeles Entertaiment Law Journal* 651 (1997).

74 *FAQ about fan fiction*   Electronic Frontier Foundation, Chilling Effects Clearinghouse, maintained by the Stanford Center for Internet and Society, at http://www.chillingeffects.org/fanfic/faq.cgi.

74 *Fan fiction background*   Camille Bacon-Smith, *Enterprising Women: Television Fandom and the Creation of Popular Myth* (Philadelphia: University of Pennsylvania Press, 1992); and Ariana Eunjung Cha, "Harry Potter and the Copyright Lawyer," *Washington Post*, June 18, 2003, p. A1.

75   *Fan quotations* Lewis Ward, "The Wrath of Viacom: Star Trek Fans Fight
     for the Right to Fair Use," *San Francisco Bay Guardian* [undated], at http://
     www.sfbg.com/Extra/Features.trek.html.

75   *Gaines quotation* Jane M. Gaines, *Contested Culture: The Image, the Voice and
     the Law* (Chapel Hill: University of North Carolina Press, 1991), p. 228,
     cited in Tushnet.

76   *Account of www.fandom.com* Sarah Kendzior, "Who Owns Fandom?" *Salon
     .com*, December 13, 2000, at http://www.salon.com/tech/feature/2000/
     12/13/fandom.

Who Owns Video-Game Characters?

76–79 T. L. Taylor, "'Whose Game Is This Anyway?': Negotiating Corporate
     Ownership in a Virtual World," available at http://www.itu.dk/~tltaylor/
     papers/Taylor-CGDC.pdf. See also documents relating to a conference,
     "The State of Play: Law, Games and Virtual Worlds," sponsored by the
     Institute for Information Law and Policy at New York Law School and
     the Information Society Project at Yale Law School, November 13–15,
     2003, accessible at http://www.nyls.edu/pages/777.asp.

PART TWO
TRADEMARKING PUBLIC LIFE

81   *Scott McNealy quotation* "The Default Language," *Economist*, May 15, 1999,
     p. 67.

81   *Dreyfuss quotation* Rochelle Cooper Dreyfuss, "Expressive Genericity:
     Trademarks as Language in the Pepsi Generation," 65 *Notre Dame Law
     Review* 397.

82   *Coombe quotation* Rosemary Coombe, *The Cultural Life of Intellectual Prop-
     erties: Authorship, Appropriation and the Law* (Durham, N.C.: Duke Univer-
     sity Press, 1995), p. 66.

4: Trademark Owners Whine,
"No Making Fun of Me!"

83   *Dreyfuss quotation* Rochelle Cooper Dreyfuss, "We Are Symbols and
     Inhabit Symbols, So Should We Be Paying Rent? Deconstructing the
     Lanham Act and Rights of Publicity," 20 *Columbia-VLA Journal of Law
     and the Arts* 123 (Winter 1996).

The Legal Lockdown of Barbie

85   *"Barbie Girl" song by Aqua* *Mattel, Inc. v. MCA Records, Inc.*, 296 F.3d 894
     (2002), and 28 F. Supp. 2d 1120 (C.D. Cal. 1998); also, Lisa Bannon,
     "This Suit for Barbie is More Flattering Than Song's Lyrics," *Wall Street*

Journal, September 12, 1997; Nick Driver, "Calling Barbie a Bimbo Is Free Speech," *San Francisco Examiner*, July 25, 2002.

85   *Evolution of trademark law*   Alex Kozinski, "Trademarks Unplugged," 68 *New York University Law Review* 960 (October 1993); Jessica Litman, "Breakfast with Batman: The Public Interest in the Advertising Age," 108 *Yale Law Journal* 1717 (1999).

86–87   *Mark Napier's Web site on The Distorted Barbie*   http://potatoland.org/bbhold/censored/censored.htm. Also, Steve Silberman, "Mattel's Latest: Cease-and-Desist Barbie," *Wired News*, October 28, 1997, at http://www.wired.com/news/culture/0,1284,8037,00.html.

87   *"Dungeon Barbie" litigation*   *Mattel v. Pitt*, 229 F. Supp. 2d 315 (2002). See also *New York Law Journal*, November 8, 2002, vol. 228, p. 29; Associated Press, "Judge: Sexed-up Barbie Doll Does not Seem to Violate Mattel Copyright," November 13, 2002.

87   *Mattel's litigation against Miller's*   Tracie L. Thompson, *California Lawyer*, July 2001, pp. 41–45; Denise Gellene, "Barbie Protesters Aren't Playing Around," *Los Angeles Times*, May 10, 1997; and Doug Clark, "Litigation Barbie, Made by Mattel," *Spokesman-Review* (Spokane, Wash.) October 5, 1997, p. A1.

87   *"Pink Anger" rebellion*   Denise Gellene, "Barbie Protesters Aren't Playing Around," *Los Angeles Times*, May 10, 1997.

88   *Books about Barbie*   M. G. Lord, *Forever Barbie: The Unauthorized Biography of a Real Doll* (New York: Avon, 1995); *Adios, Barbie* [later renamed *Body Outlaws*]: *Young Women Write About Body Image and Identity* (Seattle: Seal Press, 1998/2000); Mary F. Rogers, *Barbie Culture* (Thousand Oaks, Calif.: Sage, 1999); Jeannie Banks Thomas, *Naked Barbies, Warrior Joes and Other Forms of Visible Gender* (Urbana: University of Illinois Press, 2003).

89–93   *Tom Forsythe case*   *Mattel v. Walking Mountain Productions*, 353 F.3d 792 (2003). Personal correspondence and telephone interview, Tom Forsythe, August 15, 2002, and November 2, 2003. Interview with Douglas Winthrop and Simon Frankel of Howard Rice Nemerovski, November 26, 2003. Bill Werde, "Rebuking Barbie's Manufacturer, Judge Says Artist Can Make Fun of Dolls," *New York Times*, June 28, 2004, p. A10.

89   *Tom Forsythe's Web site*   http://www.creativefreedomdefense.org.

Straight Eye for Queer Trademark Intimidation

93–94   *Billy Parcel Service*   Andrew Keegan, "Gay Doll Stripped of Uniform," *Washington Blade*, January 25, 2002.

94   *Pink Panther Patrol*   *MGM-Pathé Communications Co. v. Pink Panther Patrol*, 774 F. Supp. 869, 21 U.S.P.Q. 2d 1208 (S.D.N.Y., 1991). See also Constance L. Hays, "Gay Patrol and MGM in Battle Over Name," *New York Times*, May 27, 1991, p. A21.

Bully-Boy Fruit of the Loom Doesn't
Think Underwear Is Funny

94–97   *Prehensile Tales Web site*   http://www.prehensile.com/does/fruitloom.htm;
interview with Styn, June 26, 2003.

Superspy Shakedown: James Bond
Roughs Up Austin Powers

97–98   *Trade press articles about the Austin Powers parodies*   Marcus Errico, "007
Dis(Gold)members Austin Powers," *E! Online News*, at http://www.eonline
.com/News/Items/0,1,9430,00.html; Greg Kilday, "NL Squabble Over
Next 'Powers' Title," *Hollywood Reporter*, January 28, 2002; Joseph Gross-
berg, "New Line Defends Its Mojo," *E! Online News*, January 29, 2002,
at http://www.eonline.com/News/Items/pf/0,1527,9440,00.html; Mark
Armstrong, "Austin Powers Says 'Member' Again," *E! Online News*,
April 9, 2002, at http://www.eonline.com/News/Items/pf/0,1527,0783,00
.html; Josh Spector, "Austin Powers Has His Gold Back, Baby," *Hollywood Reporter*, April 12, 2002.

97–98   *Law review article*   Kristen Knudsen, "Tomorrow Never Dies: The Protec-
tion of James Bond and Other Fictional Characters Under the Federal
Trademark Dilution Act," 2 *Vanderbilt Journal of Entertainment Law &
Practice* 13 (2000).

The Grave Threat of Goofy T-Shirts

98   *Yonover quotation*   Geri J. Yonover, "The 'Dissing' of Da Vinci: The Imaginary Case of Leonardo v. Duchamp: Moral Rights, Parody and Fair
Use," 29 *Valparaiso University Law Review* 935 (Spring 1995), pp. 978–79.

98–103   *Legal scholarship on the expressive use of trademarks*   Arlen W. Langvardt,
"Trademarks Rights and First Amendment Wrongs: Protecting the
Former without Committing the Latter," 83 *Trademark Reporter* 633
(September/October 1993); Arlen W. Langvardt, "Protected Marks and
Protected Speech: Establishing the First Amendment Boundaries in
Trademark Parody Cases," 36 *Villanova Law Review* 1 (1991); Steven M.
Cordero, "Cocaine-Cola, the Velvet Elvis, and Anti-Barbie: Defending the
Trademark and Publicity Rights to Cultural Icons," 8 *Fordham Intellectual
Property Media & Entertainment Law Journal* 599 (Winter 1998); Robert J.
Shaughnessy, Trademark Parody: A Fair Use and First Amendment
Analysis, 77 *Trademark Reporter* 177, 204–206 (1987).

99–100   *T-shirt cases:*

"Mutant of Omaha" T-shirts   *Mutual of Omaha Insurance Company v. Novak*,
836 F.2d 397, 5 U.S.P.Q. 2d 1314 (Ca. 8, 1987), *cert. denied*, 488 U.S. 933
(1988).

Miller Lite/"Killer Lite" T-shirts Wayne E. Green, "Miller Doesn't See Humor in T-Shirts Mocking 'Lite' Ads," *Wall Street Journal*, October 13 1989, p. B3; also *Wall Street Journal*, March 8, 1990, p. B8.

"This Beach is for You" T-shirt Anheuser-Busch, Inc. v. L & L Wings, Inc., 962 F2d 316, U.S.P.Q. 2d 1502 (Ca. 4, 1992), *cert. denied*, 113 S. Ct. 206, (1992).

101 *"Genital Electric" novelty underwear* General Electric Company v. Alumpa Coal Company, Inc., 1979 U.S. Dist. LEXIS 9197; 205 U.S.P.Q. (BNA) 1036.

101 *Jordache v. Lardashe jeans litigation* Jordache Enterprises, Inc. v. Hogg Wyld, Ltd., 828 F.2d 1482, 4 U.S.P.Q. 2d 1216 (Ca. 10, 1987).

101 *"Enjoy Cocaine" poster case* Coca-Cola Co. v. Gemini Rising, Inc., 346 F. Supp. 1183, 175 U.S.P.Q. 56 (E.D.N.Y., 1972).

101 *Pendergrast quotation* Mark Pendergrast, *For God, Country and Coca-Cola: The Definitive History of the Great American Soft Drink and the Company That Makes It*, 2d ed. (New York: Basic, 2000).

101–102 *Pregnant Girl Scout poster case* Girl Scouts of the United States of America v. Personality Posters Mfg. Co., Inc., 304 F. Supp. 1228 (1969).

102 *Cabbage Patch dolls v. Garbage Pail Kids stickers* Original Appalachian Artworks, Inc. v. Topps Chewing Gum, Inc., 642 F. Supp. 1031, 231 U.S.P.Q. 850 (N.D. Ga., 1986).

103 *Wonder Wench and Super Stud parody* D.C. Comics Inc. v. Unlimited Monkey Business, 598 F. Supp. 110 (1984).

103 *"Pretty Woman": 2 Live Crew and Roy Orbison* Campbell v. Acuff-Rose Music, Inc., 114 S.Ct. 1164 (1994).

Another Dangerous Art Form: Bawdy Spoofs

103–109 *Legal treatises dealing with obscene parodies* Bruce P. Keller and David H. Bernstein, "As Satiric as They Wanna Be: Parody Lawsuits under Copyright, Trademark, Dilution and Publicity Laws," 85 *Trademark Reporter* 239 (May/ June 1995); Richard J. Greenstone, "Protection of Obscene Parody as Fair Use," 4 *Entertainment and Sports Lawyer* 3 (Winter/Spring 1986).

103–104 *"When Sunny Sniffs Glue" parody* Marvin Fisher v. Rick Dees et al., 794 F.2d 432 (1986).

104 *"I Love Sodom" parody* Elsmere Music, Inc. v. NBC, 482 F. Supp. 741 (1980).

104–105 *"Cunnilingus Champion of Company C" parody* MCA, Inc. v. Earl Wilson, 425 F. Supp. 677 F.2d 180 (1981).

105 *Screw magazine parody* Pillsbury Co. v. Milky Way Productions, Inc., 215 U.S.P.Q. (N.D. Ga., 1981).

106 *Dallas Cowgirls porn film* Dallas Cowboys Cheerleaders, Inc. v. Pussycat Cinema, Ltd., 604 F.2d 200, U.S.P.Q. 1612 (Ca. 2, 1979).

106 109   *Air Pirates' parodies of Disney characters*   *Walt Disney Productions v. The Air Pirates et al.*, 581 F.2d 751 (1978). See also Bob Levin, *The Pirates and the Mouse: Disney's War Against the Counterculture* (Seattle: Fantagraphic Books, 2003).

106–109   *Ownership of fictional characters*   Leslie Kurtz, "The Independent Legal Lives of Fictional Characters," *Wisconsin Law Review* (May/June 1986), pp. 429–524.

5: The Corporate Privatization of Words

110   *Judge Edith Jones comment about Polo Ralph Lauren*   *Westchester Media v. PRL Holdings Inc.*, 214 F.3d 658 (2000).

Who Owns "Casablanca"?
Groucho Takes On the Studio Lawyers

111   *Vaidhyanathan quotation*   Siva Vaidhyanathan, *Copyrights and Copywrongs: The Rise of Intellectual Property and How It Threatens Creativity* (New York: New York University Press, 2001), pp. 1-2; see also Groucho Marx, *The Groucho Letters: Letters to and from Groucho Marx* (New York: Simon & Schuster, 1967).

McDonald's "Ownership" of 131 Words and Phrases

111–112   *McDonald's trademarked phrases*   Michael Manoochehri, "Black History Makers of Tomorrow®—This Phrase Owned by McDonalds!"; Kate Silver, "Serving Up the McDictionary," *Las Vegas Weekly*, April 26, 2001, available on Alternet.org, at http://alternet.org/story.html?StoryID=10900.

You Must Be Socially Acceptable
to Use the Word "Olympics"

112–114   *News accounts and commentary on the case*   Stuart Taylor, Jr., "Supreme Court Roundup: Justices Uphold U.S. Panel's Ban Against Gay Olympics Title," *New York Times*, June 26, 1987, p. A14; Rosemary J. Coombe, *The Cultural Life of Intellectual Properties: Authorship, Appropriation and the Law* (Durham, N.C.: Duke University Press, 1998), pp. 136–38.

113   *Supreme Court ruling*   *San Francisco Arts & Athletics, Inc. v. United States Olympic Committee*, 483 U.S. 522.

114   *Judge Kozinski dissent at Ninth Circuit*   781 F.2d 733.

114   *Salt Lake City Olympics*   Bob Mims, "Web Site Raises Eyebrows at SLOC," *Salt Lake Tribune*, November 9, 2000, p. C1; Rebecca Walsh, "Warning: 'O' Word is a No-No; SLOC Jealously Guards Brand Names, Symbols," *Salt Lake Tribune*, January 5, 2001, p. C1.

Only Fox News Can Claim
to Be "Fair and Balanced"

114–117   *Franken/Fox dispute over "fair and balanced"—general news coverage*   Susan
          Saulny, "'Fair and Balanced'? For Fox and Al Franken, Fighting Words,"
          New York Times, August 12, 2003; *New York Times*, "Windfall Publicity for
          Al Franken's Book," August 13, 2003; Howard Kurtz, "Al Franken: Throw-
          ing Punches and Punch Lines," *Washington Post*, August 28, 2003, p. C1.

   116   *Salon.com coverage*   Michelle Goldberg, "Franken Bests Fox," *Salon.com*,
          August 23, 2003, at http://www.salon.com/news/feature/2003/08/23/
          Franken_fox; Erin McClam, Associated Press, "Fox News Drops Lawsuit
          Against Al Franken," *Salon.com*, August 25, 2003, at http://www.salon
          .com/news/wire/2003/08/25/fox_news_suit; Laura McClure, "They
          Can Dish It Out, But They Can't Take It," *Salon.com*, August 27, 2003, at
          http://www.salon.com/news/feature/2003/08/27/Franken.

Who Came First—Ralph Lauren
or the Equestrians?

117–118   *Legal case*   United States Polo Association v. Polo Fashions, Inc., 1984 U.S. Dist.
          LEXIS 21908; *Westchester Media v. PRL Holdings, Inc.*, 214 F.3d 658 (2000).

117–118   *News coverage*   Allison Fass, "Polo Ralph Lauren Sues Jordache Over Sport
          Emblem," *New York Times*, August 11, 2000, p. C19; "New Round in Polo
          v. Polo," *New York Post*, June 23, 2001, p 8; John T. Fakler, "Polo Logo
          Feud Is Still in Fashion," *South Florida Business Journal*, April 12, 2002.

   118   *Web site of USPA Properties, Inc., the licensing arm of the U.S. Polo Association*
          http://www.uspaproperties.com/home.html.

Patrolling the Boundaries of Mental Association

119–120   *Victor's Little Secret case*   Moseley and Cathy Moseley v. V. Secret Catalog, Inc.,
          537 U.S. 418 (2003).

119–120   *News accounts*   Linda Greenhouse, "Ruling on Victor vs. Victoria Offers
          Split Victory of Sorts," *New York Times*, March 5, 2003; Associated Press,
          "High Court to Hear Victoria's Secret Case," April 15, 2002; Tony
          Mauro, "Victoria's Trademark May Carry the Day," *Legal Times*, Novem-
          ber 18, 2002, p. 6.

The Value of Godzilla? Priceless!

   120   *Nader and "Priceless" ads*   Posting on the "Random Bits" listserv: http://lists
          .essential.org/pipermail/random-bits/2000-August/000262.html; http://
          lists.essential.org/pipermail/random-bits/2000-September/000309.html;
          Cable News Network, "Nader: 'Priceless' Ads Will Run Despite MasterCard

Suit," August 17, 2000; Associated Press, "Federal Judge Refuses to Block 'Priceless' Parody Ads," September 14, 2000.

121–122 *"Entrepreneur"* Dawn Rivers Baker, "[*Entrepreneur Magazine*] Allegedly Pursues More Entrepreneurs," *The MicroEnterprise Journal*, November 10, 2003. See also *Entrepreneur Media Inc. v. Smith*, 279 F.3d 1135 (2002).

122 *"USA 2003"* Larry Neumeister, Associated Press, "Nike Sues Over Trademark Rights to Soccer," September 23, 2003.

122–123 *Village Voice versus Beachwood Voice* "Stupid Newspaper Lawyer Tricks," *New York Press*, available at http://www.nypress.com/16/17/news&columns/feature.cfm; Seth Rolbein, "Is Anyone Really Confused?" *Cape Cod Voice*, November 21, 2002, available at http://www.capecodvoice.com/vvimages/theme1121.html.

123 *Three-peat* Michael Hunt, "Kidd's Triple-Double Not Enough to Stop Lakers," *Milwaukee Journal-Sentinel*, June 6, 2002.

123–124 *Davezilla v. Godzilla* David F. Gallagher, "And Now the Sequel: Every-zilla Meets the Lawyers," *New York Times*, August 19, 2002. See also www.davezilla.org. Toho's cease-and-desist letter: http://www.davezilla.com/index.php?p=1292.

The Internet and the Rise of Super-Trademarks

125 *eToys.com versus etoy* Adam Wishart, Alexander Broadie, and Regula Bochsler, *Leaving Reality Behind: Etoy vs. etoys.com and Other Battles to Control Cyberspace* (Hopewell, N.J.: Ecco, 2003); Andrew Leonard, "Toys Were Us," *Salon.com*, March 4, 2003, http://www.salon.com/tech/feature/2003/03/004/toys/print.html.

125 *Geist quotation* "Domain Name Policy Absurd When It Comes to Trademarks," *Globe and Mail* (Toronto), July 25, 2002.

125 *Newspaper articles* Jerry Markon, "You Can Get Anything You Want—Except the Name, 'Alice's Restaurant,'" *Wall Street Journal*, April 19, 2001; Caroline E. Mayer, "No Bend on Brand Names," *Washington Post*, January 29, 2004, p. E1.

125 *Misha Glouberman,* "Trademark Wars on the Web," Web site about trademark disputes, last updated December 20, 1996, available at http://www.web.net/~misha/trademark.html.

126 *Lindows.com* Press release, Lindows.com, "Lindows.com Gains Double Victory in Microsoft Trademark Case," February 10, 2004, available at http://www.lindows.com; Associated Press, "Lindows Changes Name of Operating System," April 14, 2004; Lindows comment on name change, http://www.linspire.com/lindows_michaelsminutes_archives.php?id=111.

126–127 *Froomkin quotation* A. Michael Froomkin, "The Collision of Trademarks, Domain Names and Due Process in Cyberspace," *Communications of the ACM*, vol. 44, no. 2 (February 2001), pp. 91–97.

127 *"Kirby" and "SpiritInside"* Caroline E. Mayer, "No Bend on Brand Names," *Washington Post*, January 29, 2004, p. E1.

127–128   *Warner Bros. and Harry Potter trademark*   Stephanie Grunier and John Lippmann, "Warner Bros. Claims Harry Potter Sites," *Wall Street Journal Online*, December 20, 2000, at http://zdnet.com.com/2102-11-503255 .html; Kieren McCarthy, "Warner Brothers Bullies Girl Over Harry Potter Site," *Register* (London), August 12, 2000, at http://www.theregister .co.uk/content/archive/15324.html; Graham Lea, "Warner Threatens Harry Potter Fan Sites," *Register* (London), September 2, 2000, at http:// www.theregister.co.uk/content/archive/9146.html.

The Forbidden Words: "This Corporation Sucks!"

128   *Domain names with "sucks"*   Carolyn Said, "Dot-Complaints," *San Francisco Chronicle*, July 25, 2000.

128   *Nissan domain-name dispute*   *Nissan Motor Co. v. Nissan Computer Corporation*, 231 F. Supp. 2d 977 (2002); Uzi Nissan's side of the story: www .ncchelp.org; Public Citizen press release in support of Uzi Nissan, March 5, 2003, at http://www.citizen.org/pressroom/release.cfm?ID=1349.

129   *WIPO arbitration on "bodacious-tatas" and "crew" domain names*   WIPO Arbitration and Mediation Center, Administrative Panel Decision, *Tata Sons Ltd. v. D & V Enterprises*, Case No. D2000-0479, August 18, 2000; *J. Crew International, Inc. v. crew.com*, Case No. D2000-0054, April 20, 2000.

130–131   *Taubmansucks.com*   Press release issued by Paul Alan Levy, Public Citizen Litigation Group, March 11, 2002. Archive on Taubman domain-name case at http://www.taubman.sucks.com and on politech listserv at http:// www.politechbot.com/cgi-bin/politech.cgi?name=taubman. Levy is one of the leading public-interest attorneys fighting bullying of users who use trademarks in domain names; http://www.citizen.org.

130   *Vivendiuniversalsucks.com dispute*   WIPO Arbitration and Mediation Center ruling, at http://arbiter.wipo.int/domains/decisions/html/2002/d2001-1121 .html.

6: Property Rights in Public Image

131   *Jack Nicholson quotation*   Jib Fowles, *Starstruck: Celebrity Performers and the American Public* (1992), p. 84, cited in Michael Madow, "Private Ownership of Public Image: Popular Culture and Publicity Rights," 81 *California Law Review* 125 (January 1993).

131   *First publicity rights case*   *Haelan Lab. Inc. v. Topps Chewing Gum, Inc.*, 202 F.2d 866 (2d Cir.), *cert. denied*, 346 U.S. 816 (1953).

132   *Nimmer quotation*   Melville B. Nimmer, "The Right of Publicity," 19 *Law & Contemporary Problems* 203 (1954).

132   *Elizabeth Taylor quotation*   Tamar Lewin, "Whose Life Is It, Anyway? Legally, It's Hard to Tell," *New York Times*, November 21, 1982, Section 2, p. 1.

132–133   *Madow quotations*   Michael Madow, "Private Ownership of Public Image: Popular Culture and Publicity Rights," 81 *California Law Review* 125

(January 1993). I am indebted to Madow's insightful and comprehensive overview of this topic. Another useful general overview is Adam Liptak, "The New Protected Class?" *Brill's Content*, Fall 2001, pp. 57–63.

133   *Judge Kozinski quotation*   Alex Kozinski, "Trademarks Unplugged," 68 *New York University Law Review* 960 (October 1993).

Evoking Celebrity Personalities Is Prohibited

134   *Elroy "Crazylegs" Hirsch case*   *Hirsch v. S.C. Johnson & Son, Inc.*, 280 N.W. 2d 129 (Wis. 1979).

134   *Guy Lombardo case*   *Lombardo v. Doyle, Dane & Bernbach, Inc.*, 396 N.Y.S. 2d 661 (App. Div. 1977).

134   *Spike Lee suit against Viacom over "Spike TV"*   "Judge Temporarily Blocks Name of Spike TV," *Washington Post*, June 13, 2003, p. C7; Jim Rutenberg, "Spike Lee Is Expected to Settle Suit Over Spike TV," *New York Times*, July 8, 2003.

134–135   *Ginger Rogers versus Ginger and Fred*   *Rogers v. Grimaldi*, 875 F.2d 994 (1989).

135   *Paul Newman is HUD*   Paul Newman, "Paul Newman is Still HUD," *New York Times*, August 19, 2003, p. A21.

135   *Bill Wyman and Bill Wyman*   Associated Press, "Ex-Stone Wyman: Stop Using My Name," *Washington Post*, November 17, 2002.

135–136   *"Here's Johnny!" case*   *Carson v. Here's Johnny Portable Toilets, Inc.*, 698 F.2d 831 (6th Cir. 1983).

136   *Vanna White case*   *Vanna White v. Samsung Electronics America, Inc.*, 971 F.2d 1395 (1992).

137   *Judge Alarcon's dissent*   971 F.2d 1402 (1992).

137   *Judge Kozinski's dissent*   989 U.S. F.2d 1512 (1993).

137–138   *Publicity rights claims by Saddam Hussein, Uri Geller, Paul Prudhomme and others*   Eben Shapiro, "Rising Caution on Using Celebrity Images," *New York Times*, November 4, 1992, p. D20; *Lucasfilm Ltd. v. High Frontier*, 622 F. Supp. 931 (D.D.C. 1985); *Geller v. Fallon McElligott*, No. 90-Civ-2839 (S.D.N.Y. July 22, 1991); *Prudhomme v. Procter & Gamble Co.*, 800 F.Supp. 390 (E.D. La. 1992).

139   *Cheers case*   *George Wendt and John Ratzenberger v. Host International and Paramount Pictures Corporation*, 197 F.3d 1284 (1999) and 125 F.3d 806 (1997). See also Michael J. Albano, "Nothing to 'Cheer' About: A Call for Reform of the Right of Publicity in Audiovisual Characters," 90 *Georgetown Law Journal* 253 (November 2001).

Can the Girl from Ipanema Call Herself "The Girl from Ipanema"?

139–140   *Quotations*   Larry Rohter, "Still Tall and Tan, a Muse Fights for a Title," *New York Times*, August 11, 2001, p. A1; Ann Woolner, "Rosa Parks and

Barbie Battle for Their Names," *Taipei Times*, August 18, 2001, available at http://www.taipeitimes.com/news/2001/08/18/print/0000099148.

Rosa Parks Battles Rappers for Cultural Control

141–142   *Legal case   Rosa Parks v. LaFace Records*, 76 F. Supp. 2d 775 (1999), *cert. denied*, 329 F. 3d 437 (6th Cir. 2003). See also, LaFace Records, Petition for a Writ of Certiorari.

141–142   *Commentary on the Rosa Parks/OutKast litigation*   Jesse Walker, "Copy Cat-fight," *Reason Online*, March 2000, available at http://reason.com/0003/fe.jw.copy.shtml; and Jabari Asim, "Rosa Parks v. 'Rosa Parks,'" *Washington Post*, December 15, 2003.

Making a Statement with Larry, Curly, and Moe

142–143   *Three Stooges case   Comedy III Productions, Inc. v. Gary Saderup, Inc.*, 25 Cal. 4th 387 (2001). Also, Maura Dolan, "What is Art? Three Stooges Case to Help Decide," *Los Angeles Times*, April 23, 2001, p. A1.

144   *Tiger Woods case   ETW Corp. v. Jireh Publishing, Inc.*, 99 F. Supp. 2d 829 (N.D. Ohio 2000). See also http://www.morganesq.com/news/LanhamTigerWoods.htm.

PART THREE
THE COPYRIGHT WARS AGAINST AN OPEN SOCIETY
7: The Theft of the Public Domain

147   *Law review articles on the public domain*   James Boyle, ed., *Collected Papers: Duke Conference on the Public Domain*, 66 *Law and Contemporary Problems*, 1 and 2 (Winter/Spring 2003); Jessica Litman, "The Public Domain," 39 *Emory Law Journal* 965 (Fall 1990); David Lange, "Recognizing the Public Domain," 44 *Law and Contemporary Problems* 4 (1981).

147   *Other resources on the public domain*   David Bollier, "Why the Public Domain Matters: The Endangered Wellspring of Creativity, Commerce and Democracy" [report] (Washington, D.C.: New America Foundation, 2002); Public Knowledge Web site: http://www.publicknowledge.org.

Incentives to Dead Authors:
The Copyright Term Extension Act

148–152   *Eldred case   Eldred v. Ashcroft*, 537 U.S. 186 (2001), F.3d 849 (2001).

148–152   *Legal archive on case at Harvard Law School's Berkman Center on Internet and Society*   http://cyber.law.harvard.edu/openlaw/eldredvashcroft. See also the Wikipedia entry on the case: http://en.wikipedia.org/wiki/Eldred_v._Ashcroft.

148–152 *Profiles of Eldred, Lessig, and the litigation* Daren Fonda, "Copyright Crusader," *Boston Globe Magazine*, August 29, 1999; David Streitfeld, "The Cultural Anarchist vs. the Hollywood Police State," *Los Angeles Times Magazine*, September 22, 2002, pp. 10–13 et seq.; Ariana Eunjung Cha, "Determining the Life of Corporate Copyrights," *Washington Post*, July 4, 2003, p. E6; Siva Vaidhyanathan, "After the Copyright Smackdown: What Next?" *Salon.com*, January 17, 2003, at http://www.salon.com/tech/feature/2003/01/17/copyright.

148–152 *New York Times accounts of case (chronological)* Linda Greenhouse, "Justices to Review Copyright Extension," February 20, 2002, p. C1; Seth Schiesel and Bill Carter, "Court Ruling May Change Landscape for Media," February 20, 2002, p. C1; Amy Harmon, "Debate to Intensify on Copyright Extension Law," October 7, 2002, p. C1; Linda Greenhouse, "20-Year Extension of Existing Copyrights Is Upheld," January 16, 2003; Amy Harmon, "A Corporate Victory, But One That Raises Public Consciousness," January 16, 2003.

Stealing Classical Music from the Public Domain

152 *Conductors' lawsuit* David Horrigan, "Conductors Pose First Challenge to Copyright Law," *National Law Journal*, November 26, 2001, at www.law.com. Also, Marc Shulgold, "Copyright Fight Transcends Cat and Mouse," *Rocky Mountain News*, October 4, 2002.

153 *Golan v. Ashcroft case page (at Stanford Law School Center for Internet and Society)* http://cyberlaw.stanford.edu/about/cases/golan_v_ashcroft.shtml. See also the Web page for "OpenLaw, *Golan v. Ashcroft*," at the Harvard Law School Berkman Center for Internet and Society, at http://cyber.law.harvard.edu/openlaw/golanvashcroft; *Golan v. Ashcroft*, 310 F. Supp. 2d 1215 (2004).

Who Owns the Dewey Decimal Classification System?

154 E-mail from OCLC to Paul Jones of www.ibiblio.org online library, September 15, 2000; e-mail from Paul Jones to Andrew Goldman of Public Knowledge, September 21, 2000; Associated Press, "Dewey Decimal Owner Sues 'Library' Hotel," September 20, 2003. Also, "OCLC and The Library Hotel Settle Trademark Complaint" [OCLC press release], November 24, 2003, at http://www.oclc.org/news/releases/20031124.htm. Interview with George Buzash, June 16, 2004.

West Publishing's Claim to Own
Page Numbers—and the Law

156–158 *News accounts of the case* Gary Wolf, "Who Owns the Law?" *Wired*, May 1994, p. 98; Reuters, "Justices, Judges Took Favors from Publisher with Pending Cases," *Washington Post*, March 6, 1995; John J. Odlund, "Debate

Rages Over Who Owns the Law," *Minneapolis Star Tribune*, March 5–6, 1995, reprinted in the *Congressional Record*, July 28, 1995 (Senate), pp. S10847–55; David Cay Johnston, "West Publishing Loses a Decision on Copyright," *New York Times*, May 21, 1997, p. D1; David Segal, "West Loses Copyright Challenge," *Washington Post*, November 5, 1998, p. D1.

156–158   *Law review articles about the copyrighting of court opinions*   L. Ray Patterson and Craig Joyce, "Monopolizing the Law: The Scope of Copyright Protection for Law Reports and Statutory Compilations," 36 *UCLA Law Review* 719 (1989); David Nimmer, "Copyright in the Dead Sea Scrolls: Authorship and Originality," 38 *Houston Law Review* 1 (Spring 2001), esp. Sections IV and V.

156–158   *Memo giving excellent history of the West case*   Jol Silversmith, "Universal Citation: The Fullest Possible Dissemination of Judgments," originally published in the now-defunct *Internet Legal Practice Newsletter* in May 1997, now available online at http://www.thirdamendment.com/citation .html. See also Melissa Barr, Cuyahoga County Public Library, "Democracy in the Dark: Public Access Restrictions from Westlaw and Lexis-Nexis," 11 *The Searcher* 1 (January 2003), available at http://www.infotoday .com/searcher/jan03/barr.htm.

156   *Laura Gasaway quotation*   Gary Wolf, "Who Owns the Law?" *Wired*, May 1994, p. 100.

157   *James Love's Web site on public access to judicial information*   http://www.cptech .org/legalinfo/legalinfo.html.

158   *West Publishing case   Matthew Bender & Company, Inc. v. West Publishing Co.*, 158 F.3d 674 (1998), *cert. denied*, 526 U.S. 1154 (1999).

Selling Monopoly Access to the Law

159   *Veeck v. Southern Building Code Congress International, Inc.* (5th Cir. Ct.), available at http://www.ca5.uscourts.gov/opinions/pub/99/99-40632-cv0.htm

159   *Legal documents related to the case, from Peter Veeck's Web site*   http://regionalweb .texoma.net/cr.

159   *SBCCI home page*   http://www.sbcci.org.

159   *Quotation about citizens being the author of the law   State of Georgia v. Harrison Co.*, 548 F. Supp. 110, 114 (N.D. Ga. 1982).

160   *Peter Suber quotation*   Peter Suber's Free Online Scholarship newsletter (now Open Access News), at http://www.earlham.edu/~peters/fos/ newsletter/06-25-01.htm, and http://www.earlham.edu/~peters/fos/ 2002_06_09_fosblogarchive.html#a77616668.

160   *Law review article on "owning the law"*   L. Ray Patterson and Craig Joyce, "Monopolizing the Law: The Scope of Copyright Protection for Law Reports and Statutory Compilations," 36 *UCLA Law Review* 719, 749 (April 1989).

Private Ownership of Sports Scores, Game Photos, and Best-Seller Lists

161   *NBA lawsuit over use of real-time scores on portable beepers*   *National Basketball Association v. Motorola*, 105 F.3d 841 (2nd Cir. 1997); Lane Rose, "Technical Foul: The NBA Double Dribbles on Intellectual Property," *Wired*, January 1997, available at http://www.wired.com/wired/archive/5.01/cyber_rights.html.

162   *NBA dispute with New York Times over sports photos*   Felicity Barringer, "Times is Sued By N.B.A. Over Sale of Photos," *New York Times*, July 11, 2000; Felicity Barringer, "Those Who Want to Control Information Find an Ally in a Public That Seems to Accept Restrictions," *New York Times*, April 9, 2001, p. C12; "The National Basketball Association and The New York Times Company Enter Into Marketing Agreement," Business Wire, Inc., April 9, 2001.

163   *Amazon.com dispute with New York Times over best-seller list*   George Anders, "Amazon.com Seeks Ruling on Free Use of the New York Times' Best-seller List," *Wall Street Journal*, June 7, 1999; "Barnes & Noble Dumps New York Times List," *Wall Street Journal*, September 14, 1999; "Amazon, New York Times Settle Suit Over Book List," *Wall Street Journal*, August 10, 1999.

How Spurious Copyrights Steal the Public Domain

163–165   *Heald story*   Paul J. Heald, "Payment Demands for Spurious Copyrights: Four Causes of Action," 1 *Journal of Intellectual Property Law* 259 (Spring 1994); Heald, "Reviving the Rhetoric of the Public Interest: Choir Directors, Copy Machines and New Arrangements of Public Domain Music," 46 *Duke Law Journal* 241 (1996). See also Jason Mazzone, "Too Quick to Copyright: Companies Cheat the Law and the Public by Claiming Ownership Over Too Much Stuff," *Legal Times*, November 17, 2003, p. 62.

The Next Form of Private Property—Facts?

165–166   *General overview*   Public Knowledge critique of the Database and Collections of Information Misappropriation Act, HR 3261, available at http://www.publicknowledge.org. See also Kim Zetter, "Hands Off! That Fact is Mine," *Wired News*, March 3, 2004, at http://www.wired.com/news/business/0,1367,62600,00.html; and Consumer Project on Technology Web Site, at http://www.cptech.org/ip/database.

166   *Weather forecasting*   National Research Council, *Fair Weather Effective Partnership in Weather and Climate Services* (Washington, D.C.: National Academy Press, 2003).

8: Stifling Public Dialogue through Copyright

167   *Brennan quotation*   *Harper & Row v. Nation Enterprises*, 471 U.S. 539 (1985).

Gerald Ford Uses Copyright Law to Stifle the News

168–169   *Commentary on case*   George Will, "Leftist Journal Was Not Right," *New York Times*, May 31, 1985; "High Court Rules for Copyright Award Reinstated on Ford Memoir Infringing," *Chicago Tribune*, May 21, 1985; *The Nation*, May 1, 1985.

Extra, Extra—Newspapers Snuff Out Free Expression!

170   *Legal case*   *Los Angeles Times v. Free Republic*, United States District Court for the Central District of California, 2000 U.S. Dist. LEXIS 20484. Amended final judgment is posted on the Free Republic's Web site at http://www.freerepublic.com/focus/news/707390/posts.

170   *Law review articles on copyright and First Amendment*   Yochai Benkler, "The Free Republic Problem: Markets in Information Goods vs. the Marketplace of Ideas," Yale Law School Conference on Private Censorship, available at http://webserver.law.yale.edu/censor/benkler.htm; C. Edwin Baker, "First Amendment Limits on Copyright," 55 *Vanderbilt Law Review* 891 (April 2002); Wendy J. Gordon, "Toward a Jurisprudence of Benefits: The Norms of Copyright and the Problem of Private Censorship," 57 *University of Chicago Law Review* 1009 (1990); Lawrence Lessig, "Copyright's First Amendment," 48 *UCLA Law Review* 1057 (June 2001); and Neil Weinstock Netanel, "Locating Copyright Within the First Amendment Skein," 54 *Stanford Law Review* 1 (October 2001).

International Olympics Committee Legally Locks Up the News

171   *Newspaper articles*   Felicity Barringer, "Leery of the Web, Olympic Officials Set Limits on News," *New York Times,* September 25, 2000, p. A1; Felicity Barringer, "Damming the Flow of Free Information," *New York Times*, May 7, 2000, Section 4, p. 6.

I Have a Dream . . . That Someday *All* of Public Life Will Be Copyrighted

174   *Legal case*   *Estate of Martin Luther King, Jr., Inc. v. CBS, Inc.*, 194 F.3d 1211 (1999). Also, *Plaintiffs Brief in Support of Its Motion for Summary Judgment*, U.S. District Court, Northern District of Georgia, Atlanta, Civil Action File No. 1:96-CV-3052-WCO, November 3, 1997.

174   *News articles*   David Firestone, "Tears and a Confession from Another Rev. King," *New York Times*, January 16, 2001. For an interesting story along

similar lines, see "Tushar Backs Out of 'Gandhi Brand' Deal," *India Times*, February 9, 2002, available at http://economictimes.indiatimes .com/articleshow.asp?art_id=473602.

175   *Alcatel print ad*   *New York Times*, April 10, 2001, p. C22. Also, Vanessa O'Connell, "Alcatel Has a Dream—and a Controversy," *Wall Street Journal*, March 30, 2001.

175   *Van Munching parody*   Philip Van Munching, "The Devil's Adman," *Brandweek*, June 4, 2001, p. 30.

Uppity Alice Randall and the Cultural Icon Protection Act

176   *The books*   Margaret Mitchell, *Gone with the Wind* (1936); Alice, Randall, *The Wind Done Gone* (New York: Houghton Mifflin, 2001).

177   *Legal case*   *Suntrust Bank v. Houghton Mifflin Company*, 268 F.3d 1257 (11th Cir. 2001).

177–179   *New York Times* coverage of *The Wind Done Gone* controversy, by David D. Kirkpatrick, by date:
April 21, 2001: "Court Halts Book Based on 'Gone With the Wind.'"
April 26, 2001: "A Writer's Tough Lesson in Birthin' a Parody."
May 26, 2001: "'Wind' Book Wins Ruling in U.S. Court."
May 10, 2002: "Mitchell Estate Settles 'Gone With the Wind' Suit."
Reportage and commentary on case   Lessig, Lawrence, "Let the Stories Go," *New York Times*, April 30, 2001; William Safire, "Frankly, My Dear. . ." *New York Times*, May 14, 2001; McDonald, R. Robin, "'The Wind Done Gone' Copyright Ruling May Have Lasting Impact," *Fulton County Daily Report*, October 12, 2001; Sara Nelson, "A PEN Divided," *Salon .com*, May 2, 2001.

9: The DMCA's Attacks on Free Speech

180–182   One of the leading critics and litigators against the DMCA is the Electronic Frontier Foundation. Its Web site, http://www.eff.org/dmca is a rich source of material about the DMCA and lawsuits challenging it. See especially its report "Unintended Consequences: Five Years Under the DMCA," 2003, available at http://www.eff.org/IP/DMCA/unintended_consequences .php. In Washington, Public Knowledge (www.publicknowledge.org) is active in lobbying Congress to roll back the DMCA. There is also an anti-DMCA Web site: http://www.anti-dmca.org.

There is a rich legal literature on the DMCA. Useful articles include Glynn S. Lunney Jr., "The Death of Copyright: Digital Technology, Private Copying and the Digital Millennium Copyright Act," 87 *Virginia*

Law Review 813 (September 2001); Arnold P. Lutzker, "Primer on the Digital Millennium Copyright Act and the Copyright Term Extension Act Mean for the Library Community," at http://www.arl.org/info/frn/copy/primer.html; Free Expression Policy Project, "'The Progress of Science and Useful Arts': Why Copyright Today Threatens Intellectual Freedom—A Public Policy Report" (New York, 2003), available at http://www.fepproject.org/policyreports/policyreports.html.

   Legislative history of the DMCA   See Jessica Litman, *Digital Copyright* (Amherst, N.Y.: Prometheus Press, 2001), chapter 9, pp. 122–50.

New Genres of Forbidden Science and Speech

182   *Background*   Electronic Frontier Foundation, "Unintended Consequences: Five Years Under the DMCA," 2003; Free Expression Policy Project, "'The Progress of Science and Useful Arts': Why Copyright Today Threatens Intellectual Freedom—A Public Policy Report" (New York, 2003), pp. 25–27.

182   *Scientific researchers and the DMCA*   "Tortured Tale," *Wall Street Journal*, May 24, 2001, p. B6; Andrea L. Foster, "The Making of a Policy Gadfly," *Chronicle of Higher Education*, November 29, 2002; Pamela Samuelson, "Anticircumvention Rules: Threat to Science," *Science* vol. 293, pp. 2028–31 (September 14, 2001), available at http://www.sciencemag.org/cgi/reprint/293/5537/2028.

184   *Dutch cryptographer Neils Ferguson*   Neils Ferguson, "Censorship in Action: Why I Don't Publish My HDCP Results," August 15, 2001, available at http://www.macfergus.com/niels/dmca/cia.html.

184   *Blackboard Inc. and the DMCA*   John Borland, "Court Blocks Security Conference Talk," CNET News, April 14, 2003, at http://news.com.com/2100-1028-996836.html.

184   *Lawrence Lessig quotation*   Lessig, "Jail Time in the Digital Age," *New York Times*, July 30, 2001, p. A7.

You May Not Teach Your Robot Dog New Tricks

185   *Articles about Aibo*   David Labrador, "Teaching Robot Dogs New Tricks," *Scientific American*, January 21, 2002, available at http://www.sciam.com/explorations/2002/012102aibo/; Brendan I. Koerner, "Play Dead," *American Prospect*, January 1, 2002; Dave Wilson and Alex Pham, "Sony Dogs Aibo Enthusiast's Site," *Los Angeles Times*, November 1, 2001, available at http://www.latimes.com/business/la-000086726nov01.story?coll=la-headlines; Barnaby Feder, "A Robotic Pet Gains an Independent Streak," *New York Times*, October 17, 2002.

185   *AiboPet Web site*   http://www.aibopet.com and www.aibohack.com.

These Words May Not Be Read Aloud

187   *Lessig quotations*   Lawrence Lessig, "Adobe in Wonderland," *Industry Standard*, March 19, 2001, available at http://cyberlaw.stanford.edu/lessig/content/standard/0,1902,22914,00.html.

The Ingenious Use of Copyright Law to Squelch Competition

189   *Lexmark case*   Frank Ahrens, "Caught by the Act," *Washington Post*, November 12, 2003, p. E1; Associated Press, "Toner Case: Ruling Favors Lexmark," February 28, 2003; See also the Electronic Frontier Foundation Web site for an archive on the *Lexmark v. Static Control* case.

190   *Remote controls for garage door openers*   Katie Dean, "Garage Doors Raise DMCA Questions," *Wired News*, September 17, 2003, at http://www.wired.com/news/technology/0,1282,60383,00.html; *Chamberlain Group v. Skylink Technologies,* district court: http://www.eff.org/Cases/Chamberlain_v_Skylink/20031113_opinion_granting_summ_judgmt.pdf; circuit court: http://www.eff.org/legal/cases/Chamberlain_v_Skylink/20040831_Skylink_Federal_Circuit_Opinion.pdf.

Those Notorious Weapons of Piracy— the Shift Key and the Magic Marker!

190   *Commentary on copy-protection systems*   Mike Godwin, "What Every Citizen Should Know About Digital Rights Management: A 'DRM' Primer," November 2003, available at www.publicknowledge.org; John Gilmore, "What's Wrong With Copy Protection," February 16, 2001, available at http://www.toad.com/gnu/whatswrong.html.

191   *Alex Halderman's paper about flaws in MediaMax CD-3 software*   http://www.cs .princeton.edu/~jhalderm/cd3/; SunnComm press release criticizing Halderman report: http://www.sunncomm.com/press/printpr.asp?prid=200310091000.

191   *Newspaper accounts*   Josh Brodie, "Threat of Lawsuit Passes for Study," *Daily Princetonian*, October 10, 2003, available at http://www.dailyprincetonian.com/archives/2003/10/10/news/8797.shtml; Katie Dean, "Shift-Key Case Rouses DMCA Foes," *Wired News*, October 11, 2003, at http://www.wired.com/news/print/0,1294,60780,00.html.

192   *Sony Key2Audio copy protection*   Reuters, "CD Crack: Magic Marker Indeed," May 20, 2002, available at http://www.wired.com/news/technology/0,1282,52665,00.html.

192–194   *Diebold case*   Electronic Frontier Web site, http://www.eff.org/Activism/e-voting; Kim Zetter, "Diebold Backs Off Legal Challenge," *Wired News*, December 2, 2003.

PART FOUR
ABSURD NEW FRONTIERS OF CONTROL

196   *Charles F. Gosnell quotation*   Cited in A. Kent and H. Lancour, editors, *Copyright: Current Viewpoints on History, Laws and Legislation* (New York: Boker, 1972), p. 63.

10: The Quest for Perfect Control

TV Executive: You Are *Required* to Watch the Ads

198   *Sony Betamax case*   *Sony v. Universal City Studios*, 464 U.S. 417 (1984).

198   *Jamie Kellner quotations*   Staci D. Kramer, "Content's King," *Cableworld*, April 29, 2002, available at http://www.kagan.com/archive/cableworld/2002/04/29/cwd141724.shtml.

199   *PVR usage report*   Next Research report, *Special Release: The PVR Monitor*, April 2003, http://www.nextresearch.com, reported by Tobi Elkin, "Impact of PVRs Dramatically Less Than Expected," *AdAge.com Online Edition*, January 1, 2003. See also, Jefferson Graham, "PVRs Change the Broadcast Picture; Networks Sue Over Ad Skipping," *USA Today*, August 13, 2002, p. 1A; Dan Gillmor, "Paranoia, Stupidity and Greed Ganging Up on the Public," *SiliconValley.com*, May 4, 2002.

200   *Top Ten New Copyright Crimes*   Ernest Miller, "Top Ten New Copyright Crimes," LawMeme, May 2, 2002, available at http://research.yale.edu/lawmeme/modules.php?name=News&file=article&sid=198.

Senator Hatch: Destroy the Computers of Infringers

201   *Hatch and Saaf quotations*   Associated Press, "Hatch Wants to Fry Traders' PCs," June 28, 2003, as distributed by *Wired News* at http://www.wired.com/news/print/0,1294,59298,00.html.

202   *Hatch speech*   Senator Orrin Hatch, "The Price Tag for Free Music," speech to National Press Club, October 3, 2003, available at http://www.senate.gov/~hatch/index.cfm?FuseAction=Speeches.Detail&PressRelease_id=212804&Month=10&Year=2003.

202   *Survey results*   Harris Interactive News, "Americans Think Downloading Music for Personal Use is an Innocent Act, According to Harris Interactive Survey," January 28, 2004.

202   *Copyright enforcement report*   Committee on Economic Development, "Promoting Innovation and Economic Growth: The Special Problem of Digital Intellectual Property" [report], March 1, 2004. See also John Schwartz, "Report Raises Questions About Fighting Online Piracy," *New York Times*, March 1, 2004, p. C2.

The Great Cultural Lockdown

203   *Salkever quotation*   Alex Salkever, "Guard Copyrights, Don't Jail Innovation," *Business Week*, March 27, 2002.

203   *"Fritz Hit List" on Ed Felten's "Freedom to Tinker" Web log*   September 23–December 8, 2002, http://www.freedom-to-tinker.com/archives/cat_fritzs_hit_list.html.

204–205   *Johansen and Corley cases*   Electronic Frontier Foundation, "Unintended Consequences: Five Years Under the DMCA," 2003; Free Expression Policy Project, "'The Progress of Science and Useful Arts': Why Copyright Today Threatens Intellectual Freedom—A Public Policy Report" (New York, 2003), available at http://www.Pepproject.org/policyreports/policyreports.html.

205   *Region coding*   Mike Godwin, "What Every Citizen Should Know About Digital Rights Management: A 'DRM' Primer," November 2003, available at www.publicknowledge.org; John Gilmore, "What's Wrong With Copy Protection," February 16, 2001, available at http://www.toad.com/gnu/whatswrong.html.

206   *"RIAA Wants Background Checks"*   *Technology News*, October 29, 2001, available at http://www.bbspot.com/news/2001/10/riaa.html.

The Morality Lectures of Industry Virtuecrats

207   *Chernin quotation*   Declan McCullagh, "Media Chief Decries Net's Moral Fiber," August 21, 2002, on McCullagh's Politech listserv, www.politech.org, and at http://news.com/com/2100-1023-954651.html.

208   *Richard Parsons quotation*   Chuck Philips, "Piracy: Music Giants Miss a Beat on the Web," *Los Angeles Times*, July 17, 2000, p. A1.

208   *Jack Valenti quotation*   Testimony of Jack Valenti, President, Motion Picture Association of America, Inc., Home Recording of Copyrighted Works: Hearing on H.R. 4783, H.R. 4794, H.R. 4808, H.R. 5250, H.R. 5488, and H.R. 5750 Before the Subcommittee on Courts, Civil Liberties and the Administration of Justice Subcommittee of the Committee on the Judiciary, 97th Congress, 2d Session, 1983.

208   *Statistics for DVD and videocassette sales and box-office receipts*   Adams Media Research, as cited in "Romancing the Disc—Hollywood Loves the DVD," *Economist*, February 7, 2004. Sales and rentals of DVDs account for two-fifths of the film industry's revenues.

208–209   *Jack Valenti speech*   "Some Comments on the Moral Imperative," Remarks by Jack Valenti, Chairman and CEO, Motion Picture Association of America, at Duke University, Durham, North Carolina, February 24, 2003, available at http://www.mpaa.org/jack/2003/2003_02_24.htm.

209   *Pat Schroeder quotation*   "Pat Schroeder's New Chapter. The Former Congresswoman Is Battling for America's Publishers," *Washington Post*, February 7, 2001.

210   *Judith Platt quotation*   Lisa Bowman, "Library 'Radicals' Targeted in Latest Copyright Battles," CNET News, July 12, 2001, available at http://news.com.com/2009-1023-269775.html?legacy=cnet.

11: Intellectual Property Goes Over the Top

As Difficult as A®, B®, C®

211   *Owning letters*   Adam Liptak, "Legally, the Alphabet Isn't as Simple as A, B and C," *New York Times*, September 2, 2001.

211   *McDonald's claims to own "Mc"*   Naomi Klein, *No Logo: Taking Aim at the Brand Bullies* (New York: Picador, 1999), pp. 177–78; *Quality Inns International, Inc. v. McDonald's Corporation*, 695 F. Supp. 198 (1988); Stephen Howard, "McChina Food Chain Wins Trade Name Battle," Press Association News (UK), November 27, 2001; "Big Trouble in Little McChina," *Brand Strategy*, February 1, 2002; Elissa Elan, "What's in a McName? As Far as McDonald's Trademarks Are Concerned—Everything," *Nation's Restaurant News*, December 10, 2001, p. 19; Tamzin Lewis, "McHaggis Quick Off Trademark," *Sunday Mirror* (UK), January 28, 2001, p. 9.

212   *"Aunt Jemima doctrine"*   *Aunt Jemima Mills Co. v. Rigney & Co.*, 247 F. 407 (2d Cir. 1917), *cert. denied*, 245 U.S. 672 (1918).

213   *Magazine title dispute*   ABC News/Mr. Showbiz, "Erotica Mag Sues Oprah Over Trademark," August 22, 2001, available at http://www.abcnews.com; Jeff Bercovici, "Oprah Puts Lash to German Fetish Title," *Media Life*, July 15, 2002, available at http://www.medialifemagazine.com/news2002/jul02/jul15/1_mon/news3monday.html; "German Erotic Magazine Sues Oprah Over Title," *Ananova*, August 22, 2001, available at http://www.ananova.com/entertainment/story/sm_380212.html.

214   *"U" and "2"*   Negativland, *Fair Use: The Story of the Letter U and the Numeral 2* (Concord, Calif.: Seeland, 1995). See also Rod McCarvel, "Every Artist is a Cannibal: The Strange Saga of Negativland, the Letter U, and the Numeral 2," at http:www.seanet.com/~rod/cannibal.html.

215   *WWF*   *Guardian Unlimited* (London), "Charity Wins Legal Bout Over WWF," August 10, 2001; Matthew Beard, "WWF—The Wildlife Fund—Stops Wrestlers Muscling In On Its Name," *Independent* (London), August 11, 2001.

215–216   *WWJD*   Damien Cave, "What Would Jesus Do—About Copyright?" *Salon.com*, October 25, 2000, at http://www.salon.com; Ron George,

"What Would Jesus Do Words in a Trademark Battle," Scripps Howard News Service, July 1, 1998; "What Would They Do? Get a WWJD Patent," Religion News Service, September 5, 1998.

A Legal Monopoly over Silence

217–218 *Newspaper articles* Davis Lister, "Big Noises At Odds over the Sound of Silence," *Independent* (London), June 21, 2002, available at http://www.independent.co.uk/story.jsp?story=307449; Ben Mattison, "King of Crossover Balks at Paying the Price for Silence," *Andante* (online classical music Web site), June 25, 2002, at http://www.andante.com/magazine/print.cfm?id=17428; Associated Press, "The Right to Remain Silent: Composer Reaches Settlement with John Cage Publisher," September 23, 2003; BBC News, "'Silent works' do Battle," July 17, 2002; "Silent Music Dispute Resolved," September 23, 2002.

Owning the Smell of Freshly Cut Grass

219 *Harley-Davidson's attempt to trademark its "hog" sound* Anna D. Wilde, "Harley Hopes to Add Hog's Roar to Its Menagerie of Trademarks," *Wall Street Journal*, June 23, 1995; Michael B. Sapherstein, "The Trademark Registrability of the Harley-Davidson Roar: A Multimedia Analysis," 1998 Boston College Intellectual Property & Technology Forum 101101 (online journal), at http://www.bc.edu/bc_org/avp/law/st_org/iptf/articles/index.html; Cecil Adams, "The Straight Dope" syndicated column, September 15, 2000, available at http://www.straightdope.com/columns/00915.html. To listen to the "hog roar" online, go to http://newsport.sfsu.edu/archive/f96/sounds/pending.html.

219 *Color trademark case* Qualitex Co. v. Jacobson Products Co., Inc., 54 U.S. 159 (1995). See also Karin S. Schwartz, "It Had to be Hue: The Meaning of Color 'Pure and Simple,'" 6 *Fordham Intellectual Property, Media and Entertainment Law Journal* 59 (Fall 1995).

220 *Scent marks* In re Clarke, 17 U.S.P.Q. 1240 (TTAB 1990); Faye M. Hammersley, "The Smell of Success: Trade Dress Protection for Scent Marks," 2 *Marquette Intellectual Property Law Review* 105 (1998); Florent Latrive, "The Smell of Cut Grass Privatized," *Liberation*, December 6, 2003, available at the Truthout Web site, http://www.truthout.org; C. Classen et al., eds., *Aroma: The Cultural History of Smell* (New York: Routledge, 1995).

221 *Tattoos and intellectual property* Marisa Kakoulas, "The Tattoo Copyright Controversy," bmezine.com [*Body Modification Ezine*] (Tweed, Ontario, Canada), December 8, 2003, available at http://www.bmezine.com/news/guest/2003/1208.html. See Elayne Angel's service mark registration at http://ringsofdesire.com/wingsregistration/index.htm.

No Photos, Please, of the Inside of a Starbucks

221 *Professor Lawrence Lessig's Web log entry for Starbucks no-photo incidents* http://www.lessig.org/blog, May 23, 2003.

221 *Second account of no-photo incident* Web log entry, March 31, 2002, at http://www.nedbatchelder.com/blog/200203.html#e20020331T163851.

222 *Newspaper article* Margie Boule, "Focus on Starbucks: Are Snapshots OK Along with Coffee Shots?" *Oregonian*, July 10, 2003.

223 *Starbucks photos Web site* http://www.starbucksphotos.com.

223–224 *Starbucks' reported response to no-photo complaints* http://wwwbumperactive.org, May 27, 2003.

Send in the Yoga Police!

224 *Bikram Yoga Web site* http://www.bikramyoga.com.

224–227 *Background on the case* James Greenberg, "Asana TM," *Yoga Journal*, December 2003, pp. 97–101; Vanessa Grigoriadis, "Controlled Breathing, in the Extreme," *New York Times*, July 6, 2003; *Open Source Yoga Unity v. Bikram Choudhury, Joint Case Management Conference Statement*, November 13, 2003 [Case No. C 03-3182 PJH]; "The Litigious Yogi," *Economist*, June 19, 2004, p. 64.

227 *Open Source Yoga Unity Web site* http://www.yogaunity.org.

227 A growing body of case law deals with copyright claims in spiritual and religious disciplines. See, e.g., *Michael Foundation, Inc. v. Urantia Foundation v. Harry McMullan, III* (10 Cir. Ct. App.), 2003 U.S. App. LEXIS 4232. Also, Walter A. Effross, "Owning Enlightenment: Proprietary Spirituality in the 'New Age' Marketplace," 51 *Buffalo Law Review* 483 (Summer 2003). The generic nature of "Pilates" was determined by a federal court in 2000 in *Pilates Inc. v. Current Concepts*, 96 Civ. 43 (MGC) (S.D.N.Y. 10/19/00); see also John Aquino, "Trademarks 'Pilates' Mark Generic, New York Court Holds," 6 *Intellectual Property Strategist* 7 (November 2000).

Patenting Side-to-Side Swinging

227 Patents can be reviewed at Web site of U.S. Patent and Trademark Office http://patft.uspto.gov.

228 *Smucker's crustless sandwich patent* David Lawsky, "Smuckers Protects Peanut Butter-Jelly Sandwich Patent," Reuters, January 25, 2001. Also, U.S. Patent and Trademark Office Web site.

228 *Mrs. Smith's latticework pie crust* Jarred Schenke, "Mrs. Smith's Latticework Pie Crust Top," *Atlanta Business Chronicle*, September 14, 2001, available at http://atlanta.bizjournals.com/atlanta/stories/2001/09/17/newscolumn7.html.

229 *Web links of wacky patents* http://www.patent.freeserve.co.uk/othersites.html.

229 *Criticism of patents* Denise Caruso, "Patent Absurdity," *New York Times*, February 1, 1999; James Gleick, "Patently Absurd," *New York Times Magazine*, March 12, 2000; Gregory Aharonian, Internet Patent News Service [newsletter]; Sabra Chartrand, "Federal Agency Rethinks Internet Patents," *New York Times*, March 30, 2000; Sabra Chartrand, "Patents: A Web Site Invites Bounty Hunters to Disprove Ownership of Ideas, Even Those of Its Founders," *New York Times*, October 23, 2000; Internet Patent News Service Web site on patent issues at http://www.bustpatents.com.

229 *Online fund-raising patent* *Ziarno v. American National Red Cross*, 2001 U.S. Dist. LEXIS 25433 (N.D. Ill. Nov. 13, 2001), 2003 U.S. App. LEXIS 234.

230 *Patenting rare-disease genes* Matt Fleischer, "Patent Thyself," *American Lawyer*, June 21, 2001; James Boyle, *Shamans, Software and Spleens: Law and the Construction of the Information Society* (Cambridge, Mass.: Harvard University Press, 1996), especially chapter 9.

231 *Patenting a Harvard scientist* Adam Scott, "Patenting the Harvard Scientist," *357 Magazine*, June 2002, available at http://www.gwilly.ca/357.

12: Just Kidding or Dead Serious :-(?

Who Owns the "Frowny" Emoticon?

232 *Despair Web site* Press releases at http://www.despair.com. Email from Justin Sewall of Despair Inc., June 11, 2003.

Freedom of Expression™

234 *Kembrew McLeod Web site* http://www.kembrew.com; see also Kembrew McLeod, "Copyrighting Freedom of Expression™," Alternet.org, January 27, 2003, available at http://www.alternet.org. See also, Nat Ives, "Advertising: When Marketers Trip Over Trademarks, the Fun Begins," *New York Times*, January 22, 2003, p. C4; interview with Kembrew McLeod, January 20, 2004.

Dialing for Dollars: Licensing the "Music" of Phone Tones

237 *Magnus-Opus Web site* http://www.magnus-opus.com.

237–240 *Press coverage of Magnus-Opus* Rick Karr, "Australian Musicians Copyright Their Compositions," National Public Radio, November 2, 2001; Claire O'Rourke, "Phoney Art Now at Your Fingertips," *Sydney Morning Herald*, October 1, 2001.

Tanzania Loses Name to Tanning Salon
Company, and Other Spoofs

240   *Tanzania spoof*   "Tanzania Loses Name to Tanning-Salon Company," *The Onion*, September 2, 2003, p. 1.

241   *Matt Groening and Binky the Rabbit*   "Interview with Noel Tolentino," *Zines*, vol. 1, available at http://www.researchpubs.com/books/zine1exc3 .shtml.; Brian Doherty, "Interview with Matt Groening," *Mother Jones*, March/April 1999, available at http://www.snpp/com/others/interviews/ groening99e.html.; *Suck* online, December 1, 1995, available at http:// www.suck.com/daily/95/12/01/daily.html.

242–243   *The Simpsons episode*   John Swartzwelder, "The Day the Violence Died," *The Simpsons* cartoon series, Production Code 3F16, original airdate in North America, March 17, 1996. Script available at http://www.snpp .com/episodes.

242   *Mickey Mouse's debt to Oswald the Rabbit*   Russell Merritt and J. B. Kaufman, *Walt in Wonderland: The Silent Films of Walt Disney* (Baltimore: Johns Hopkins University Press, 1993).

Conclusion: Reclaiming the Cultural Commons

245   *The politics of copyright law*   Robert S. Boynton, "The Tyranny of Copyright?" *New York Times Magazine*, January 25, 2004; Lawrence Lessig, *Free Culture* (New York: Penguin, 2004); Siva Vaidhyanathan, *The Anarchist in the Library* (New York: Basic Books, 2004).

246   *Web sites of interest*
      Public Knowledge: http://www.publicknowledge.org
      Electronic Frontier Foundation: http://www.eff.org
      American Library Association, Washington Office: http://www.ala.org/ ala/washoff/oitp/oitpofficeinformation.htm
      Future of Music Coalition: http://www.futureofmusic.org
      Consumer Project on Technology: http://wwwcptech.org
      Berkman Center for Internet and Society: http://cyber.law.harvard.edu/ home
      Creative Commons: http://creativecommons.org
      Negativland Web site: http://www.negativland.com
      The Thing: http://bbs.thing.net
      ®™ ARK: http://www.rtmark.com
      Lawrence Lessig's Web log: http://www.lessig.org/blog
      Edward Felten's Web log: http://www.freedom-to-tinker.com
      Siva Vaidhyanathan's Web log: http://www.nyu.edu/classes/siva
      Ernest Miller Web log: http://www.corante.com/importance

ChillingEffects.org: http://www.chillingeffects.org

LawMeme at Yale Law School: http://research.yale.edu/lawmeme

Donna Wentworth, Copyright: http://www.copyfight.org

WIPOUT essay contest: http://www.uea.ac.uk/~j013/wipout/

ALA's Information Commons Web site: http://www.info-commons.org

David Bollier on the commons: http://www.bollier.org and http://www.onthecommons.org

249   *Committee for Economic Development report*   Committee for Economic Development, Digital Connections Council, *Promoting Innovation and Economic Growth: The Special Problem of Digital Intellectual Property* [report], March 2004, at http://www.ced.org/docs/report/report_doc.pdf; John Schwartz, "Report Raises Questions About Fighting Online Piracy," *New York Times,* March 1, 2004, p. C2.

Toward a New Language of the Commons

251   *Benkler essay*   Yochai Benkler, "Coase's Penguin, or Linux and the Nature of the Firm," 112 *Yale Law Journal* 369 (2002), available at http://www.benkler.org.

252   *The paradigm of the commons*   David Bollier, *Silent Theft: The Private Plunder of Our Common Wealth* (New York: Routledge, 2002); John Clippinger and David Bollier, "A Renaissance of the Commons" [essay], in Rishab Aiyer Ghosh, ed., *CODE: Collaboration, Ownership and the Digital Economy* (Cambridge, Mass.: MIT Press, 2004); essays and other literature at http://www.onthecommons.org.

Bibliography

Alford, William P. *To Steal a Book Is an Elegant Offense: Intellectual Property Law in Chinese Civilization* (Stanford, Calif.: Stanford University Press, 1995).

Bollier, David. *Silent Theft: The Private Plunder of Our Common Wealth* (New York: Routledge, 2002).

Boyle, James, ed. *The Public Domain,* a collection of essays from the Duke Conference on the Public Domain, November 2001, published in 66 *Law and Contemporary Problems,* vols. 1 and 2 (Winter/Spring 2003).

————. *Shamans, Software, and Spleens: Law and the Construction of the Information Society* (Cambridge, Mass.: Harvard University Press, 1996).

Coombe, Rosemary J. *The Cultural Life of Intellectual Properties: Authorship, Appropriation and the Law* (Durham, N.C.: Duke University Press, 1998).

Fishman, Stephen. *The Public Domain: How to Find and Use Copyright-Free Writings, Music, Art and More* (Berkeley, Calif.: Nolo Press, 2000).

Gaines, Julie. *Contested Culture: The Image, the Voice and the Law* (Chapel Hill, N.C.: University of North Carolina Press, 1991).

Horovitz, Jed, prod. *Willful Infringement* [DVD](Hadddonfield, N.J.: Fiat Lucre LLC, 2003).

Lessig, Lawrence. *The Future of Ideas: The Fate of the Commons in a Connected World* (New York: Random House, 2001).

————. *Free Culture: How Big Media Uses Technology and the Law to Lock Down Culture and Control Creativity* (New York: Penguin, 2004).

Litman, Jessica. *Digital Copyright* (Amherst, N.Y.: Prometheus, 2001).

McLeod, Kembrew. *Owning Culture: Authorship, Ownership and Intellectual Property* (New York: Peter Lang, 2001).

McSherry, Corynne. *Who Owns Academic Work? Battling for Control of Intellectual Property* (Cambridge, Mass.: Harvard University Press, 2001).

National Research Council. *The Digital Dilemma: Intellectual Property in the Information Age* (Washington, D.C.: National Academy Press, 2000).

Negativland. *Fair Use: The Story of the Letter U and the Numeral 2* (Concord, Calif.: Seeland, 1995).

Perelman, Michael. *Steal This Idea: Intellectual Property Rights and the Corporate Confiscation of Creativity* (New York: Palgrave, 2001).

Vaidhyanathan, Siva. *Copyrights and Copywrongs: The Rise of Intellectual Property and How It Threatens Creativity* (New York: New York University Press, 2001).

————. *The Anarchist in the Library: How the Clash between Freedom and Control Is Hacking the Real World and Crashing the System* (New York: Basic Books, 2004).

Index